MYCENAEAN GREECE AND THE AEGEAN WORLD

In this book, Kramer-Hajos examines the Euboean Gulf region in Central Greece to explain its flourishing during the postpalatial period. Providing a social and political history of the region in the Late Bronze Age, she focuses on the interactions between this "provincial" coastal area and the core areas where the Mycenaean palaces were located. Drawing on network and agency theory, two current and highly effective methodologies in prehistoric Mediterranean archaeology, Kramer-Hajos argues that the Euboean Gulf region thrived when it was part of a decentralized coastal and maritime network, and declined when it was incorporated in a highly centralized mainland-looking network. Her research and analysis contributes new insights to our understanding of the mechanics and complexity of the Bronze Age Aegean collapse.

Margaretha Kramer-Hajos has taught at the University of Michigan and at Indiana University. She is the recipient of the Award for Excellence in College Teaching from the Classical Association of the Middle West and South. Her articles have appeared in *Hesperia*, the *Journal of Hellenic Studies*, and *Kadmos*; a monograph was published with British Archaeological Reports in 2008. Her research focuses on Mycenaean Central Greece.

Mycenaean Greece and the Aegean World

The Aegean World

Palace and Province in the Late Bronze Age

MARGARETHA KRAMER-HAJOS

CAMBRIDGE
UNIVERSITY PRESS

CAMBRIDGE
UNIVERSITY PRESS

One Liberty Plaza, 20th Floor, New York, NY 10006, USA

Cambridge University Press is part of the University of Cambridge.

It furthers the University's mission by disseminating knowledge in the pursuit of
education, learning, and research at the highest international levels of excellence.

www.cambridge.org
Information on this title: www.cambridge.org/9781107107540

© Margaretha Kramer-Hajos 2016

First published 2016

Printed in the United States of America by Sheridan Books, Inc.

A catalogue record for this publication is available from the British Library.

Library of Congress Cataloguing in Publication Data
Kramer-Hajós, Margaretha Theodora, 1970–
Mycenaean central Greece and the Aegean world : palace and province in the late Bronze
Age / Margaretha Kramer-Hajós.
New York, NY : Cambridge University Press, 2016. | Includes bibliographical
references and index.
LCCN 2016013899 | ISBN 9781107107540 (hardback : alkaline paper)
LCSH: Euboea Island Region (Greece) – Antiquities. | Civilization, Mycenaean. | Civilization,
Aegean. | Bronze age – Greece – Euboea Island Region. | Excavations (Archaeology) – Greece –
Euboea Island Region. | Palaces – Greece – Euboea Island Region – History – To 1500. | Coastal
settlements – Greece – Euboea Island Region – History – To 1500. | Social archaeology –
Greece – Euboea Island Region. | Coastal archaeology – Greece – Euboea Island Region. |
BISAC: SOCIAL SCIENCE / Archaeology.
LCC DF261.E9 K73 2016 | DDC 938/.401–dc23
LC record available at https://lccn.loc.gov/2016013899

ISBN 978-1-107-10754-0 Hardback

CONTENTS

List of figures   *page* vii
List of tables   ix
Acknowledgments   xi

1 INTRODUCTION TO THE REGION AND THEORETICAL
   APPROACHES   1

   The Euboean Gulf coasts and Central Greece: an overview of previous
      research   5
   Brief gazetteer of important sites   8
   The natural landscape of the Euboean Gulf area   12
   Network analysis: a brief introduction   19
   Agency and iconography   28
   Summary   31

2 THE ETHOS OF THE SWORD: THE CREATION OF EARLY
   MYCENAEAN ELITE CULTURE   33

   Swords for heroes   33
   Warrior tombs in the Euboean Gulf area   39
   The warrior's beauty   44
   Chariots: part of the warrior package   46
   Feasts and feasting   49
   Ships and coastal raiding   50
   Conclusions: the Euboean Gulf coasts in the early Mycenaean period   54

3 THE ROLE OF ELITE NETWORKS IN THE MYCENAEANIZATION OF THE
   PROVINCES   56

   Emerging centers: early Mycenaean networks   56
   The microscale: pottery production at Mitrou   67
   Conclusions   68

4 SEALS AND SWORDS AND CHANGING IDEOLOGIES   70

   The creation of a small-world network in LH IIIA1   70

Changing ideologies   76
The disappearance of chariots on seals   77
Symbols of power outside the Peloponnese   84
Evidence for provincial aspirations to elite status   94
The domestication of the warrior   100
Conclusions   105

5   PREHISTORIC POLITICS: THE CREATION OF THE PERIPHERY. 107
From maritime to land-based networks   108
Destructions and abandonment   113
Orchomenos, Gla, and the Kopais   115
Conclusions   125

6   PALATIAL CONCERNS: SHIPS AND EXOTICA 128
Missing ship and seafaring iconography   128
Palatial monopolies on elite goods   141
Conclusions   147

7   REACTIONS TO COLLAPSE: THE RISE OF A SAILOR-WARRIOR
    CULTURE 149
Reactions against palatial domination   149
Kraters for warriors   152
The Mycenaean galley revisited   157
Weapons and armor   161
Return of the warrior tombs   163
Conclusions   165

8   MODELING COLLAPSE AND REVIVAL 166
Galleys and the formation of new long-distance networks   171
Postpalatial trade   174
Conclusions   178

9   CONCLUSIONS 180

Bibliography   187
Index   207

FIGURES

1.1   Map of Central Greece   *page* 2
1.2   The Euboean Gulf area in Central Greece   3
1.3   Map of East Lokris   6
1.4   View of the headland of Skroponeri   16
1.5   View of the tidal islet of Mitrou   17
1.6   The mound of Lefkandi from the west   18
1.7   The mound of Kynos from the west   18
1.8   Examples of network architecture 1   20
1.9   Examples of network architecture 2   21
1.10 PPA models for the Early Bronze Age Cyclades   25
2.1   Depiction on Grave Stele V, Shaft Grave V, Mycenae   34
2.2   Impression of an early Mycenaean gold cushion seal from
      Shaft Grave III, Grave Circle A, Mycenae, showing a duel
      between a sword-bearing and a spear-bearing warrior.   34
2.3   The "Battle in the Glen," impression of an early Mycenaean gold
      signet ring from Shaft Grave IV, Grave Circle A, Mycenae.   35
2.4   Impression of an early Mycenaean gold cushion seal from
      Shaft Grave III, Grave Circle A, Mycenae, showing a heroic
      warrior fighting a lion.   37
2.5   Antler horse bridle piece from Mitrou   46
2.6   Ship from the "Flotilla Fresco," south wall of the West House in Akrotiri 51
2.7   Fragment of the silver Siege Rhyton, Shaft Grave IV   52
3.1   MH sites in Central Greece   57
3.2   MH III-LH IIA sites in Central Greece   57
3.3   Chalkis-Trypa, LH IIA stirrup jar with three handles and figure-8 shield
      decoration   60
3.4   Schematic representation of MH and LH I sociopolitical network
      dynamics along the Euboean Gulf   62
4.1   Schematic representation of changes in sociopolitical network structure
      between LH I-II and LH IIIA   72
4.2   Krater from Ugarit   76
4.3   Carnelian seal from Kalapodi-Kokkalia Tomb I. Drawing of impression
      showing a lion attacking a bull   89

4.4   Look-alike lentoid seals from Kalapodi, Tanagra, and Nichoria
        showing griffins   90
4.5   A pair of griffin cushion seals from Routsi   91
4.6   Sealing from Thebes, made by an MPG seal   95
4.7   Worn MPG seals from Chalkis and Tanagra, Ledeza   97
4.8   Two MPG seals from Megaplatanos-Sventza   98
4.9   Major categories of Aegean swords   102
5.1   Hypothetical territories of Thebes and Orchomenos   108
5.2   Chalkis-Trypa, tall-bodied, straight-sided alabastra   109
5.3   Chalkis, large and giant alabastra   109
5.4   Simplified model of Mycenaean redistribution of staples
        and wool products   110
5.5   Transition from decentralized to centralized network between
        LH IIIA1 and LH IIIA2-B   111
5.6   LH IIIB fortifications in the Euboean Gulf area   113
5.7   Cyclopean masonry at Larymna (a) and Gla (b)   121
6.1   Mast and rigging of a traditional sailing ship on fresco fragments
        from Pylos   129
6.2   Mycenaean galley on an LH IIIC Middle stirrup jar from Skyros   131
7.1   LH IIIC Light on Dark "Griffin pyxis" from Lefkandi   150
7.2   Two joining pictorial krater sherds from LH IIIC Middle Kynos,
        depicting a shipboard battle   153
7.3   Pictorial krater fragments from LH IIIC Middle Kynos, depicting
        warriors on ships   155
7.4   Pictorial krater fragment from LH IIIC Middle Kynos, depicting
        a warrior on a galley   156
7.5   Sea battle between Egyptians and Sea Peoples, Medinet Habu   158
8.1   Transformation of sociopolitical network structures during
        the LH IIIB-C transition in the Euboean Gulf   167
8.2   Changes in site density and distribution between LH IIIB and LH IIIC
        in Central Greece   168

TABLES

1.1   Chronological framework for the Mycenaean period (adapted from
Shelmerdine 2008a, 4 fig. 1.1 and 5 fig. 1.2)   *page* 2

4.1   Numbers of amber beads (after Harding et al. 1974)   71

4.2   Minoan and Mycenaean chariot seals   79

4.3   Seals with lions attacking bulls   86

4.4   Numbers of selected "power depictions" on various types of seals
(after Laffineur 1990)   87

4.5   Seals at Kalapodi-Kokkalia   88

4.6   Condition of MPG seals from the Euboean Gulf coasts   97

8.1   Imports in the Perati tombs   175

ACKNOWLEDGMENTS

The seed for this book was planted in 2009, when my husband, Jozsef Hajos, gave me Barabási's book *Linked* (2009) to read on a long flight and I realized that the collapse of the Mycenaean civilization at the end of the Bronze Age could be perfectly described and explained by applying concepts from network theory. Subsequent discussions with him have been instrumental in sparking ideas and formulating arguments. The germination of these ideas into a book has benefited greatly from the input of several colleagues who have shared their offprints or drafts, commented upon my drafts, directed my attention to useful bibliography or comparanda, answered my questions, corrected some of my more egregious errors, or were willing to brainstorm with me. I wish to thank here especially John Bintliff, John Coleman, Anastasia Dakouri-Hild, Evi Gorogianni, Richard Janko, Alex Knodell, Olga Krzyszkowska, Bartek Lis, Tom Palaima, Marie-Nicole Pareja, Laetitia Phialon, Jeremy Rutter, Philip Stockhammer, Thomas Tartaron, Salvatore Vitale, Michael Wedde, Judith Weingarten, and John Younger. The anonymous readers for Cambridge University Press provided many comments that helped shape the arguments in this book, and Asya Graf and Mary Bongiovi have been excellent and patient editors. I thank Cyprian Broodbank, Alex Knodell, and Barry Molloy for sharing their illustrations. Generous funding from the Edward A. Schrader Archaeological Research Fund at Indiana University has made several research trips to Greece possible. I am grateful to the ephors, epimeletes, archaeologists, and guards of the Greek Archaeological Service who allowed me into their storerooms, onto their sites, and generously shared their time and knowledge, including Vassilis Aravantinos, Ioannis Fappas, Rozina Kolonia, Maria-Photeini Papakonstantinou, and Angelos Ritsonis.

1

INTRODUCTION TO THE REGION AND THEORETICAL APPROACHES

Not so long ago, the Euboean Gulf area (Figures 1.1; 1.2) was seen as rather marginal to the study of Mycenaean culture and archaeology: although the site of Lefkandi, excavated in the 1960s, had provided unexpected evidence of a thriving LH IIIC settlement,[1] Lefkandi seemed the exception in a region otherwise unknown for its Mycenaean remains. In recent years this has changed, with excavations at Mitrou informing us about the earlier Mycenaean phases, and those at Kynos confirming the importance of the LH IIIC period and the transition to the Early Iron Age in the Euboean Gulf area. In addition, excavations of the cemetery at Elateia and the sanctuary at Kalapodi, both further inland but in areas equally "provincial," indicate that in the interior, too, there was virtually no break between the end of the Bronze Age and the beginning of the Early Iron Age. This stands in stark contrast to the situation in, for example, the Argolid, Messenia, and central Boeotia.

These major excavations have ensured that the Euboean Gulf area is nowadays rightfully considered an area of paramount importance for the understanding of several crucial phases of the Late Bronze Age: the transition from the MH to the LH and the accompanying "Mycenaeanization" outside the core areas of the Argolid and Messenia, the transition from the palatial period (LH IIIA2–IIIB) to the postpalatial LH IIIC period, and the transition from the Late Bronze Age to the Early Iron Age. Despite this recent increased interest, the Euboean Gulf area has not been subject to the amount of scholarly investigation and interpretation as, for example, the Argolid, Messenia, or even Attica. This book is the first attempt to write a social-historical analysis of this area and its relation to the main centers of the Mycenaean world (Mycenae, Thebes) in the Late Bronze Age.

[1] See Table 1.1 for the Mycenaean chronology. The absolute dates for the earlier part of the sequence (MH-LH IIIA1) are disputed, with an alternative "high chronology" favoring a starting date of LH I closer to 1700 BCE; see Shelmerdine 2008a for a brief overview. I follow here the traditional "low chronology."

TABLE 1.1. *Chronological framework for the Mycenaean period (adapted from Shelmerdine 2008a, 4 fig. 1.1 and 5 fig. 1.2)*

Cultural phase	Pottery phase	Calendar dates BCE
Prepalatial (ca. 1750–1400)	Middle Helladic III (MH III)	1700–1600
	Late Helladic I (LH I)	1600–1500
	Late Helladic II A (LH IIA)	1500–1430
	Late Helladic II B (LH IIB)	1430–1390
	Late Helladic III A1 (LH IIIA1)	1390–1370/60
Palatial (ca. 1400–1200)	Late Helladic III A2 (LH IIIA2)	1360–1300
	Late Helladic III B (LH IIIB)	1300–1200
Postpalatial (ca. 1200–1000)	Late Helladic III C (LH IIIC)	1200–1070
	Submycenaean	1070–1000

FIGURE 1.1. Map of Central Greece, with places mentioned in the text indicated.

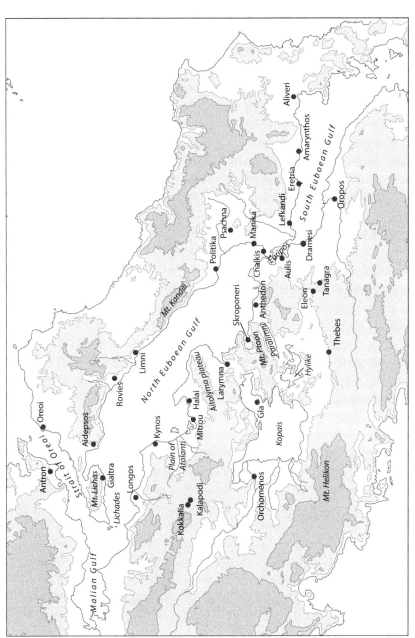

FIGURE 1.2. The Euboean Gulf area in Central Greece, with places mentioned in the text indicated. Elevation lines at 200 m and 600 m. The Kopaic Basin is shown in its original (undrained) state.

It is also the first to draw attention to and attempt to provide a holistic explanation for the drastically different trajectories of the coasts compared to the interior of Boeotia. Employing a coastscape approach (see Pullen and Tartaron 2007), it juxtaposes the coasts with the interior, exploring the relationship between the core areas of the Mycenaean world (the Mycenaean palatial areas) with more marginal areas, the coasts of the Euboean Gulf.

In the cosmopolitan world of the Late Bronze Age, the Euboean Gulf coasts were strategically located, with ready maritime access to distant resources. It is therefore unsurprising that in the early Mycenaean period they followed the same trajectory as, for example, the Argolid. Yet, they suffered cultural decline during the palatial period. They flourished again only in the postpalatial period, after the collapse of the palaces. It is evident that somehow the palaces were responsible for the decline of the coasts in the palatial period, and this makes Mycenaean Central Greece fertile ground for investigating power dynamics and cultural interaction models. In this book, the Euboean Gulf area is used as a case study for investigating the reactions of the "hinterland" to the emergence of organized states, the manners in which these states attempted to incorporate or marginalize the province, and the violence, but also the vibrant creativity, which may result from a sudden collapse of the organized state. By looking at the Euboean Gulf region of Central Greece, important questions bearing on the emergence of Mycenaean identity outside the Mycenaean core areas, the interaction between palaces and provinces, and the end of the Bronze Age are thus addressed.

In order to understand the changes that happen over time in the relative status of the Euboean Gulf coasts, and the curiously "out of sync" pattern mentioned earlier, this book invokes aspects of network theory. It focuses especially on the transitions between network types to illuminate the changes in social-political structures taking place between periods. I will argue that large-scale changes in culture and society (such as the emergence of an identifiable Mycenaean identity, the emergence of palaces, their collapse, and the new order that forms after their collapse) can be understood by analyzing changes in network structure, diameter, and orientation.

To understand the reasons for these changes in network types, I turn to the rich iconographic record of Mycenaean Greece. Artifacts like frescoes, engraved seals, and display pottery project the values of the elites commissioning and using them, and understanding these values aids in understanding changes in society. The same is true for exotic imports: changes in import consumption throughout time reflect changing ideologies, concerns, and relations. Using the two approaches together then allows us to link actors: in network theory the individuals or groups constituting nodes that may have various links to each other, with agents, the individuals or groups responsible for introducing new technological, artistic, or cultural changes in agency theory. Reconstruction of networks allows us to see the relations between actors, whereas agency theory allows us to formulate agents' motives. Together, the two approaches allow for as comprehensive a reconstruction of social histories as one may hope for in prehistoric societies.

THE EUBOEAN GULF COASTS AND CENTRAL GREECE: AN OVERVIEW OF PREVIOUS RESEARCH

The coverage of fieldwork in the area has been rather uneven. Major recent excavations are limited to the mainland (Kynos, Mitrou, Kalapodi, Gla, Thebes, and Eleon) and to Central Euboea (Lefkandi); several other sites have been excavated either earlier or are published rather unevenly (Orchomenos, Tanagra).[2] In addition to these major excavations, the Greek Archaeological Service has in previous decades undertaken many rescue excavations of Mycenaean chamber tombs especially in East Lokris (Figure 1.3; Kramer-Hajos 2008, 35–72). Although these have so far been published only in preliminary reports, they have done much to illuminate the history of Mycenaean settlement in that area, illustrating burial customs, ideologies, and the degree of incorporation of the area into the Mycenaean koine. In most cases, associated settlements are yet to be located, but these cemeteries, many of which are large and relatively wealthy, suggest that the interior of East Lokris was densely populated.

For North Euboea the picture is worse: the only excavations of Mycenaean sites that have taken place have been poorly published, either because they took place early in the twentieth century (tombs around Chalkis),[3] or because publication is limited to perfunctory annual reports (the settlement at Aidepsos).[4] Therefore, the major source of information for Mycenaean North Euboea remains, unfortunately, the half-century-old survey report by Sackett and his colleagues (Sackett et al. 1966).

Several other surveys have taken place in the area, some in conjunction with established excavations or as preliminaries to excavation. Extensive one-man surveys by Fossey in the 1980s covered East Lokris and Boeotia.[5] The Cambridge/Bradford Boeotian Expedition, directed by John Bintliff and Anthony Snodgrass, focused between 1978 and 1999 on diachronic landscape use of large swaths of Boeotia (Bintliff and Snodgrass 1985, 1988; Bintliff et al. 2007); it was followed in 2000 by the Leiden-Ljubljana Ancient Cities of Boeotia Project that is ongoing as of 2016 (yearly reports are published in *Pharos*, the journal of the Netherlands Institute at Athens). Since both

---

[2] References for each site are given on pp. 8–11.
[3] Papavasileios 1910, pp. 21–24, 52, 60, 65, and 71–72; Hankey 1952.
[4] *AR* 49 [2002–2003] p. 48 and *AR* 51 [2004–2005] p. 52.
[5] Fossey 1988, 1990a. The entire area is also covered by Hope Simpson and Dickinson (1979).

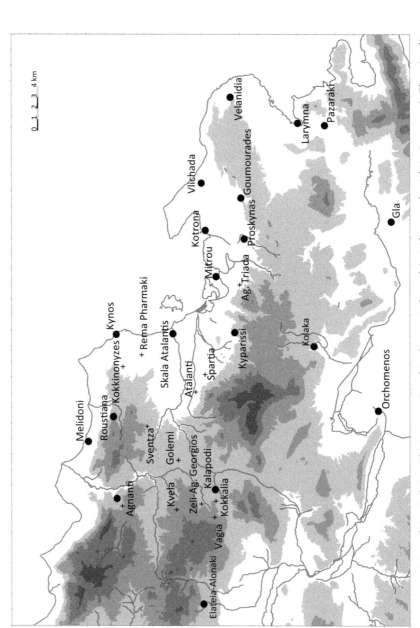

FIGURE 1.3. Map of East Lokris with sites mentioned in the text indicated (+ indicates a burial site/cemetery). Elevation lines at 200 m intervals.

projects focus on the historical periods and on theoretical questions and approaches, their use for the Late Bronze Age is largely limited to questions of landscape use and settlement density (e.g., Bintliff forthcoming). Similarly, the intensive Oropos Survey Project, directed by Michael Cosmopoulos, focused on the rural history of ancient Greek city-states, although the final publication does present and discuss data pertaining to the Late Bronze Age (Cosmopoulos 2001). A small-scale survey by the Cornell Halai and East Lokris Project (CHELP) in 1988–1989 of the area around Halai did not yield many results for the Mycenaean era, except for the part of this survey focusing on the site of Mitrou.[6] The Eastern Boeotia Archaeological Project (EBAP) started out with a survey of the plains surrounding the modern towns of Arma, Eleon, and Tanagra (Burke 2007) before commencing excavation at Eleon.

Although Karystos appears in Linear B tablets from Thebes (as ka-ru-to), the southernmost area of Euboea is conspicuously lacking in significant Mycenaean material: after several surveys, a mere five LH II–IIIA Mycenaean sherds have been identified, all from Agios Nikolaos, northeast of Karystos (Tankosić and Mathioudaki 2009, 2011, 135–136). The dearth or complete lack of Mycenaean material is noted by the South Euboea Exploration Project (SEEP), active since 1984 and directed until 1995 by Donald Keller and the late Malcolm Wallace; the Norwegian Archaeological Survey in the Karystia (NASK), started in 2012 under the direction of Žarko Tankosić; and the Plakari Archaeological Project, focusing on the site of Plakari near Karystos since 2009 and directed by Jan Paul Crielaard and, until 2014, the late Maria Kosma (Crielaard et al. 2012, 96; Cullen et al. 2011, 38, 2012; Talalay et al. 2005; Tankosić and Chiridoglou 2010; Wallace et al. 2006).

Several recent studies attest to the emergence of Central Greece onto the scholarly scene. Farinetti discusses the long-term Boeotian settlement landscape by integrating archaeological, historical, and environmental data in a GIS-based approach (Farinetti 2011). Phialon gives a thorough and up-to-date overview over all of Central Greece in the early Mycenaean periods (MH III–LH IIIA; Phialon 2011). Knodell picks up where Phialon leaves off, and gives a synthesis of the entire area from the Mycenaean palatial period through the Early Iron Age (Knodell 2013). Less detailed regarding the empirical evidence, the strength of this dissertation is its use of network theory to interpret the evidence. Knodell's observations and interpretations regarding the LH IIIB and IIIC periods correspond well to the arguments in this book. Two other studies are limited to smaller areas within Central Greece:

---

[6] The extensive CHELP survey of the Halai area is unpublished. It should be noted that informal excursions by John Coleman in recent years have led to the chance discovery of several sites (Vlichada, Goumourades, Kotrona) in this area (Kramer-Hajos 2008, 49, 51, and 53). For the intensive survey of Mitrou, see Kramer-Hajos and O'Neill 2008.

Kramer-Hajos provides a synthesis of Late Bronze Age East Lokris (Kramer-Hajos 2008), and Privitera treats the Mycenaean period in Attica in admirable detail (Privitera 2013). Lemos gives a useful brief overview focusing on Euboea and Central Greece in the postpalatial period (Lemos 2012).

BRIEF GAZETTEER OF IMPORTANT SITES

Since most of the arguments in this book are based on evidence from a select number of sites, this section gives a brief archaeological and historical account of these key sites, going from north to south. Other relevant sites will be introduced throughout the text.

Kynos (Pyrgos Livanaton) was excavated between 1985 and 1995 by the Greek Archaeological Service under the direction of Fanouria Dakoronia.[7] It is a high mound site located directly on the coast, inhabited from the Early Helladic to the Byzantine period. The most significant evidence excavated dates to the LH IIIC Middle period, when Kynos was a thriving settlement with household production of pottery, metals, and textiles; a transport stirrup jar attests to connections with Crete (Stockhammer 2007, 280). Locally produced pictorial pottery, predominantly with depictions of warriors and ships (Dakoronia 1987, 1996b, 1999), shows stylistic and thematic similarities with pottery from Volos, Kalapodi, Lefkandi, and Amarynthos; impressed pithoi are similar to those found at Mitrou and Kalapodi (Lis and Rückl 2011). Evidence for levels predating LH IIIC is not as clear, but the LH IIIC settlement was built at a different angle than that of the preceding IIIB settlement, suggesting a break in habitation. It has been suggested that Kynos served as harbor for the nearby site of Palaiokastro or possibly Roustiana (Dakoronia 1993, 125–126; see also Kramer-Hajos 2008, 72), located several kilometers inland from Kynos, in a pattern that is also prevalent in Greece today, with a main settlement having a subsidiary settlement on the coast. Whether or not this was the case, the main settlement would have been close enough to the coast to be part of the coastal sphere and would be closely linked to its harbor.

Mitrou has been excavated since 2001 by the Mitrou Archaeological Project, codirected by Aleydis Van de Moortel and Eleni Zahou.[8] The site is located on a small tidal islet in a bay; in the Bronze Age, it would have been

---

[7] Kynos has been published only in preliminary reports: see Dakoronia 1987, 1993, 1996a, 1996b, 1999, 2002b, 2003, 2006, 2007a; Dakoronia and Kounouklas 2009; and the annual reports in the *Archaiologikon Deltion* (*ArchDelt*) and the *Archaeological Reports* (*AR*).

[8] Preliminary reports: Van de Moortel and Zahou 2005, 2011; Rutter 2007; Van de Moortel 2007, 2009; Vitale 2008, 2009, 2011, 2013a, 2013b; Lis 2009; Lis and Rückl 2011; Maran and Van de Moortel 2014; and the annual reports in the *AR* for the years 2004–2005 through 2010–2011. The results of the earlier surface survey are published in Kramer-Hajos and O'Neill 2008.

a peninsula (Kramer-Hajos 2008, 23–28).[9] The site was continuously inhabited from the Early Bronze Age through the Early Iron Age. Especially the early Mycenaean evidence is important, as settlement remains from this period are relatively rare. Mitrou flourished during the early Mycenaean period, with evidence for emerging elites, monumental architecture, and a purple dye industry (Vykukal 2011). During the LH IIIA2 period the settlement was destroyed and afterward not rebuilt in the same location: although roof tiles and palatial-style pottery (Vitale 2013b) suggest the continued importance, including monumental architecture, of the site, the locus for this building has not yet been found. In LH IIIC, a new monumental building was built directly on top of the earlier destroyed structure, suggesting a conscious reverting to prepalatial symbols of power. Despite a thriving settlement in LH IIIC, Mitrou lacks so far pictorial pottery or imports in this period. It becomes a rural settlement in LH IIIC Late.

The sanctuary of Kalapodi was continuously in use from at least LH IIIA1 (and possibly as early as MH) through the Archaic period and is therefore one of the most important sites with evidence for Bronze Age–Early Iron Age continuity. The site was excavated between 1973 and 1982 and again from 2004 by Rainer Felsch and Wolf-Dietrich Niemeier.[10] Initially identified as the sanctuary of Apollo Hyampolis and Artemis Elaphebolos, Niemeier has now identified the temple as that of Apollo of Abai (*AR* 53 [2006–2007], 41). Under the Archaic temple of Apollo, successive strata have revealed an uninterrupted sequence going back to Mycenaean times. The Mycenaean evidence consists of the remains of a temple (South Temple 1; *Chronique des Fouilles* 2012) built of large limestone blocks, including an altar and offering table; seals and beads are among the votives, and numerous pottery fragments date this temple to LH IIIA1–2. After its destruction, an LH IIIB temple (South Temple 2) was built in its place, with a horseshoe shaped clay altar, probably for libations, and a wooden offering table. The temple continued into LH IIIC but was violently destroyed in the eleventh century BCE, judging from the spread of sherds belonging to a bovine figure dating to the LH IIIC phase (*Chronique* 2011). An early (LH IIA–IIIA1) chamber tomb cemetery at the nearby site of Kokkalia provides evidence, consisting of weapons and jewelry, for the presence of early Mycenaean elites (Dakoronia 2007b; Kramer-Hajos 2008, 59–60).

[9] This inspires a cautionary note: it is possible that parts of the Late Bronze Age coastline are now submerged because of local tectonic activity; this may be one of the reasons that it is so difficult to identify Bronze Age harbor installations (Tartaron 2013, 140–143).

[10] See Felsch 1996, the annual reports in the *AR* for the years 2004–2005 through 2008–2009, and the *Chronique des Fouilles* 2005–2012.

The palace of Orchomenos is of paramount importance in the northern part of Mycenaean Boeotia. Heinrich Schliemann excavated a monumental tholos tomb, the so-called Treasury of Minyas, in 1880 (Schliemann 1881); subsequently Heinrich Bulle and Adolf Furtwängler conducted excavations in 1903–1905 (Bulle 1907). Theodoros Spyropoulos excavated at the palace in 1970–1973 (annual reports in the *Arch. Delt.*). Given the early date of some of these excavations and the preliminary character of publications on the more recent excavations, Orchomenos is a difficult site to understand. The tholos tomb, rivaled only by the so-called Treasury of Atreus at Mycenae and probably, like it, dating to LH IIIB, suggests Orchomenos' status as first-order center, and LH IIIB fresco fragments depicting warriors and chariots, a boar hunt, and possible bull leapers (Immerwahr 1990, 195; Spyropoulos 2015) are indicative of palatial status; however, no traces of Linear B tablets or monumental palatial architecture have been found. Both Knodell and Maggidis have suggested that Orchomenos may have shifted its center of political power in the thirteenth century BCE to Gla, designating Orchomenos mainly as an ancestral burial ground (Knodell 2013; Maggidis 2014).

The palatial site of Gla, first excavated in 1893 by T.A. de Ridder, continues to pose new questions and to inspire new field projects. The initial excavation was followed by excavations in 1955–1961 by I. Threpsiades and in 1981–1983 and 1990–1991 by Spiridon Iakovidis (Iakovidis 1989, 1998, 2001). This work showed that the Cyclopean citadel of Gla was built early in LH IIIB and destroyed at the end of this period, about a century later, after which it was no longer inhabited. Buildings included storage rooms and rulers' or administrators' quarters (a "melathron" consisting of two wings of roughly equal size and layout), and among the finds were fresco fragments, horns of consecration, and roof tiles. Yet, the large citadel seemed largely devoid of buildings. Recent work, directed by Christofilis Maggidis for the Dickinson Excavation Project and Archaeological Survey of Glas (DEPAS), has discovered a large number of hitherto unknown structures (including residential buildings, a cistern, and sally ports) within the citadel walls (Maggidis 2014). Another recent project, Archaeological Reconnaissance of Uninvestigated Remains of Agriculture (AROURA), directed by Michael Lane and Vassilios Aravantinos, investigated the rural polder landscape around Gla in a geophysical survey between 2010 and 2012 (Lane 2011, 2012).

Mycenaean Thebes is located under the modern town of the same name, on a low hill in the alluvial plains of eastern Boeotia; excavations have taken place since 1900 in various areas of the modern town (Dakouri-Hild 2010, 690–691).[11] They have revealed a site of major importance, where in the early Mycenaean period elites were buried with swords and prestige goods in

---

[11] Dakouri-Hild 2010 gives a succinct overview over the site and lists the extensive relevant literature.

much the same manner as in the shaft graves at Mycenae (Dakouri-Hild 2010, 696); during LH IIIA–B the site housed a large, pear-shaped Mycenaean palace, the Kadmeion. The surrounding hills (nowadays part of the modern town) were in this period used as burial grounds. Evidence for workshops (specializing in, e.g., ivory, gold, and stone), exotic imports, and Linear B tablets (Aravantinos et al. 2001)[12] show that the "House of Kadmos" was unrivalled in LH IIIA–B Central Greece.

The mound site of Eleon, located in the fertile plains of eastern Boeotia, is the subject of ongoing excavations, currently codirected by Brendan Burke, Bryan Burns, and Alexandra Charami.[13] Known from Theban Linear B tablets as an important secondary center, this status is borne out by finds of LH IIIB pottery and, spectacularly, a steatite jewelry mold, presented at the AIA Annual Meeting in 2015, for the sort of gold jewelry found at Thebes and its cemeteries (see Aravantinos 2010, 75). The nearby Mycenaean cemeteries of Tanagra were excavated between 1969 and 1984 by Theodoros Spyropoulos and published in preliminary reports; they are best known for their decorated larnakes (Kramer-Hajos 2015).

In Central Euboea, Lefkandi is a prominent high mound site, situated between two harbors directly on the coast, controlling the maritime traffic through the Euripos. The site was first excavated in the 1960s by Mervyn Popham and Hugh Sackett; excavation continues today under the direction of Irene Lemos.[14] As at Kynos, the LH IIIC levels are impressive, giving evidence for contact with Italy as well as with Cyprus, the Levant, and Egypt, and with pictorial pottery attesting to a similar warrior ethos as at Kynos. Since the LH IIIC levels cut down into the LH IIIB levels on the site, here, too, the extent and character of the earlier inhabitation is less clear than that of the LH IIIC period.

A few other sites are, although not strictly speaking part of the Euboean Gulf coasts, nevertheless closely connected to them. Near Volos, several sites (Kastro, Dimini, and Pefkakia) less than 5 km from each other constituted important centers at the head of the Pagasitic Gulf that were organized in heterarchical fashion (Pantou 2010).[15] Pantou argues that tholos tombs at Kastro, Dimini, and Kazanaki, and built chamber tombs at Pefkakia, suggest

---

[12] For critical reviews of the publication of the Linear B material from Thebes, which should be consulted together with the main publication, see, e.g., Palaima 2003; Deger-Jalkotzy and Panagl 2006.

[13] Preliminary reports: Burke 2007; Aravantinos et al. 2009, 2012; Burke et al. 2013; Charami et al. 2015.

[14] The main publication for the Mycenaean periods is Evely 2006, focusing on the LH IIIC levels. See also the annual reports in the *AR* for the years 2003–2004 through 2004–2005 and 2006–2007 through 2009–2012, and Lemos 2012.

[15] Adrimi-Sismani (2006) has interpreted the site of Dimini as the ancient palatial site of Iolkos. Pantou (2010) argues convincingly for a heterarchical organization in which Dimini, Kastro, Pefkakia, and perhaps Kazanaki were centers of similar status and with overlapping functions.

several elite centers rather than a single dominant center. Dimini was important, with evidence for two megara, ceremonial drinking practices, metal working, Linear B inscriptions (though not on tablets), and a sanctuary, but recently identified Linear B tablets from Kastro (Stamatopoulou 2011, 77–78) strengthen Pantou's heterarchical model (in addition, Kastro has evidence for metal working and drinking ceremonies, and architecture is possibly more impressive than at Dimini). At Pefkakia, a possible megaron, evidence for purple dye industry, and a sherd with an incision in Cypro-Minoan script indicate a third important center.

On the coast of Attica, south of the Euboean Gulf, the sites of Perati and Thorikos provide evidence for, respectively, the postpalatial period and the early Mycenaean period.[16] The chamber tomb cemetery of Perati was in use in the postpalatial period and consists of quite small and not very well constructed tombs that usually held only one or two burials (Iakovidis 1969);[17] numerous imports, from the Levant, Egypt, and Cyprus, are distributed over a large number of these tombs.

Thorikos, located in the southeastern part of Attica on the Petalian Gulf (south of the entrance to the South Euboean Gulf), benefited from its position just east of the metalliferous Laureion ridge: soil dated to the end of the sixteenth century BCE contains evidence for cupellation (the method for separating lead and silver from the argentiferous lead ore) in the form of fragments of litharge (the residue of the cupellation process; Laffineur 2010, 712). Almost contemporaneous is the first of four monumental tombs that neatly illustrate the evolution of the tholos tomb at Thorikos. The first of these (Tomb V) is a built chamber tomb covered by a tumulus, dating to the MH–LH I transition; the last two (Tombs I and III) are tholoi, in use from LH IIA onward (Laffineur 2010). It is likely that the exploitation of the metal ores was a catalyst for the emergence of elites at Thorikos. At Marathon-Vrana, somewhat further to the north, two tumuli covered monumental tombs as well, and a nearby tholos dating to LH II is known for its interment of two horses in the dromos.

THE NATURAL LANDSCAPE OF THE EUBOEAN GULF AREA

This book juxtaposes the area where the Central Greek palaces emerged (Thebes and Orchomenos, both firmly land-based) with the coasts (the so-called provinces, to indicate that they are culturally Mycenaean, but largely

---

[16] For Perati, see Iakovidis 1969; for Mycenaean Thorikos see Servais 1968, 1969; Spitaels 1982; Servais and Servais-Soyez 1984; Mountjoy 1995. Laffineur 2010 gives a succinct overview.

[17] A similar change to more poorly constructed tombs occurs at the cemetery of Elateia and seems characteristic for the postpalatial period. Together with the introduction of occasional cremation burials, it may signal the transition to individual burial in the Early Iron Age.

lacking in palatial culture and rather marginal to the palaces).[18] This may require explanation, since the Euboean Gulf coasts are traditionally viewed as the outer borders of the landmasses of which they are a part: as the fringes of Attica, Boeotia, East Lokris, and the island of Euboea itself (Figure 1.1).[19] There are several causes for this, administrative (these four areas are administered as separate *eparchiai*) as well as historical (in the modern world, people traveling in cars on paved roads are able to traverse almost any mainland area quickly and effortlessly). Viewed from the land, the Euboean Gulf coasts, intersected by ranges of high hills and mountains, appear as a disjointed series of "dead ends." However, modern administration and traveling methods are, of course, irrelevant when trying to reconstruct Bronze Age circumstances, and in the case of the Mycenaean Euboean Gulf a "coastscape approach," advocated by Pullen and Tartaron in 2007, is more useful. The coastscape approach makes the coast central rather than peripheral, shifting the perspective from land-based, with the coast as border, to the coasts themselves, as spaces connecting land and sea and connected to each other by water (Tartaron 2013, 9). The coast is a liminal zone, the edge where sea and land meet and where the microclimate is different from interior regions; an area also where because of its peculiar location people have somewhat different lifestyles, subsistence bases, and cultural identities than people further inland. The coastscape approach has been successfully employed to explain, for example, the lack of a palace in the Corinthia (Pullen and Tartaron 2007) and to draw attention to the non-palatial character of regions during palatial times (Tartaron 2010).

When viewed as a coastscape, the Euboean Gulf area makes the impression of two self-contained bodies of water, connecting the coasts of Attica, Boeotia, and East Lokris with those of Euboea. Virtually closed off from the open sea at its northern and southern points, the Euboean Gulf is generally calm, never giving the impression of a large open body of water: the Euboean Gulf is at all points narrow enough that the opposite coast is clearly visible. A view from the coast into the hinterland, on the other hand, is often blocked by ranges of hills and mountains (Figures 1.2; 1.4). From a phenomenological point of view, the coastal communities are thus oriented to the opposite coast, rather than to the hinterland; they have this in common with communities along the Saronic Gulf (Tartaron 2010, 173). But also from a practical viewpoint, coastal sites were easier to reach – via a quick hop across the Euboean Gulf – than many inland sites, which could only be reached by

---

[18] To date, no palace has been found along the coasts of the Euboean Gulf or on Euboea. Although it is possible that future work will change this – witness the recent discovery of a palace at Agios Vasileios in Laconia (*AR* 2010–2011, 23; 2012–2013, 31) – we have to work with the evidence we have, and I assume throughout this book that Euboea lacked a palace.

[19] A notable exception is Crielaard 2006. Maps are based on the modern maps of the area. No attempt has been made to reconstruct the ancient shoreline.

traversing hills or circumventing mountain ranges. This can be demonstrated most clearly for Skroponeri, a site that is enclosed by steep, barely accessible mountains, but has an unencumbered view on (and easy maritime access to) the large, fertile, densely inhabited plain of Psachna on Euboea. Many sites on north Euboea (e.g., Gialtra, Rovies, Limni) have a similar insular character, albeit less dramatically so, and this pattern of orientation toward the sea is true in varying degrees for all sites along the Euboean Gulf.

The Euboean Gulf coasts are highly fragmented: whereas the North and South Euboean Gulf are separated by the Euripos, at the narrow strait at Chalkis, the shores are separated by mountains and lakes. The most formidable obstacle is formed by Mt. Kandili on Euboea, rising out of the sea with sheer cliffs and reaching a height of 1,246 m. This mountain effectively separates the coasts of North Euboea from those of Central Euboea. Its sheer presence makes sailing an easier option for the traveler from, e.g., Politika to Limni, although sudden violent storms at all times of the year make this part of the Euboean Gulf dangerous for small craft (Sackett et al. 1966, 49). To the southwest, on the mainland, Mt. Ptoon, though no more than 724-m high, creates a similar obstacle because of its sheerness and the fact that it reaches all the way to the sea. Further inland, to the southwest and west of Mt. Ptoon, lakes Hylike and Kopais continue the barrier, creating a natural border between the territories of Thebes and Orchomenos. In short, there is a zone about a quarter up from the Euripos into the North Euboean Gulf, which functions as a barrier of sorts. On Euboea, Mt. Kandili is insurmountable. Off the Euboean coast, sailing can be treacherous. On the mainland, the landscape is dissected by cliffs and lakes, making travel arduous. This barrier effectively divides the North Euboean Gulf into two parts, and this natural barrier separates clusters of coastal settlements to its north from those to its south (Figure 1.2). The Euboean Gulf coastal sites thus constitute a series of "small worlds" in the sense that Broodbank (2000, 175–210) used the term: "microregions" in which settlements are visually, and inevitably closely, connected with each other. In this respect the Euboean Gulf region is similar to the Saronic Gulf.

On the other hand, the Euboean Gulf is actually a strait passing between the east coast of the mainland of central Greece (Attica, Boeotia, and East Lokris) and the west coast of the large island of Euboea. In this respect the Euboean Gulf differs from the three areas discussed in some detail by Tartaron in his book on Mycenaean coastal worlds (the Saronic Gulf, the Lamian Gulf, and the Bay of Volos: Tartaron 2013). The Euboean Gulf functioned as a major maritime route, connecting the southern Aegean (Crete, the Cyclades) with the Gulf of Volos, the northernmost extension of the Mycenaean core area, and beyond. The Euboean Gulf was thus of paramount importance in receiving and disseminating influences from the entire Aegean. This is visible as early as in the Early Bronze Age, when the site of Manika shows Cycladic and Trojan connections. Metal oxhide ingots found off Euboea suggest that trading ships sailed through these waters in the Bronze Age (Wachsmann 1998, 209); and in the Early Iron Age, links between Lefkandi and the Near East suggest a continued importance of the Euboean sailing route. The sheltered waters of the Euboean Gulf, with ample anchorage along the route, were preferable over the open sea east of Euboea, where the coast is mostly sheer and rocky.

The natural resources of the Euboean Gulf are abundant: much of the soil is fertile, consisting of light and easy-to-till Tertiary deposits and of coastal plains with heavy but fertile alluvium, and fresh water springs are numerous, especially in the northern part of the area. The largest of the alluvial plains on the Euboean Gulf shores are the Lelantine Plain between Chalkis and Eretria, the Plain of Psachna, and the Plain of Atalanti in East Lokris. Unsurprisingly, most evidence for habitation in the Mycenaean period is centered on these plains. In addition, there are smaller coastal plains at Rovies and the westernmost part of the Lichas peninsula on Euboea, and opposite Chalkis and at Longos on the mainland. Even smaller are the strips of land at Limni, Loutra Aidepsou, and Anthedon.

Prehistoric coastal settlements on both sides of the Euboean Gulf are primarily, if not exclusively, located on promontories and low mounds: Skroponeri (Figure 1.4), Mitrou (Figure 1.5), Manika, and Chalkis are head-lands protruding into the sea, while Dramesi, Lefkandi (Figure 1.6), Anthedon, Vlichada, Kynos (Figure 1.7), Melidoni, Gialtra, and Rovies represent substantial mounds or natural hills selected for settlement.[20] Coastal settlements are in all cases located near rivers (which are plentiful in northern and central Euboea as well as on the mainland shore), and are often separated from each other by hill ranges.

On the mainland, coastal sites are located at quite regular distances from each other: Anthedon, Skroponeri, Larymna, Vlichada, Mitrou, Kynos, and Melidoni form a string of Mycenaean sites located directly on the coast. Coastal centers, so recognized either by their remains (Larymna, Mitrou, Kynos) or by their position on a prominent mound (Anthedon, Vlichada, Kynos, Melidoni) were spread out at around 10 km (a two-hour walk) from each other. Because of the mountainous character of the Euboean coast, the dispersal of sites here is less regular: sites are limited to the plains or strips of flat land along the sea. Nevertheless, here, too, Lichas and Gialtra, as well as Aidepsos, Rovies, and Limni, and Politika/Mnima and Chalkis are at about 10 km distance from each other. Sites are found mostly at places that are still inhabited nowadays, suggest-ing either stable long-term settlement patterns dictated by natural resources or a recovery pattern that is to a high degree dependent on modern human activity.

In addition, a denser network of smaller sites on the mainland (Drosia, Skroponeri, Goumourades, Kotrona, Proskynas, Skala-Atalantis) existed at

[20] In the Strait of Oreoi, a mound at Oreoi continues the pattern to the northeast.

FIGURE 1.4. View of the headland of Skroponeri from the west, with Mt. Kandili on the Euboean coast in the background (a) and from southeast (b).

about 4 km (or an hour's walk) from the major sites and from each other. A two-tier inter-settlement hierarchy is thus readily apparent. The density of these sites on the better surveyed mainland and their contrasting paucity on North Euboea suggest that many of these smaller settlements (some of them identified on the basis of just a few sherds) have not so far been recognized on Euboea.

Settlement is concentrated in two areas: one to the northwest and one to the southeast of the "barrier zone" between Mt. Kandili and Mt. Ptoon. The southern concentration is centered on the plain of Oropos in Boeotia

FIGURE 1.5. View of the tidal islet of Mitrou from the southwest, with the Euboean coast around Rovies in the background (a) and from the east (b).

and the plain of Psachna and the Lelantine Plain on Euboea, while the northern cluster centers on the mainland plain of Atalanti. Important sites are however not limited to these two centers of settlement: Gialtra was likely an important center, with high-quality pottery similar to that of Chalkis and sight lines to Mitrou, Kynos, Melidoni, Rovies, and Limni (Sackett et al. 1966, 38).

This book examines how the Euboean Gulf area functioned in relation to the wider Mycenaean world, especially the Argolid (Mycenae) and the interior of Boeotia (Thebes) during three distinct Late Bronze Age periods: the early Mycenaean period of LH I–II (Chapters 2–3), the palatial period of LH

FIGURE 1.6. The mound of Lefkandi from the west.

FIGURE 1.7. The mound of Kynos from the west.

IIIA2–B (Chapters 5–6), and the postpalatial period of LH IIIC
(Chapters 7–8). Chapter 4 deals with a number of ideological changes and
transitions between the prepalatial and palatial periods. By paying attention
to the natural landscape as well as to the crucial roles of the palatial polities of
Thebes and Orchomenos and their interactions with the Euboean Gulf
region, both naturally determined geographical factors and human agency
can be seen to have played important roles in shaping the history of the
Euboean Gulf coasts.

NETWORK ANALYSIS: A BRIEF INTRODUCTION

This book will draw on insights from network analysis to gain understanding of the mechanics behind the ascendance, decline, or collapse of settlements, microregions, and regions in Central Greece. Barabási (2002) makes a strong case for viewing familiar evidence and problems through "network glasses," and one of the aims of this book is to do just that. This shift of perspective has the power to reveal how large-scale changes in society are inextricably linked with changes in networks.

A set of selected tools from the toolbox of social network analysis will be applied to study sociocultural, sociopolitical, and socioeconomic relationships between coastal societies, and between coastal societies and palaces along the Euboean Gulf during the Late Bronze Age. These tools will be used in a qualitative rather than quantitative manner: definitions of network parameters will be explained in words to reach an understanding of what they represent. I will thus focus on network architecture by visualizing, analyzing, and comparing network topology and by examining network dynamics with an emphasis on transitions between network types.

A network is made up of a finite set of nodes and the relations between them. These relations are the collections of links (also called edges, ties, or connections, and indicated by lines in a visual representation of the network) of a specified kind. Examples of links, the social connections between nodes, are movement of raw materials and finished goods, transfer of technology, and formal relations (such as authority or kinship). Nodes (also called vertices or system actors, and indicated as dots in a visual representation) are discrete social units, such as inhabitants of a settlement, a group of traders, or an individual administrator. In this book, nodes are typically communities making up a settlement or a small group of elites within a settlement, whereas links are mostly transfers of materials, goods, or technologies. A graph visualizes a network; it is defined here as a model for a social network where a link is either present or absent between each pair of nodes. It has to be emphasized that neither the geometric position of the dots representing nodes, nor the length and shape of lines graphically representing links within a graph carry any information: although the nodes may represent settlements, the graphs do not represent maps. Nor are they static: the links are not "roads" used whenever convenient; instead, the travel of goods or individuals *constitutes* the network, the links *are* the exchanges. This means that links require active maintenance; if neglected, they cease to exist. Thus networks change constantly, as some interactions intensify while others are neglected.

Graphs visualize, among other things, the speed and ease with which travel through the network is possible. A single link between two nodes indicates a direct connection. Other nodes can be reached by following a number of links. The shortest path between two nodes (also called the geodesic) is the path with the least number of nodes between two nodes (the lowest degree of separation), and represents therefore the easiest travel between two nodes.[21] The number of links required to travel to reach any given node is not dependent on geography: nodes that are geographically far removed from each other may nevertheless be connected by a single link (in the case of direct contact), whereas nodes that are geographically more proximal may not be linked directly.[22] The size of a network or graph (also called the characteristic path length) is the average shortest path length; the diameter of a graph is the length (number of links) of the largest distance between any two nodes of the graph.

There are various types of networks, characterized by different network architecture allowing for different speeds of communication. A mesh-like network (ordered lattice, or grid) is a distributed network with a high degree of clustering (i.e. there is an increased probability of two nodes being directly connected to each other if they share a nearest neighbor). Its most symmetrical form, the regular lattice, is characterized by a constant node degree (e.g., always three nearest neighbors). We can take as an example of a regular lattice-type network a circle of nodes where each of the nodes is connected to their nearest four neighbors (Figure 1.8a). Such networks emerge, for example, when applying Proximal Point Analysis (PPA), when each site is mechanically connected to a fixed number of nearest neighbors. The distributed network in Baran's graphs is a more realistic model of a mesh-like network, in which nodes are connected to a variable number of nearest neighbors (Figure 1.9a).

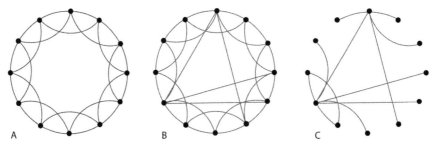

FIGURE 1.8. Examples of network architecture 1: distributed network, ordered lattice (a), small-world network (b), decentralized, scale-free network (c). Adapted from Barabási 2002, fig. 4.2.

---

[21] A path is a sequence of links between two nodes, where no nodes can be reached more than once. The length of a path is the number of links it contains; the distance (also called geodesic distance) between two nodes is the length of the shortest path. A trail is a sequence of links in which no link can be repeated, and a walk is an unrestricted sequence.

[22] This is something not taken into account in applying Proximal Point Analysis (PPA) and is one of the intrinsic weaknesses of PPA.

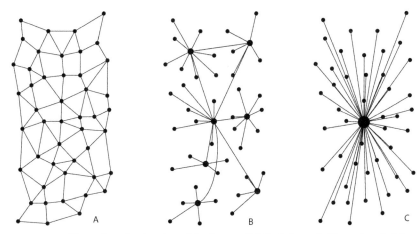

FIGURE 1.9. Examples of network architecture 2: distributed, mesh-like network (a), decentralized, scale-free network (b), centralized network (c). Adapted from Baran 1964.

Small-world networks can be derived from a mesh-like network by the addition of a few extra links connecting distant nodes. The long-range links that are added connect nodes with a high degree of separation and thus act as shortcuts, drastically decreasing the size of the network and thus creating a small world (Figure 1.8b). Although the geographical distance between each two nodes is the same, the speed with which goods and especially ideas (including technologies) travel between most nodes is manifold, since the idea does not have to be understood, accepted, and internalized by every node before traveling on to the next node: there are fewer degrees of separation. The size of a small-world network increases very slowly with the number of nodes, as most pairs of nodes are connected by a short path through the network. Small-world networks, similar to mesh-like networks, show high clustering. The node degree distribution of a small-world network follows a normal (Poissonian) distribution or bell curve: many nodes have an average number of links, while fewer nodes have either more or fewer links.[23]

Nodes having long-distance ties have an advantage over nodes lacking those and will tend to attract new links by preferential attachment (also referred to as cumulative advantage), as new links are generated preferentially to those nodes that are already well connected (in other words: existing nodes create ties to well-connected nodes, a phenomenon also referred to as "the rich get richer" phenomenon: links attract more links). When this happens, we speak of a scale-free (heavy-tail) network. An important feature of scale-free networks is the relative frequency of nodes with a node degree

[23] Small-world networks were first described by Milgram (1967); the first account of the "degrees of separation" concept can be found in Karinthy's short story "Chains" (1929). The mathematical model of small-world networks was developed by Watts and Strogatz (1998).

greatly exceeding the average node degree: node degree distribution follows a power law (that is, very few nodes have very many links, while almost all other nodes have very few links).[24] The nodes with the highest degrees are often referred to as hubs. Scale-free networks are vulnerable to the removal of a few of its highly connected hubs, while featuring robustness against the removal of nodes or links at random. In archaeology, scale-free networks represent hierarchical settlement patterns. Baran's decentralized network (Figure 1.9b) corresponds to a stage of a small-world network in which increasing preferential attachment is accompanied by a loss of links between nodes that are not hubs, resulting in a scale-free network.

A centralized network (Figure 1.9c) is a network in which a single central node has direct links to all other nodes, which are not connected to each other.[25] Centralized networks may emerge by condensation. They are highly vulnerable against coordinated attacks: if the central hub is removed, the network falls apart completely.

Networks are rarely, if ever, completely distributed or completely centralized; they tend to fall somewhere on a scale between the two. However, the degrees to which networks are centralized or distributed make a large difference, and are especially important to explain societal structures and changes in the archaeological record.

In the ideal distributed network no single node is more important than any other single node: if a node starts becoming more important, it will attract more connections, and the structure of the network will change from distributed (mesh-like) to decentralized (scale-free). Thus this type of network represents a heterarchical, egalitarian society as often envisioned for the earlier part of the MH period, for example. Such an organization represents a "large world" (the average shortest path length is high) in which ideas travel slowly: in order for a new idea to travel between two distant nodes, the idea has to pass through many other nodes (i.e. there are many degrees of separation). Since no nodes are isolated (they are all part of the same large network) but ideas travel slowly, such networks are characterized by homogeneous, somewhat stagnant, cultures. The removal of a high number of nodes (or links) is required to disrupt the network: it is unlikely that local disruption or decline affect the network as a whole. Therefore, such networks are stable over long periods of time.

As Baran's graphs illustrate, the speed of communication has an inverse relation to the vulnerability of the network (Figure 1.9). More robust networks are characterized by slow communication (changes happen slowly),

---

[24] The mathematical model for scale-free networks was developed by Barabási and Albert (1999); the first description of the phenomenon is by De Solla Price (1965).

[25] It should be noted that a mesoscale centralized network could be connected with one or several long links to other such centralized networks, creating a decentralized network on a macroscale.

while increasing centralization allows for faster communications (and there-fore faster rates of change), but also renders the network more vulnerable to coordinated attack. The stability of the distributed network depends to a high degree on the number of links between nodes: if the distributed network is characterized by high node and link connectivity (node connectivity being the smallest number of nodes to be removed to disconnect the graph, link connectivity the smallest number of links to be removed to disconnect the graph), it is stable, since removing any node does little to affect the network as a whole, and even failure of a number of random nodes still keeps the network as a whole functioning. With fewer connections between nodes, and fewer nodes (i.e. in a smaller-scale network) the distributed network is more vulnerable: failure of a number of random nodes can fracture the system into non-communicating islands.

How does a site become a hub (in other words: why do certain nodes attract more links than others)? Various factors play a role in this. One is the carrying capacity of the site: the more local resources a site has, the more attractive it becomes for other sites to connect to it. Such a hub is a central place (Renfrew 1977). The Mycenaean palaces are all characterized by plenty of access to fertile farmland, the basis for wealth according to the Mycenaean economy (Galaty et al. 2014). Another factor is the site's place in the network: a site that occupies a crucial place in the network, connect-ing various parts (clusters) of the network and thus acting as a bridge (if the bridge is broken, connectivity of the network is damaged), is a hub as well; such a site has "betweenness centrality" (Knappett et al. 2013). An example is the site of Akrotiri (Knappett et al. 2011); Broodbank argues convincingly that the importance of Daskaleio-Kavos, a site with marginal resources, can be attributed to betweenness centrality (Broodbank 2000, 223–246). Such sites are compelling evidence of the influence of networks on site impor-tance. Finally, we should not overlook the scenario in which a community actively creates new links (e.g., when a group of sailors ventures into new territories and sets up trade connections). Because of preferential attach-ment, the forging of new links will attract more links, transforming a node into a hub.

In archaeology, material culture is used to infer social, economic, or political interactions. A hub is a central place, "a locus for exchange activity" through which more of any material passes per head of population than through a smaller settlement (Renfrew 1977, 85): hubs are recognizable by the amounts and variety of material. The links (interactions, connec-tions) in networks are detectable by the presence or absence of certain diagnostic material. At the most basic and straightforward level, analysis of sealings (Weingarten 2010a) or of personal names occurring in the Linear B tablets from Pylos (Nakassis 2013) may reveal connections of individuals traveling between various settlements. Somewhat less tangible but more relevant for Central Greece is, for example, the presence of a common material culture (a koine) in a region, suggesting a network in which sites in a region are all densely connected; if, on the other hand, certain materials – for example, imports, or seals, or a specific type of pottery – are concentrated only in a few sites, those sites participate in particular import, seal, or pottery networks while other sites in the region are excluded. A "trickle down" of goods, whereby fewer of the goods turn up the farther a node is removed from the distributing hub, suggests the location of hubs and the topology of a scale-free network. Multiple networks (e.g., of pottery, metals, or seals) of different topology may operate simultaneously. A diachronic change in network structure is then detectable if, for example, certain materials that are earlier found throughout a region now become concentrated in a single site (or when, conversely, diagnostic materials that are first limited to one site now disseminate to other sites in the region). Networks can also change diameter (that is, the number of sites and links that make up a network may increase or decrease), either because the absolute number of nodes changes (nodes appear or disappear) or because existing nodes change their ties (neglecting and eventually severing their existing ties in favor of linking to other nodes). Much of the scientific network literature is concerned with the mechanics of network growth, but from the perspective of an archaeologist, the decline and collapse of networks are equally interesting.

Although network theory has been around for decades, Aegean and Classical archaeologists have begun to apply methods explicitly taken from network science only relatively recently. The growing popularity of the term "network" is reflected in a number of recent titles (Malkin et al. 2009; Malkin 2011; Brysbaert 2011; Knappett 2011, 2013; Tartaron 2013; and Rebay-Salisbury et al. 2014, for example); the *Journal of Archaeological Method and Theory* came out with a special issue (22[1], March 2015) about application of network theory in archaeology. The way networks are used as a heuristic device in these publications is however strikingly varied, ranging from the casual (the use of the phrase "network" as virtually synonymous with "interaction"; e.g., Brysbaert 2011; Rebay-Salisbury et al. 2014) to the heavily theoretical (e.g., Knappett 2011). A similar range of the application of network analysis can be found in some of the works that have pioneered network approaches for the prehistoric and classical Aegean. Broodbank used aspects from social network theory to illuminate settlement patterns and understand the relative importance of individual sites in the Early Bronze Age Cyclades (Broodbank 2000); more recently, Tartaron applied similar aspects of network theory to his discussion of Mycenaean coastal worlds (Tartaron 2013). Malkin's approach, similarly rooted in sociology, aimed to understand Greek identity formation throughout the Mediterranean (Malkin 2011), while Knappett's sophisticated modeling is closer to that of colleagues in the physical sciences

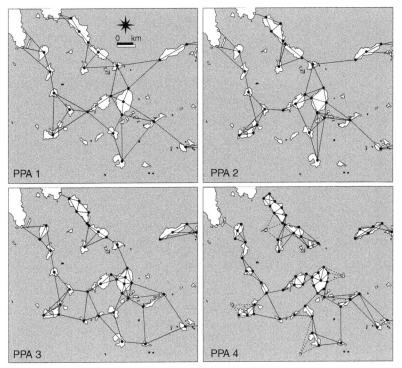

FIGURE 1.10. PPA models for the Early Bronze Age Cyclades: PPA 1–4 (courtesy of Cyprian Broodbank).

(Knappett et al. 2008, 2011). Given the lack of a unified network theory, Knodell eschews the phrase "network theory" in his dissertation (2013) in favor of "network thinking" (Knodell 2013). This is in effect what Barabási rallied for, and it is the approach taken in this book as well.

This alleviates a problem with applying network theory to archaeological datasets: these datasets are invariably incomplete. Any network model based on settlement maps runs the risk of incorrectness because of incompleteness of datasets. For this reason, Broodbank (2000, 180–186) provides Proximal Point Analysis (PPA) for four different, hypothetical settlement density scenarios (Figure 1.10) to tease out patterns, rather than trying to create a model based on a single, fixed, "known" and "real" settlement map. This model illustrates how, when using a fixed number of nearest neighbors, an increase in known sites results in the splitting off of parts of a network that used to be connected but have now become "islands" of dense interaction within themselves, but much less frequent interaction with other clusters. Knappett et al.'s model (2008) represents an improvement over the mechanical PPA: the latter draws connections based solely on geographical proximity, whereas the newer model takes a number of variables into account – not only the geographical distance but also the site's intrinsic carrying capacity, the site's relative importance, and the expenditure that a site puts into its interaction with any other site. However, this model works because Knappett and his colleagues make the fairly safe assumption that the 34 sites they include in their model "constitute a reasonable approximation of what would have been the most significant settlements in the period" in the Middle Bronze Age Aegean. This sort of modeling works very well on a large scale[26] (on which we may assume that most important centers are known); on a smaller regional scale they may reflect more the amount of work that has been done in a region than historical reality. The "gravity feature" of the model allows for uncertainty on the local level, when the model is applied to large regions; it does not ameliorate when the scale of the model is closer to the local scale, or when entire regions are virtually unexplored.

An example from Central Greece illustrates that even regional centers can be easily "missed." When Hope Simpson and Dickinson published their Gazetteer of Mycenaean sites in 1979, East Lokris seemed a truly peripheral area, with suspected or confirmed Late Bronze Age sites limited to Kynos, Skala Atalantis, Kyparissi, Melidoni, and Agnanti (Hope Simpson and Dickinson 1979, 262–263). Nowadays, however, major sites at Mitrou and Kalapodi have dwarfed the importance of Skala Atalantis, Kyparissi, and Agnanti, and no fewer than six cemeteries between Kalapodi and Agnanti represent additional dense settlement (Figure 1.3; Kramer-Hajos 2008, 59–69). Any network reconstruction must look strikingly different as a result. In addition to missing entire sites, problems of dating and hierarchical importance multiply for smaller, lesser-known sites. Thus smaller-scale networks are bound to reveal not so much the actual Late Bronze Age reality, as the current state of our knowledge. Especially for North Euboea, where barely any work has been done since the 1960s survey by Sackett and his colleagues and many lower-level sites probably remain to be detected, this picture may well change in the future, with inevitable repercussions for the reconstructed network.

In short, this sort of modeling, invaluable as it is, suggests a level of detailed knowledge and a level of certainty regarding the number, location, importance, and phases of sites, which in reality is simply non-existent. The more abstract "network thinking" approach, on the other hand, is fairly independent of exact knowledge of all representative sized site locations.

---

[26] Knappett (2011) defines three scales: the microscale, dealing with proximate interactions such as those between people and objects within the household; the mesoscale, dealing with interactions between households in a community and between communities in a region; and the macroscale, dealing with interregional interactions. As Knappett notes, this division is a rough guideline: both the borders of these scales and their number are by no means fixed or predetermined (2011, 98). This book deals primarily with the mesoscale of regional interactions; Knappett et al.'s model deals with the macroscale (Knappett et al. 2008).

Therefore I follow in the footsteps of Broodbank, Tartaron, and Knodell by drawing on network approaches to explain phenomena across various scales, rather than attempting to model the intensity or frequency of interactions.

Since this book is concerned with analyzing the social structure of prehistoric societies, the modeling used here is abstract, matching graph structures with societal structures and relations rather than with geographic realities (see also Leidwanger et al. 2014). This has the advantage of clarifying how changes in network topology affect society. Although I examine interaction networks in a specific geographic area and the analysis therefore involves to some extent "linking network dynamics and actual space" (Malkin 2011, 17), it should be stressed that it is by no means necessary to do so. An example that largely divorces space from the network is the fourteenth-century BCE Uluburun ship, which sank off the coast of southern Turkey, in an area with unpredictable winds and submerged cliffs (Pulak 1997, 1998). It carried a huge cargo consisting of raw metals (10 tons of copper ingots, a ton of tin ingots) as well as raw and processed luxury goods such as fine pottery, pomegranates, terebinth resin, ebony logs, elephant and hippopotamus tusks, glass, amber, and stone beads, and olive oil. Its diverse cargo links the shipwreck to Cyprus, the Levant, Egypt, Crete, and the Mycenaean mainland: in network terms, the ship and its crew formed a well-connected node, even a hub. Yet it is obviously not fixed in place but changing position while roaming the eastern Mediterranean continuously. In other words, the crew of this ship would not sell from and import to one harbor, their home port (which would make their home port a hub). Ships like these not merely maintained links but they functioned as moving hubs. It is important to keep in mind that although a network can in some cases be overlaid onto a map, such geographic correspondence is not a given.

The networks modeled and visualized here conform, for theoretical and practical reasons, to a set of restrictions. By definition they are undirected (representing directionless, symmetric relationships), unweighted (the importance of a node solely derives from the number of links with other nodes), simple (multiple links between the same pair of nodes as well as links connecting a node to itself are forbidden), sparse (there are fewer links than in a fully connected complete, saturated graph, in which all theoretically possible links between nodes are present), and connected (continuous, reachable), as any node can be reached from any other node within the network by following a path consisting of a finite number of links). Although imposing such restrictions inevitably leads to certain simplification, it results in simple and clear models that highlight the salient features of the network; in addition, a lack of knowledge about, for example, frequency of interaction and level of reciprocity makes more complex (weighted and directed) network models more speculative.[27]

Although graphs in this book do thus not represent weighted links, I do apply concepts from "the strength of weak ties" theory (Granovetter 1973). With its origins in sociology, the strength of weak ties is an important concept that emphasizes the impact of infrequent contacts that are not shared with neighboring nodes: occasional contacts with an outsider facilitate the introduction of new knowledge and ideas, whereas frequent interaction with the same group of neighbors tends to result in stagnation of knowledge, attitudes, and behavior. The occasional contact (weak tie) with the outside world has thus greater effect on a culture than its frequent internal contacts. This concept will be important in, for example, the early Mycenaean period (see Chapter 3), when the exploitation of weak ties results in the creation of early Mycenaean culture; if weak ties connect to a node in a small-world network, change may pervade the network rapidly.[28]

An inherent limitation of network theory is that it focuses on the connections (the ties between the nodes) at the exclusion of the actors: it does not necessarily reveal the identity, let alone the motives, of the actors creating and maintaining the network. In other words, network thinking does not explain the reasons behind any of the network changes. It analyzes the structure of interactions; it does not address questions of agency. In order to get to this level, I turn to another approach, which is commonly used in art historical analysis and iconography.

AGENCY AND ICONOGRAPHY

Agency is – like network theory – a concept that has its origins in fields outside archaeology. In sociology and philosophy, it refers to the capability of individuals to make their own choices, and is tied up with the debate of "free will." In archaeology, it is often understood more loosely, and therefore has been applied in various ways. In Brumfiel's definition, agency "refers to the intentional choices made by men and women as they take action to realize their goals" (Brumfiel 2000, 249); in Dornan's succinct summary, "people purposefully act and alter the external world through [their] actions"

---

[27] See Knappett et al. 2008, 2013 for sophisticated modeling of Middle Bronze Age Aegean directed and weighted networks.

[28] It should be noted that networks operate and can be analyzed - on different scales. For example, on the regional scale of Central Greece contact with the Argolid may constitute a weak tie. Zooming out, however, many such weak ties seem to constitute the links between regions in a decentralized network. Looking at this from the perspective of nodes rather than ties, Thebes may seem like the central hub on the regional scale, but when zooming out, it appears as one of numerous nodes in a decentralized network.

(Dornan 2002, 3–4). Agency is then, in origin, opposed to structure: it allows for individual decisions and actions to change the status quo. As Whitley puts it, "structure is what lends a period, people, or culture coherence; agency is what enables that structure to change, and history to enfold" (Whitley 2012, 581). Unsurprisingly, it is debated if and to what extent individuals in prehistoric societies would have acted counter to the established norms and societal expectations: are the social goals that agents pursue cross-culturally valid, or are they deeply embedded in cultural traditions and moral commitments (Brumfiel 2000, 249; Voutsaki 2010b, 65)? Do concepts of agency, with their emphasis on individual action and will, perhaps merely reflect current Western mentalities (Dobres and Robb 2000, 10–13; Voutsaki 2010b)?

Several theories attempt to bridge the gap between human agency and societal structure and thus alleviate concerns about the validity of agency concepts in prehistoric societies somewhat: according to these theories, it is possible to practice agency within the structure of society. Practice theory views the two as inextricably connected. A key concept of practice theory is *habitus*, the internalized social structures and norms guiding individual human behavior and thought (Bourdieu 1977, 1990). Social change can then emerge from individual actions that are in line with the established *habitus* but over time lead to change, for example, when individuals encounter other cultures and take over (material) aspects of that culture (and *habitus*); or it can be the result of a change in *habitus* itself, caused, for example, by influx of a new population with a different *habitus*. Structuration theory represents another attempt to reconcile structure and agency, which structuration theory views as inseparable: neither is more important than the other, and social structures are both the cause and the result of social actions (Giddens 1984). Moreover, Giddens' actors are knowledgeable social actors: they may manipulate and use structural institutions to their advantage and transform the rules that govern their behavior (Giddens 1979).

In this work, I use agency in its most basic meaning as the driving force for social and cultural change, as a result of actions by individuals or communities. I assume that prehistoric individuals (or groups of individuals) made decisions and took actions that made sense within their own societal and cultural framework (within their own *habitus*); by doing so, they purposefully or inadvertently altered their world and *habitus*.[29] For example, if the cultural framework dictates that status is enhanced by the conspicuous consumption of exotica, elites would reasonably try to increase their own consumption of exotica while prohibiting others from doing so. This application is close to Giddens' "Knowledgeable Social Actor" and Bell's "Rational Actor" concepts (Giddens 1979; Bell 1992) in that it envisions individuals

---

[29] "Irrational" decisions and actions must have occurred as well, but I assume that for an action to be repeated frequently enough to result in visible change, the action must have had a rational basis or a positive outcome or both.

making calculated decisions to increase their prestige. Assuming rationality behind acts that cause change allows for reasonable guesses as to the reasons for the changes, as well as to the identity and intention of the agents.[30] Thus, I use the concept of agency to investigate the reasons behind changes in the material record; in other words, to try to explain *why* (rather than how) network structure and orientation changed between the four periods with which this book is concerned.

Not only people have agency: objects, too, exert their influence and therefore have agency, a concept explored in Gell's "Anthropological Theory" of art and agency (Gell 1998). Gell argues that (art) objects are in their origin far from the untouchable, isolated pieces we admire in museum vitrines but were objects crafted with a purpose, intended to be used and handled, and entangled in a social and historical web of human relations. Hodder sums this entanglement up nicely:

> "Humans depend on things. [...] Things depend on other things. [...] Things depend on humans. [...] The defining aspect of human entanglement with made things is that humans get caught in a double-bind, depending on things that depend on humans." (Hodder 2011, 154)

According to agency theory, objects cannot be seen objectively: they acquire and change meaning depending on circumstances. For example, an heirloom is not merely valuable for its own sake but is imbued with personal historical meaning: it has an object biography (Gosden and Marshall 1999). Similarly, gifts have added value because of their biography.

The same is true for exotic objects: their foreign origin and relation to exotic "others" increases their value and prestige, making their impact (their agency) on recipients the more powerful (see Helms 1988). If objects exert agency on humans, the moment an individual acquires, consumes, or conspicuously displays exotica, that individual and anybody else who interacts with these exotica is subjected to the agency of these foreign objects. Thus, logically, the affected humans change as a result of interaction with this exotic material. This is the reason that it is impossible for a culture to interact with another culture and not be changed in the process: the established *habitus* must change upon interaction with another culture.

Swords are excellent examples of objects with agency. A Bronze Age sword was never meant to be merely examined visually; it was meant to be handled and carried (or even "worn"), as an extension of the warrior's body (Malafouris 2008), as well as admired from a distance, and the special emphasis on swords in the early Mycenaean period (see Chapter 2), as well

---

[30] Although it should be noted that purposeful actions may not always have had the intended results (Shanks and Tilley 1987, 116).

as the Early Iron Age custom of "killing" swords before their deposition in a burial, suggests that swords were imbued with almost magical powers. Thus swords evoked strong reactions and led to strong actions (not only "killing" the sword in the Early Iron Age, but also covering it in gold in the Shaft Graves [see Chapter 2 and Harrell 2012]). Many other objects, too, can be readily seen to alter individuals' perceptions. For example, in addition to their real defensive function, the Cyclopean walls of the Mycenaean citadels can be assumed to have acted upon individuals viewing them in various ways, evoking possible feelings of awe, pride, fear, or resentment depending on the relation of the individual to the palatial power. Similarly, palatial frescoes showing cultural ideals of palatial elites would have reinforced, but also created, the sense of what it meant to belong to the palatial elite and, more generally, what it meant to be Mycenaean (see Davis and Bennett 1999). Such frescoes could be manipulated by palatial elites in a conscious identity-forming process: agency of objects and agency of human actors are inextricably linked.

Other objects with pictorial decoration, too, exerted their agency upon the viewers, and it is for this reason that in this book I link agency strongly with iconography. I follow the line of thought that iconographic analysis has the potential to reveal ideologies. Especially pictorial frescoes in palaces are usefully regarded as vehicles of social-political propaganda and ideologies: after all, these paintings are not utilitarian, are fixed in place, and associated with the highest elites (Tourvanitou 2012, 723). Monumental sculpture, such as the Lion Gate at Mycenae, shares these characteristics. But other prestige objects, too, that are linked to elites can be interpreted in terms of displaying ideologies; most obvious in this group are small luxury goods with depictions, produced in specialized workshops: ivory plaques, metal and hard stone seals, and metal relief vessels. Pictorial kraters of the postpalatial period, too, represent some "self-advertisement," revealing ideologies of the postpalatial elites. Changes in iconography, as traced in especially Chapter 4, may then represent changes in values as well as more or less conscious attempts to manipulate ideologies. These changes in values, in turn, may underlie changes in networks.

SUMMARY

In short, this book examines the relations between the coastal "provinces" and the palatial interior of Boeotia. In order to understand the ascendance and decline of regions, microregions, and even individual sites, I turn to aspects of network theory. Network theory can provide a visualization of socio-political structures (and when it does this, it is a descriptive aid), but it can also explain how and to what extent societal structures change over time, and thus carries explanatory power. By reducing relations to their essence, network analysis provides a valuable approach for revealing network structure and actor relations. Network analysis can thus be extraordinarily useful in illuminating the mechanics of change in societal structures. To address the reasons behind these changes, this book invokes aspects of agency theory and iconographic analysis, which bring humans and human motivations into the story and result in an explanation on two levels: "how" and "why."

2

THE ETHOS OF THE SWORD
The creation of early Mycenaean elite culture

The Mycenaean culture takes its name from the assemblages discovered by Schliemann in the Shaft Graves of Mycenae. The shaft graves in Grave Circle A, dating to LH I (16th century BCE in the traditional chronology; see Table 1.1), are still the most spectacular embodiment of early Mycenaean culture, and are unique in sheer quantity of grave goods, including 15 kg of gold, and imports with origins as far away as the shores of the Baltic sea (more than 1500 amber beads; 1290 from Grave IV alone: Harding et al. 1974, 148), central Anatolia (the silver Stag Rhyton from Grave IV), and Minoan Crete (silver and stone vessels, seal stones and rings, and LM IA pottery). Apart from the wealth and the imported prestige items, a number of other characteristics are notable, especially when compared to MH graves. Most striking, perhaps, is the emphasis on warrior prowess, seen in weapons and in iconographic themes on decorated vessels and seals. Grave IV alone, burial site of three men and two women, contained at least 27 swords and 16 more sword pommels of ivory, gold, alabaster, and wood (Vermeule 1972, 89), at least five daggers and six more pommels, 16 knives, and five razors, as well as 38 arrowheads and 92 boar's tusk plates. One of the inlaid daggers shows a scene of five men hunting (or rather battling, since they carry shields) three lions. In addition, the silver Siege Rhyton depicts a battle, and two gold rings depict, respectively, a battle and a hunting scene. The horse-drawn chariot used for the latter is also popular on the grave stelae marking the graves (Figure 2.1). Quantities of bronze cauldrons, pitchers, hydriai, and kraters, along with gold and silver cups and jugs, suggest an emphasis on ceremonial feasting and drinking (Wright 2004b, 23–24).

SWORDS FOR HEROES

The sheer number of swords in Grave IV suggests that this is the weapon that defines the essence of a warrior in the early Mycenaean period; the reiteration of the same symbol signifies its importance and is a clear warning against

FIGURE 2.1. Depiction on Grave Stele V, Shaft Grave V, Mycenae.

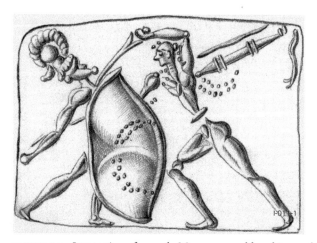

FIGURE 2.2. Impression of an early Mycenaean gold cushion seal from Shaft Grave III, Grave Circle A, Mycenae, showing a duel between a sword-bearing and a spear-bearing warrior. CMS I 11. Courtesy CMS.

a literal, biographical reading of the swords as used in battle by their owner (Whitley 2002). The prime importance of the sword, as warrior-implement par excellence, is also suggested by the way it is depicted in the art of the period: in almost every instance, a sword fighter is engaged in a duel (rather than a mass battle, for example), and is poised to win this battle. Thus on a gold cushion seal from Shaft Grave III (Figure 2.2) depicting a straightforward duel, the right warrior, unprotected by a helmet or a shield, thrusts his long sword aggressively into the throat of his opponent who despite his helmet, large shield, and long lance stands no chance against the dominating sword fighter. The force of the impact is such that the sword fighter's hair flows behind him, suspended in the air, and his scabbard is lifted up in the air behind him, parallel to his opponent's lance, which passes behind him futilely. On other seals, too, the sword fighter emerges victorious: the rules of early Mycenaean iconography demanded that the long sword be

FIGURE 2.3. The "Battle in the Glen," impression of an early Mycenaean gold signet ring from Shaft Grave IV, Grave Circle A, Mycenae. CMS I 16. Courtesy CMS.

the winning weapon. In fact, there are no unequivocal scenes from early Late Bronze Age art where a swordsman is defeated by an opponent with any other weapon.[1]

Moreover, the sword fighter typically lacks armor, whereas his opponent, armed with a different weapon, has shield and helmet. This suggests that the sword is associated with a real hero, who has no need for protection. On the famous "Battle in the Glen" ring (CMS I 16; Figure 2.3), at first sight, the dominating figure on the right, his weapon (a short dagger in this case) held high, appears to be winning the duel. Closer inspection, however, suggests that in fact the kneeling figure to the left is poised to win: he points his sword at his opponent's face, whose dagger, moreover, points at his own neck. The tip of the spear held by the leftmost figure is the third weapon to point at the looming warrior's helmet. The dagger-bearing warrior thus has three weapons (including his own) pointing at or near his head, and as if to reflect this predicament, his dagger-wielding arm is drawn far back, in a defensive rather than an offensive position. On this gold ring, then, too, the long sword is victorious, and in both cases the winner of the duel lacks helmet and shield: real heroes, it seems, have no need for protection.

Despite the presence of four figures on this ring, only two persons are actively engaged in fighting. The spearman, despite his armor and his ready spear, pointed to the head of the dagger warrior, does not actually engage in battle: all glory goes to the warrior with the long sword. The naked, bearded man perched comfortably on the right edge of the depiction appears to be a spectator, watching the battle with interest, as is suggested by the animated pose of his legs and straight posture. Although his beard and complete nudity

---

[1] A similar case is presented by the early Mycenaean chariot, which always battles an enemy on foot, and always is poised to win: Schon 2007, 140. In some cases, as on several grave stelae from Grave Circle A at Mycenae, the charioteer even wields a long sword, the foot soldier a single-edged sword (Stele V, Grave V) or a spear (Stele IV, Grave V).

mark him as of different status, there is nothing in the way he is depicted that suggests he is wounded or a bound captive. If indeed he represents a spectator, this would suggest that we are not dealing with a real battle scene, in which the two figures are shorthand for entire armies, but with a staged duel, an agonistic display between elite warriors, part spectator sport, part deadly competition. Similarly, on the stele from Shaft Grave V a warrior in a chariot is about to draw his sword to take on a single warrior on foot (Figure 2.1); no other warriors are present. Indeed, even on a much later (LH IIIA-B) larnax from Tanagra, two men duel with swords and despite the ample space on either side of them, no armies surround them; instead, they are, in a faint echo of the iconography on the LH I grave stele, flanked by two chariots. There are, in fact, no group battle scenes involving swords (Molloy 2010, 410). Thus swords in iconography are associated with individual duels, either of a virtually naked hero taking on a heavily armed opponent, or between two equally equipped swordsmen.[2] The design of the long sword supports this interpretation.

The long swords of the Aegean had been invented in the Middle Bronze Age, with the earliest examples found at Arkalochori and Mallia on Crete, at Kolonna on Aegina, and at Mycenae and Thebes on the mainland (Molloy 2010). Before the invention of the long sword, daggers were used. Although superficially similar to swords, daggers are easier to handle because of their limited size. They were suitable in close combat between individuals but had a range of other potential uses: in hunting, sacrificing, and slaughtering and butchering animals, for example. The early Aegean swords were considerably longer and required vast technological advances to produce: experiments have shown the complexities in distributing the molten bronze evenly through a long, thin mold, as well as the difficulties in producing such molds in the first place (Molloy 2010, 413). They also required a much more specialized fighting style than daggers, and were the first weapons suitable exclusively for interpersonal violence (Molloy 2010, 414): whereas daggers proclaimed an undefined masculine identity, swords characterized exclusively and specifically warriors. Although occasionally depictions show swords used against lions (Figure 2.4), this has probably more to do with the unique role of the lion as stand-in and foil for a warrior-hero in early Mycenaean iconography than with reality (more on this later). The sword is the symbol of the warrior.

There are three types of swords in the early Mycenaean period. Type A is Minoan in origin, impressive in length (up to a meter) but somewhat fragile. With thin tapering blades and a raised midrib, Type A swords are

[2] This is also familiar from the *Iliad*, where war is shown as an individual, personal matter. Homeric heroes duel while the throngs of subordinate fighters watch, much like what is shown on the ring in Figure 2.3. See Voutsaki 2010b for the idea of continuity in ethos between the early Mycenaean period and the Homeric epics.

FIGURE 2.4. Impression of an early Mycenaean gold cushion seal from Shaft Grave III, Grave Circle A, Mycenae, showing a heroic warrior fighting a lion. CMS I 9. Courtesy CMS.

more impressive visually than robust service weapons. The blades were attached to an organic hilt with rivets, but this attachment was rather weak. The pronounced midrib and narrow blade-width limited the sword's cutting potential, while the great length of these swords, their thin tapering blades, and weak handle attachment made them unsuitable for percussive strokes. They could be used in potentially lethal thrusting moves, and that is how they are shown in action on depictions. The bilateral sharp, thin cutting edges running the entire length of the blade suggest that light slicing moves may have been possible as well (Molloy 2008), but the thinness of the blade and the high midrib would have precluded making deep cuts. Cutting would thus result in bleeding from multiple wounds – a highly visible result compatible with a spectator sport – which would however not necessarily be lethal or even debilitating (Molloy 2010, 422–423). This suggests that these swords were suitable for agonistic display or, in other words, for "show duels." The fragile design of the swords means that only highly skilled warriors would be able to use them to the desired effect; too much torsion would result in bending or even breaking of the sword. Duels with these swords would thus allow for the display of great skill, as well as of sustained stamina in the face of multiple injuries.

Type B, which is heavily concentrated at Mycenae and appears to be a Mycenaean invention or adaptation, is shorter but more serviceable (Sandars 1961). It has a markedly improved handle attachment: a long, wide metal tang protrudes from the blade to form the core of the handle and makes the weapon less likely to break off from the handle because of forces of torsion. The third early Mycenaean sword was short lived: it is the single bladed sword held, for example, by the foot soldier on the stele from Shaft Grave V at Mycenae (Figure 2.1). Although experiments with replicas suggest that this is a formidable weapon (Molloy 2010), it is not attested after LH I.

As sword fighters were individuals, their swords, too, were individualized. Harrell notes that the Shaft Grave swords "display a level of distinctiveness and variety that is highly suggestive of the aim of intentional individualism" (2012, 801). Swords are truly unique weapons, possibly linked inextricably with their owner, whom they follow to the grave. Harrell even makes the tentative suggestion that the non-functional gold hilts may have replaced functional hilts only upon the warrior's death in order to mimic the latter's funeral outfit (2012, 803–804); as mentioned in the Introduction, this embellishment is a striking example of the agency the swords exerted on the people involved with them. The sword was in a sense the extension of the individual warrior's body (Malafouris 2008), the means by which the warrior could as an individual rise above other individuals or, perhaps, a mass of less individualized "commoners."

In all cases where a sword is shown used in combat, it attacks the same area: the throat/neck/head area (Figures 2.2–2.4). This is true regardless of whether the opponent is human or not. This may be practical, as the throat is an area of soft tissue not protected by the shield and a wound there would be lethal; Molloy has suggested that it may also be an echo of sacrifice scenes (Molloy 2008). The symbolic importance of the sword is often expressed in burials by associated grave goods: burials with swords are generally accompanied by more valuable goods than those with spearheads, and the more swords a burial contains, the more other rich goods are present as well (Kilian Dirlmeier 1988, 164). This suggests that excellence in warfare, symbolized by a multiplicity of swords, allows for the accumulation of wealth: status and wealth are dependent on living the life of a successful warrior-hero. These swords, new in this period, are thus likely to represent more than just a change in warfare and tactics. A symbolically charged meaning is suggested by iconography, deposition context, and the weapons themselves.

Swords deposited in graves are often highly decorated with precious materials. Moreover, although some of these weapons show wear on their blades and therefore were actually used, others show no wear at all and may have been crafted specifically for deposition in a grave (Molloy 2010). In these cases they are highly symbolic and used more to mark the exalted position – the warrior status – of the individual than representing biographical facts (see Whitley 2002). All evidence suggests that the sword was more than just another weapon in the mind of early Mycenaean warrior–elites: it was the weapon that was most charged symbolically, most indicative of high status, and most used to mark an individual as heroic. Malafouris has suggested that the sword was essentially regarded as a body part of the warrior (hence the "killing" of his sword upon a warrior's death; Malafouris 2008): the sword was as much part of the warrior as his groomed face and slender but muscular arms and legs.

The explosion of pictorial imagery visible in the art of the Shaft Graves is new on the mainland; the preceding MH period was entirely aniconic. It attests to an artistic and creative explosion probably triggered by increased contact with Minoan Crete and the Cyclades, where pictorial art flourished. Yet, the themes of this art are for the most part different from Minoan art, showing either subjects unknown from Crete at this time (for example, hunting scenes involving chariots) or, if attested, decidedly unpopular compared to other themes. The early Mycenaean emphasis on battles, duels, hunting, and similar "masculine" themes is uniquely its own. Equally unique, and different from the MH custom, is the treatment of the dead body as area for display: whereas the MH dead body was placed in a contracted position with few accompanying grave goods, in the Shaft Graves bodies are laid out and sometimes literally covered in gold in what must have been an act of extreme conspicuous consumption. This is thus an example of a change in *habitus* prompted by contact with another culture: contact with Minoans and their pictorial tradition changed the *habitus* of mainland elites to incorporate human depictions as well as treat the body as an area for conspicuous consumption.

Similar finds from elsewhere in the Argolid, Laconia, Messenia, and Central Greece suggest that the Shaft Graves were not an isolated phenomenon but that this mass deposition of prestigious objects in the graves of warrior elites happened throughout the core area of the Mycenaean world, albeit less spectacularly. In Central Greece, a built tomb in the center of the Kadmeion in Thebes contained the tightly contracted skeleton of a warrior interred with his sword, spear, knife, arrows, and boar's tusk helmet; other contemporary graves included gold jewelry and precious stones. This chapter examines to what extent the Euboean Gulf area shared in these developments and argues that, although generally somewhat later and not on the same level, emerging elites in the Euboean Gulf region followed the same strategies as the Shaft Grave princes.

WARRIOR TOMBS IN THE EUBOEAN GULF AREA

The Shaft Graves are essentially deep and large cist graves entered from a long shaft above. As such they represent a monumentalized form of the standard MH cist grave. They were large enough to hold multiple interments: a new development possibly signaling the increased importance of (symbolic) linking to the chief and elite families. The Mycenae Shaft Graves may have been inspired by the Kolonna grave (Kilian-Dirlmeier 1997), although this was strictly speaking a built tomb rather than a shaft grave. It however presaged in the MH II period the Mycenae Shaft Graves with its large and eclectic assemblage of grave goods including weapons, jewelry, and pottery imports from Crete and the Cyclades.

Along the Euboean Gulf, built tombs occurred around the MH III-LH I transition at Thorikos, Dramesi, and Lefkandi, and toward the end of the LH I phase at Mitrou. Built chamber tombs always occur before sites have been completely Mycenaeanized and differ widely in exact form and size. For these reasons, Papadimitriou has interpreted them as indigenous, local expressions of emerging elite status (Papadimitriou 2001). Their distribution along the Euboean Gulf suggests that elites emerged here around the same time as they did in the Argolid; the two tombs at Dramesi and Lefkandi, on opposite sides of the Euripos, suggest regional elite competition.

The built chamber tombs at Thorikos, Dramesi, Lefkandi, and Mitrou are all characterized by a certain degree of monumentality. At Thorikos, Tomb V is a cist grave surrounded by a rectangular structure of 7.80 x 5.80 m; the entire structure was covered by a tumulus. The built rectangular chamber in the center of a tumulus parallels the two earliest tumuli in Vrana-Marathon (tumuli I and II). Tomb V was looted, but sherds of Gray Minyan Ware, Matt Painted Ware, and Bichrome Matt Painted Ware confirm the date, and two fragments of marble jugs with MM III and LM IA parallels, and the upper part of an askos, with a good parallel in Grave Upsilon in Grave Circle B at Mycenae, suggest connections with the southern Aegean. It is noteworthy that the settlement may have been fortified at the end of the MH period. An oblong tomb with a uniquely structured vault (Tomb IV) dates to the end of LH I; it may represent a transitional phase between built chamber tomb and tholos tomb (Laffineur 2010, 714); two real tholos tombs (Tombs I and III) were in use from LH IIA onward. Though Tomb IV had been looted in antiquity, Laffineur lists a number of small gold offerings with parallels in the Shaft Graves or the southern Peloponnese (Laffineur 2010, 714).

The L-shaped built chamber tomb at Lefkandi was found robbed (Sapouna-Sakellaraki 1995); pottery dates the tomb to the MH-LH I transition. Like Thorikos, the settlement at Lefkandi received a fortification wall around this time (Popham et al. 2006, 87–92). The more monumental built tomb at Dramesi, with a 1.80-m-wide doorway, yielded "some bits of bronze weapons," including a spearhead with a parallel in Shaft Grave IV (Blegen 1949, 41), suggesting this was a warrior tomb. At Mitrou, an L-shaped built chamber tomb, with a 3-m-long dromos and a monumental (5 m x 2 m) rectangular chamber, both encompassed by a rectangular enclosure wall, was looted already in antiquity, but a Vapheio Cup fragment and fragments of a polychrome vase indicate that it was in use in the LH I period. Other finds, dating to LH I-IIB, include a gold and a silver rivet and a small amber bead.[3]

---

[3] *Archaeology in Greece* database (accessible via http://www.hellenicsociety.org.uk/frame .htm) Form ID 2009 (Mitrou 2010 report).

Although there is no evidence for a warrior burial at this early date, nine fragments from a boar's tusk helmet dated to LH IIIA from the same tomb suggest that by the fourteenth century, at least, the tomb was used by elites who had attained warrior status. Whether or not it was a warrior tomb from its inception, the rich grave goods, including boar's tusk platelets, arrowheads, and precious and semiprecious ornaments in gold, bronze, amber, etc. (Vitale 2013a, 127), and its large size indicate it was an elite tomb, conspicuously set apart from a nearby cist tomb cemetery, and enclosed by "Building D," a monumental structure measuring 13.5 m x 8.25 m with 0.7-m thick walls, of which the outer façade was constructed with large stones.[4] Building D was bordered by two roads paved with cobblestones; since two other roads followed the same orientation, the excavators have suggested the layout in this period of an orthogonal town plan (Van de Moortel and Zahou 2011, 288). The three early built tombs suggest that Dramesi, Lefkandi, and Mitrou were early centers of emerging elites, possibly emerging slightly later at Mitrou, in the northern part of the North Euboean Gulf, than near the Euripos, corroborating Hope Simpson and Dickinson's suggestion that the emergence of several regional centers was facilitated by the fragmentation of the landscape (Hope Simpson and Dickinson 1979, 235).

In addition to the centers at Dramesi, Lefkandi, and Mitrou, the cemetery at Chalkis-Trypa provides another indication of precocious development on Euboea. The earliest rock-cut chamber tombs at Chalkis-Trypa date to the end of LH I or to LH IIA and are thus contemporary with or only slightly later than Agia Anna Tomb 2, the earliest known chamber tomb at Thebes, which is dated to LH I and is very similar in dimensions to Mycenae Tomb 518 (Dickinson 1977, 63–64; Cavanagh and Mee 1998, 60, 67). Chamber tombs are typical Mycenaean tomb forms, and the tombs at Chalkis continue into LH III. They are rich: Hankey catalog beads and other ornaments of gold, amber, agate, amethyst, lead, and rock crystal, as well as bronze tools and weapons (Hankey 1952). Although most of the richer finds may belong to LH III (many tombs were looted already in antiquity, and they were published almost half a century after excavation, making it impossible in most cases to assign grave goods to specific burials), already the earliest tombs contain, for example, a bronze arrowhead (Tomb I) and an ovoid rhyton (Tomb V; Hankey 1952, 94, 61–62 no. 401), suggesting an early elite presence. In this respect, the tombs are similar to contemporary tombs in Thebes or in the Argolid, which also contain weapons, rhyta, and other elite vessels, though on a much grander scale, and it seems reasonable to assume that Chalkis was one of several strong and flourishing centers in early Mycenaean Central Euboea.

---

[4] See *AR* [2006–2007] p. 40; [2007–2008] p. 58; [2009–2010] p. 92 for Building D and the built tomb.

Somewhat later again than Mitrou's built tomb are a warrior grave on Skopelos and a pair of warrior tombs at Kalapodi. The early Mycenaean warrior grave at Cape Staphylos, in southeast Skopelos (Platon 1949), suggests that the warrior culture extended through the Strait of Oreoi to the Sporades. The large rectangular built chamber tomb yielded a long sword with gold foil decoration, a knife with duck's head hilt, a spearhead, and a dagger, as well as LH IIB pottery (Ephyraean goblets, squat alabastra: Hood 1978, 183; Mountjoy 1999, 857–860). Two warrior graves from Kalapodi in Phokis date to the same period.[5] The two burials took place in adjacent rock-cut chamber tombs (Tombs I and III) at the site of Kokkalia, within the modern village of Kalapodi; they represent the earliest rock-cut chamber tombs known from this part of Central Greece. Tombs I and III both deviate from the standard form of Mycenaean rock-cut chamber tomb by the presence of small side chambers, suggestive of a certain degree of experimentalism in this period, as well as an attempt at monumentality that rock-cut chamber tombs lost after they became more standard and widespread.[6]

Tomb I at Kokkalia contained a long bronze sword with ivory and gold inlays, a short dagger, two knives, a bronze spearhead, many arrowheads, three balance scales (used for measuring small weights), seals, a pair of tweezers, golden beads, and golden attachments (Dakoronia and Dimaki 1998, 394; Dakoronia 2007b, 59). Tomb III yielded more spectacular grave goods: golden attachments were found around and under the head of the deceased, together with golden and amber beads, vases, spindle whorls, a seal stone, two bronze knives, a bronze spearhead, some bronze arrowheads, and a silver ear scoop. Based on the presence of balance scales in Tomb I and the ear scoop in Tomb III, Dakoronia has made the suggestion that these tombs were the last resting place of warrior–physicians: both balance scales and ear scoops are found as parts of "kits" of medical equipment (Dakoronia 2007b). This is an intriguing idea in the light of Kalapodi's later status as cult place for Apollo, god of healing; however, the ear scoop could also be used for grooming (Salavoura 2012), like the tweezers, and the balance scales might be symbolic. Although elsewhere in the Euboean Gulf area warriors are interred in built tombs, here we find rock-cut chamber tombs with warrior

[5] The tombs have only been briefly published in preliminary reports, and their date is not entirely clear in these. In the report in the *ArchDelt* all four tombs excavated at Kokkalia are dated to LH IIA-IIIC, and Tombs I and III are stated to have had small side chambers and pits for secondary burial (*ArchDelt* 53; see also *AR* 51 [2004–2005] 55). However, the most recent publication (Dakoronia 2007b, 59) states that Tomb I is securely dated to LH IIB and not reused later and that the warrior burial in Tomb III dates to the same period (2007, 60).

[6] A different case of experimentalism is visible at Kokkinonyzes, near Kynos. A single monumental chamber tomb was constructed in LH IIB and in use until early LH IIIA1. This tomb is unusually large (chamber: 3.70 x 2.70 m, dromos: 8.50-m long) and well constructed, but its most unusual feature are the two wide benches running along the sides of the chamber.

interments: an interesting development suggesting that the warrior culture reached Kalapodi not before the custom of rock-cut chamber tombs.[7]

The two tombs at Kalapodi may well contain two warriors of different rank. Gold and other rich goods are abundant in both tombs: both contained high-status burials. The similarity of the tombs is further underscored by the presence of two "look-alike" seals (see Chapter 4), suggesting a close connection between the interred from both tombs. Yet the burial from Tomb III might denote a warrior of somewhat lower rank than that of Tomb I: he lacks sword and dagger and is equipped only with spear, arrows, and knives. He is thus not so much accorded warrior status as a general masculine status; if read biographically, this might be the assemblage of a hunter rather than of a warrior. Although spearmen are occasionally pitted against sword fighters in early Mycenaean iconography, bow and arrow are used to hunt the deer on the Shaft grave ring, and spears are used by hunters in palatial frescoes at, e.g., Pylos, Tiryns, and Orchomenos, as well as by a hunter in a fragment from LH I Agia Irini (Abramovitz 1980, 65 no. 83). Even the men fighting lions on the dagger from Shaft Grave IV at Mycenae do so with spears and bow and arrows, despite the fact that they are equipped with tower and figure-of-eight shields. The close association between hunting and warring has already been noted, and it seems likely that a continuum existed in which the first-rank warrior, equipped with sword, took place of pride, whereas lower-ranked warriors merged with hunters through an invisible dividing line.

Finally, at Marathon-Vrana and Thorikos on the east coast of Attica, early tholos tombs suggest the rise of elites as well. The Marathon tholos tomb contained two horse burials in the dromos and two cists in the floor, one with a gold cup; the cists are dated to LH IIB. Thorikos adopted the tholos tomb early, experimenting with shape until in LH IIA a real tholos tomb was built. Grave goods from the end of the LH I period include a gold sheet ornament in the shape of a butterfly (similar to examples from Shaft Grave III at Mycenae), two papyrus-shaped gold beads (with counterparts in Shaft Grave III), two circular gold sheets with an embossed griffin, a gold sheet with three rows of embossed spirals of a variety known from Mycenae, a small gold spoon (with counterparts in the early Mycenaean period in Messenia and Laconia), and a gold rod with octagonal section, the narrow central part of which is very similar to examples from Shaft Grave IV at Mycenae (Laffineur 2010, 714).

This brief overview suffices to show that the coasts of the Euboean Gulf area participated fully in the new warrior culture. At various sites, elites emerged and proclaimed their status by constructing monumental tombs, consuming luxury items, and emphasizing a warrior identity.

---

[7] This might in turn suggest a spread of rock-cut chamber tombs overland from Thebes, since rock-cut chamber tombs appear only later along the northern part of the Euboean Gulf.

THE WARRIOR'S BEAUTY

The occurrence of swords on the mainland coincides chronologically with the reinstatement of human depictions, which had been – with the notable exception of the Kolonna pithoi – completely absent on the mainland in the aniconic MH tradition, and was in the EH limited to coastal sites in Attica (Agios Kosmas) and Euboea (Manika), where Cycladic style figurines were occasionally interred with the deceased.

As the Type A sword was Minoan in origin, so was the common iconography. In Late Bronze Age I-II Crete seals and stone vessels commonly portray elite males with weapons or armor; the similarity in their hairstyles, dress, and emphasized musculature suggests that these males belonged to the same upper warrior class. The emphasized musculature and light, wiry body types are quintessentially Minoan and display what at the time was probably considered the ideal male body type. Although most Minoan depictions of males show this body type, exceptions such as the pudgy bronze figurine of a worshipper now in the British Museum (Higgins 1997, 137 fig. 168) show that this was not mere convention but imbued with meaning. The emphasis on the beauty of the male body, athletic, strong, and agile, is in line with the elaborate hairstyles, banded kilts, and groomed faces of these figures. Such an emphasis on external characteristics is in line with what Treherne calls the "warrior's beauty" (Treherne 1995): a warrior, as member of the elite, was recognizable not merely by his acts in combat but as much so by his appearance. Thus warrior graves often include items of personal adornment (seals, rings, and other jewelry) or grooming equipment (razors, combs); implements of grooming at Kalapodi may include a pair of tweezers and a rare silver ear scoop. Although Dakoronia argues for an interpretation of these items as medical equipment, they may also, as she notes, have been used for grooming purposes and this is perhaps more likely given the common presence of other grooming items in early Mycenaean tombs (Dakoronia 2007).

In the Shaft Graves at Mycenae, human representations are found in the form of gold death masks, and the material as well as the depositional context (including swords, ceremonial daggers, and a gold signet ring with a battle scene) indicate that here, too, wealth and prestige were dependent upon a military lifestyle (Kilian Dirlmeier 1988, 163). Indeed, since only Shaft Graves with swords contained other valuable goods, and since the number of valuable goods increases with the number of swords, an intimate connection between military prowess and wealth accumulation can be assumed (Kilian Dirlmeier 1988, 162–163): the accumulation of wealth and the accompanying claims of social and political leadership were made possible by military achievements. This "ethos of the sword" (Malafouris 2008, 5) is characteristic of the early Mycenaean period, mitigated only slightly by mechanisms of gift exchange and conspicuous consumption.

The focus on the individual is visible in the manner of burial as well. The Shaft Grave warriors were treated and fixed in death as beautiful individuals, even fixed in gold sometimes. In the Euboean Gulf area this glorification is less visible, but the two inhumations from Tombs I and III at Kalapodi were both laid out in extended position, like the Shaft Grave burials but unlike the contracted burials of the MH and, mostly, LH period in the region, allowing for a dramatic increase of the potential for individual display (Treherne 1995, 113; Sherratt 1994).

One striking feature of most warrior graves is the emphasis on weapons of attack. With the notable exception of boar's tusk helmets (which were themselves however symbolic of being a successful attacker, since the man-ufacturing of a single helmet required the killing of as many as 30 boars: Schofield 2007, 45), warrior implements found in graves are almost always of the offensive type only: sword, dagger, spear, even arrowheads are found frequently whereas the first greaves, arm protectors, and other defensive armor date to the beginning of LH IIIA1, when they accompanied the warrior in Chamber Tomb 12 at Dendra. Although it cannot be excluded that much protective armor was made of perishable materials such as leather or linen (Chadwick 1976, 160; Fortenberry 1991), the emphasis on offensive weapons is nevertheless striking and suggests that the symbolism of showing the deceased as a man of action, ready to fight, was more important than showing him as he would have appeared in real battle.

Even the actual battle costume of a Mycenaean warrior seems to have revolved around symbolism. The boar's tusk helmet suggests great hunting prowess. In addition, Fortenberry has drawn attention to the odd occurrence of single bronze greaves in Mycenaean graves as well as on fresco paintings and concludes that these greaves were worn only on the right leg as a sign of rank or status (Fortenberry 1991). The highly symbolic value of weaponry is also suggested by the discrepancy between skeletons suggesting battle damage and burials with weaponry, as noted for Mycenaean graves from Athens: six burials (five male and one female) included weaponry, whereas skeletal data suggest that three other males, from graves without weapons, suffered injuries "consistent with combat or interpersonal violence" (Kirkpatrick Smith 2009, 107). This suggests that at least at Athens, the high-status "warriors" were in fact not the ones doing the actual fighting, or at least not the fighting in actually dangerous, uncontrolled situations; that was left to lower ranking men, undistinguished in burial by any ostentatious grave goods. It seems likely that this was the common practice in the Late Bronze Age as through much of history. And if high-status warriors in fact mostly dueled with long swords in almost symbolic agonistic displays, wounds would be invisible on their skeleton. Such duels would make sense in a society in which status was tied up with being a warrior and, to some extent, fluid; the duels might be instrumental in determining individual status.

CHARIOTS: PART OF THE WARRIOR PACKAGE

An emphasis on horse-and-chariot is prominent at Mycenae, for example on several stelae from Grave Circles A (graves I, IV, V, ?VII, VIII, IX, and ?XI) and B (grave 13; see Younger 1997); the combat iconography on these stelae suggests that the importance of the horse for these early Mycenaean elites lay in its (symbolic) association with waging war, an association which may well have been taken over together with the chariot from Near Eastern elites, since the rocky Greek landscape lends itself poorly to the sort of chariot warfare that was common in Egypt and Anatolia. The horse-and-chariot has been identified as part of a "package" defining elite warrior aristocracies in the early to mid-second millennium BCE spreading from the Urals to central Europe and the Aegean (Kristiansen and Larsson 2007, 28). Although Kristiansen and Larsson have been criticized for imposing a grand narrative onto sometimes scanty evidence, and of ignoring the finer points of Aegean chronology (e.g., Harding 2006; Nordquist and Whittaker 2007), both the timing and the places where the first horse remains have been found correspond well with the idea that the horse-and-chariot was linked to the emergence of (warrior) elites. The first remains of horses themselves in Greece were found at MH Lerna in the Argolid and possibly at Nichoria and Malthi in Messenia (Drews 1988, 82), and it is tempting to suggest a link between these first MH appearances and the rise of early Mycenaean elites in these areas not much later.

Evidence from Mitrou suggests an elite interest in chariots echoing that visible in the Shaft Graves. One of the most intriguing finds from Mitrou is a northern import found in an LH I destruction layer in complex H (Maran and Van de Moortel 2014; Figure 2.5). It consists of a finely worked horse bridle piece made of deer antler; the curvilinear designs with which it is decorated suggest an origin in the Carpathian Basin (Harding 1984, 193).

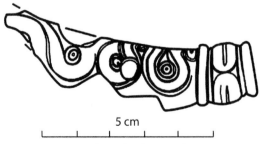

5 cm

FIGURE 2.5. Antler horse bridle piece from Mitrou, LH I. After Maran and Van de Moortel 2014, 534, figs. 6–7.

Bridle pieces such as this have been found in the Balkans and Greece, always in elite contexts, and often together with chariot pieces. In the case of the Mitrou bridle piece, the sharp serrated edges strongly suggest its use on a chariot-drawing horse (Maran and Van de Moortel 2014, 541). The bridle piece thus links the early elites at Mitrou with the pan-European phenomenon of an emerging warrior-aristocracy.

This artifact encapsulates the priorities of the early elites at Mitrou in two ways. First, it shows that its owner could afford that status symbol par excellence, the horse-and-chariot. Second, since the bridle piece was exotic, it proclaimed that these elites possessed knowledge of the world and suggested their control over long-distance exchange networks, leading automatically to an exalted status (Helms 1988). Helms' thesis, that contact with exotic regions increases local status, suggests the importance of weak ties with foreign lands. The chariot had its origins in the Near East, and Steel remarks that since the chariot motif was adapted from Near Eastern prototypes, "[i]ts popularity in the Aegean reflects the prestige and political advantage that the Mycenaean elite derived from esoteric knowledge of the lifestyle of Near Eastern royalty and nobility" (2006, 148). Although in the case of Mitrou the actual bridle piece has a northern origin, the observation that chariots were associated with esoteric knowledge remains valid. In the early Mycenaean period, the acquisition of foreign goods was an end in itself, serving to create a differentiation between those who did, and those who did not, possess them; foreign goods were by definition exotic and therefore prestigious (Burns 2010, 192–193), and they were acquired by living the life of a warrior (Kristiansen and Larsson 2007). The bridle piece thus functioned as a status symbol of a "warrior on the move" communicating with a distant other (Kristiansen and Larsson 2007; Schon 2010, 217); it would have been understood as exotic and evoked dim images of distant lands. This is an example of the exploitation of weak ties in which the weakness of the ties is a precondition for the prestige associated with them.

Horse-and-chariot iconography is not limited to battle scenes: a well-known gold signet ring from Shaft Grave IV at Mycenae depicts a chariot with two men, one of whom aims an arrow at a fleeing deer (CMS I 15). This suggests that chariots were not only associated with war, but also with hunting. That the hunt and battle were closely connected is suggested by the common headgear of both warriors and hunters in early Mycenaean iconography: the boar's tusk helmet. The common presence of boar's tusk helmets in MH III-LH I burials together with the representations of hunting suggest that prowess as a hunter was another essential quality in reaching high status in this early Mycenaean society. The significance of the boar's tusk helmet lies as much, if not more, in its symbolic message as in its protective value. Since as many as 60 tusks may have been needed for the construction of a single helmet (Schofield 2007, 45), it conveys a powerful message of masculine prowess. Male boars, with their sharp protruding tusks, are notoriously ferocious and unpredictable, and hunting them was a pastime worthy of the later Mycenaean palatial elites, as suggested by LH IIIB fresco fragments from Tiryns and Orchomenos. Thus wearing a boar's tusk helmet implied that the wearer was a skilled and fearless hunter and thus an intimidating opponent, someone to be feared in battle. Unsurprisingly, boar's tusk helmets are found in Mycenaean warrior graves (including the built tomb at Mitrou, where they date to LH IIIA) and are depicted on frescoes, seal stones, and ivory carvings from the inception of the Mycenaean culture through the high palatial period.

Just as the bridle piece symbolized knowledge of the exotic, hunting in farming societies is an activity that, since it takes place outside of the domestic, local, sphere and takes the participants into the potentially dangerous sphere of the wild outside or the sphere of the "other," provides exalted status (Helms 1993; the same is true for warriors). Thus hunters, warriors, and travelers or explorers (for lack of a better word) in general share similar associations and gain status because of their esoteric knowledge. It is therefore not surprising that boar's tusk helmets reference hunting as well as warfare; that warriors fight other warriors as well as lions (who are targets of the hunt, fierce opponents, and exotic: Thomas 1999); and that the exotic ivory may have invoked associations with boar's tusks. All these associations are entangled and wrapped up in a general masculine elite warrior package.

Ethnographically, the similarities between hunters and warriors are well attested since both are often expected to observe certain taboos (such as refraining from interaction with women) and take certain preparations (Rossman and Rubel 1989). Specific to hunters is their ability to connect the two spheres, domestic and "wild," since they bring the result of the hunt – meat – home to be consumed in a domestic setting. Given their ability to connect these two spheres, they are often seen as shamans who participate in and mediate between the two worlds (Helms 1993, 153–157). In Mycenaean iconography, hunting themes blur not only with those representing chiefs or warriors but also with those depicting "ritual makers," as Thomas has shown in a study focusing on lion hunting (Thomas 1999). Battle, the hunt, and ritual were all realms of specialized knowledge and thus of power.

It should be expected that ship captains and sailors, too, would incur high status because of their specialized knowledge allowing them to navigate to exotic places. Indeed, in the early Mycenaean period ships are, more than before, associated with warrior activities and depicted on high-status artifacts such as frescoes and metal and stone vessels (see pp. 50–54), although not to the same extent as swords, hunting, and the chariot.

FEASTS AND FEASTING

Given the symbolic importance of (game) meat, it is unsurprising that feasting, too, constitutes an important part of the elite warrior identity. In the Shaft Graves the importance of feasting and drinking is apparent from the large numbers of gold, silver, and bronze vessels and cups; an early Mycenaean fresco from Agia Irini seems to show the preparations for a feast, with cauldrons being heated above fires (Morgan 2005, 33 fig. 1.18). Other parts of the fresco show a helmeted hunter with a deer slung over a pole, and fragments from another wall show dogs pursuing deer (Morgan 1998, 204). In the scene with the tripod cauldrons, one man carries a large brown object to a kettle; although the exact identity of the amorphous object is unclear, it has been interpreted as venison by Ambramovitz (1980, 62), and the prominence of deer in the hunting scenes accompanying the tripod scene makes this a not unlikely supposition.[8] In the Euboean Gulf area, this importance of feasting and drinking manifests on a more modest scale: in pottery and bone fragments. Here the evidence from Mitrou is of great importance, since it constitutes the only evidence from a settlement context.

LH I evidence for feasting at Mitrou consists of a platform in an open area near Complex H (*AR* 2007–2008, 58). This building complex is of a size that precludes its use as a private residence: this is an example of monumental communal architecture as found on a larger scale in Kolonna's Large Building Complex, which dates to the advanced Middle Bronze Age with final use in the LH I period (Gauss and Smetana 2010). And just like the Large Building Complex at Kolonna housed large amounts of pottery and animal bones, at Mitrou the open area near Complex H served, judging from the animal bones found around it, as slaughter and preparation table for animals of different kinds, including deer. The high-quality fine tableware and the plastered floors in a large building complex (32 x 24 m) with walls made of cut field stones show that dining and drinking were serious affairs for which no effort was spared.

An LH I-IIA deposit of vessels used in communal feasting and drinking activities at Mitrou include an unpainted goblet, painted and unpainted Vapheio Cups, Aeginetan kraters, a locally made krater, and a selection of service, storage, and cooking vessels, among which are a lustrous decorated ewer, Aeginetan jugs, and a matt-painted hydria from Aegina or the Cyclades (Vitale 2013b). In this deposit, lustrous Mycenaean and Aeginetan wares dominate: the emerging elites at the site invested in state-of-the-art pottery of non-local derivation to impress their peers at symposia or similar drinking ceremonies, as they did on a grander scale at Mycenae (Wright 2004a). Since other pottery from this period is more mundane – Gray Minyan and

[8] Frescoes in LH IIIB Pylos likewise show hunters with dogs, men with tripods, and deer together.

Polychrome Matt-painted Wares continue to exist, and unpainted light-slipped Mycenaean pottery is common as well – it is clear that these symposia were the occasions where the living could display conspicuous consumption.

Ceremonial drinking and the consumption of alcohol is again part of the warrior package that is seen throughout Bronze Age Europe, and may have been one of the main means of creating and retaining a troop of warrior companions (Treherne 1995, 110). Drinking (and feasting) are common strategies for elites both to cement ties with the community and to reinforce the hierarchy (Wright 1995); it may refer to social storage (the host as provider of food and drink) but with the added implications of celebrating the host, the leader of a warrior band.

SHIPS AND COASTAL RAIDING

Although the coastal communities of the Euboean Gulf probably engaged actively in sailing, to date there is no evidence for this. Elsewhere the evidence is indirect, consisting of imported Aegean goods and pictorial references to ships and raiding. Maritime or, rather, coastal battles are popular themes on relief vessels and also occur on frescoes in the early part of the Late Bronze Age. By the LH I period, ships have made their way onto frescoes at Akrotiri and Agia Irini; bronze long boat models from Agia Irini resemble the lead models from the Early Bronze Age Cyclades (Wachsmann 1998, 102 figs. 6. 33–6.34). What is new about the way ships are depicted in the early phase of the Late Bronze Age is the narrative context in which they appear.

The miniature wall paintings from the West House in Akrotiri, dated to the Shaft Grave era, are the clearest example of this. On the north wall, long ships seem to attack a coastal settlement with a masonry building; naked warriors (enemies?) are defeated and drowning. The favorite weapon of these maritime warriors was the long lance: this is visible in the "shipwreck" scene in the North Frieze in the West House at Akrotiri. Long lances are prominently displayed: three of them are stacked in the bow of a ship, and a warrior on board holds a fourth. These long lances are also stored above the heads of the seated warriors on the South Frieze (Figure 2.6). In the *Iliad*, such maritime lances (*xusta naumacha*) appear twice, both times in book 15, and are singled out for their great length: in lines 387–389, the Greeks are "riding on their black ships, fighting up there with the long lances carried on board; these lances were well-assembled and their ends were covered with bronze." In line 677 the hero Ajax brandishes, apparently pacing the decks of several ships with long strides, a *xuston naumachon* 22 cubits (9.77 m) long made in sections and secured with metal rings. This description is reminiscent of the spear on the Battle in the Glen ring (Figure 2.3), which appears to be constructed in segments. The exaggeration of its length and the fact that the great hero Ajax uses the maritime lance suggest its importance. And although

FIGURE 2.6. Ship from the "Flotilla Fresco," south wall of the West House in Akrotiri. After Wedde 2000, no. 614.

the text of the *Iliad* is generally thought to have been fixed in its present form only in the eighth century BC, the hero Ajax "has every appearance of belonging to the early Mycenaean age" (West 1988, 158). In the Late Bronze Age pictorial record, the long lance is limited to the early Mycenaean period.

The ships are iconographically linked to the Kolonna ship (Wedde 2000); they may be the last step in an evolution of design starting with the Early Cycladic longboats (which were also probably used at least occasionally for raiding: Broodbank 1989). The south frieze shows that these ships could be paddled if needed, but since the paddlers lean awkwardly over the gunwale in order to reach the water (Figure 2.6), they were primarily meant to be sailed. The festive garlands suspended from the mast of the central ship and the conservative mode of propulsion suggest that these ships participate in a ceremonial event. Ships with awnings and a hull decoration of dolphins, as shown on the south frieze of the West House, are known from fresco fragments at Ayia Irini as well (Morgan 2005, 33 fig. 1.18). There, too, they appear in a celebratory setting: behind them, men are tending to their cauldrons.

On the North Frieze warriors, identified by their boar's tusk helmets and large body shields and carrying long spears, march in a file up to a hill where shepherds lead cattle and goats to a well that is also used by women carrying pitchers. Although these warriors carry swords in addition to spears, attention to their swords is minimal: only the ends of their scabbards are visible behind them. The role of these warriors is unclear: Warren identified them as the raiders, now diverting their attention to the cattle and the women as the objects of capture (Warren 1979), but since nobody in the fresco appears to be in the least disturbed by their presence, they may also represent intervening Mycenaean warriors who have just successfully repulsed the raiders (Morgan 1988, 153; Televantou 1994, 322–323).[9] Morris draws a parallel with the typical paratactic ordering present in the Homeric epics, with which she links the

---

[9] It should be noted that Televantou ascribes a Near Eastern, not an Aegean, locale to the events depicted on the frieze (Televantou 1994, 322–323). Morgan places it in the Aegean: 1988, 153.

FIGURE 2.7. Fragment of the silver Siege Rhyton, Shaft Grave IV. After Hood 1978, 161 fig. 155.

frieze (Morris 1989, 530–531). Either way, a story is depicted, even if its constituent elements do not always have a clear causal relationship to each other: we seem to witness a seaborne invasion involving a communal group of warriors with boar's tusk helmets.

The Akrotiri frescoes are the only frescoes depicting such seaborne raids, but the theme also appears on vessels of various materials and thus seems to have been popular elsewhere in the Aegean as well. The silver Siege Rhyton from Shaft Grave IV (Figure 2.7) suggests with its iconography a raid carried out by seafarers on a coastal town: the defenders of a walled Minoan town (horns of consecration are visible), naked (except for two figures on the right who wear body shields) and with short hair, attempt to ward off an attack with slings and bows. The creation of perspective by means of overlapping on this fragment is noteworthy: the cloaked figures seem to stand at the bottom of a hill that is placed in front of the town, partially obscuring its walls; the slingers and bowmen in turn are standing in front of the cloaked figures on cliffs.

Below the cliffs, on the bottom of the fragment, parts of five figures are preserved. The rightmost of these wears a plumed helmet and has been interpreted as punting a boat to the left (Hooker 1967, 269; the boat itself has not survived), but comparison with the Flotilla Fresco from the West House in Akrotiri suggests he may be a helmsman (see the leftmost standing figure in Figure 2.6). Four boar's tusk helmets in front of him presumably belong to occupants of the boat. These five figures, distinguished from all other figures by their helmets, have been interpreted as seaborne attackers. Although they move in the same directions as the presumed defenders, this might perhaps be explained by their being part of an invasion moving to the location of a beach, which is the target of the defenders. Without additional fragments, this remains an open question, but on a separate fragment, placed in restoration in front (i.e. our left) of the defenders, six naked figures are seen, perhaps swimming in the water. Another fragment, lower on the rhyton's body, displays a pattern representing shallow water and a rocky seabed with another swimmer (Morgan 1988, pl. 192). Thus, despite the popular name for the Siege Rhyton, what is depicted here may rather be the arrival of warriors by sea (an event that the artist seems to have placed in juxtaposition with the fight on the slope), suggesting a sudden landing by pirates and a hastily organized defense (Hooker 1967, 270). The fact that a Shaft Grave chief carried a rhyton with this theme to his grave suggests that the theme resonated with the early Mycenaean elites. The importance and value placed on this kind of activities by these Shaft Grave elites suggests at the same time one of the mechanisms by which they could accumulate much of the wealth found in their graves.

Similar raid scenes from Crete and Epidauros date probably to the same period: the inception of the Mycenaean culture.[10] An inlaid niello dagger from the Vapheio tomb (from an LH IIA context) preserves fragmentary swimmers that may represent victims of a raid (Younger 2011, 164). Inlaid daggers as a class of objects are limited to LH I-II (Papadopoulos 1998, 52) and can be taken as typical for the elite warrior culture.

Depictions on high-status artifacts from the early Mycenaean period thus suggest that coastal raiding by seaborne warriors was considered a suitable subject for depiction in the Aegean at this period. Moreover, since many of these scenes depict successful raids, the users and owners of these artifacts may have identified with the raiders, suggesting that raiding was viewed as heroic. Raiding scenes with drowning enemies, ships, and soldiers marching thus seem to have been a *topos* in the early part of the Late Bronze Age; Morris indeed links such narrative scenes with early Mycenaean epics (Morris 1989), and Ruijgh and West, to name the two most prominent exponents of the theory, have suggested that some traces of early Mycenaean epics are detectable in the *Iliad* (Ruijgh 1985, 1995, 2004; West

---

[10] See Warren 1979, 125–128. The Epidauros stone vase fragment was found in a disturbed context and may be of a later date (Sakellariou 1971, 3). Its type, style, and subject seem to connect it however to similar scenes from the beginning of the Late Bronze Age.

1988, 156–159). "Epic" in character or not, it is now for the first time that such *topoi* emerge – suddenly, it seems – and are immediately popular. These topoi link ships, warrior activities, and exotic (or otherwise high status) materials and objects.

It is likely, however, that coastal raids were not merely epic topoi but a reality in the early Mycenaean period and one of the means by which early Mycenaean elites gained riches and status. Younger adduces the presence of mundane elements such as the herders and water-carriers on the North frieze in the West House in Akrotiri to suggest that we are to imagine a real-life scene (Younger 2011, 173, 176). And although raiding is certainly not the only possible explanation for the "'hodge-podge' collection of showy trinkets" (Younger 2011) from various cultures (Minoan, Egyptian, Anatolian, Baltic) present in the Shaft Graves, it would account for this eclecticism neatly. At the very least, this eclectic character suggests that the mainland elites were themselves the drive behind these collections and collected this wealth in an anarchic system (Schon 2010): they actively created the long-distance ties. Wright conjectures that not much later they may have offered their services as warriors, either to control piracy or to increase security around the palaces (Wright 2008, 243). It is possible that such mercenaries are depicted on a later (LH IIIA) papyrus fragment from Amarna, which shows running figures wearing boar's tusk helmets; given the context of Egyptians fighting Libyans in other fragments, these figures have been interpreted as Mycenaeans fighting for the Egyptians (Schofield and Parkinson 1994). Such activities would have enabled these adventurers to amass exotic luxury items, which they then used to exalt their status at home, rising above their peer elites who did not have access to foreign luxury goods. This situation must have been highly competitive and dynamic, demanding ever increasing displays of status and conspicuous consumption.

CONCLUSIONS: THE EUBOEAN GULF COASTS IN THE EARLY MYCENAEAN PERIOD

Elites emerged at multiple centers along the Euboean Gulf following similar strategies as the better known centers in the Argolid: they built monumental tombs and accorded certain interments large amounts of movable wealth. They emphasized warrior prowess, feasts, and ceremonial drinking. Although not as spectacular as at Mycenae (or, for that matter, Thebes), Mitrou, Kalapodi, Chalkis, Lefkandi, and Dramesi all seem on a similar trajectory as these larger sites. The same is true for Thorikos, Marathon, and Skopelos.

The area of the Euboean Gulf thus shared fully in the creation of an elite Mycenaean culture in the beginning of the Late Bronze Age: sites show evidence for a warrior elite whose ethos was shared with the rest of the

Aegean. An emphasis on swords, scenes of combat, horses and chariots, and the hunt suggests an ethos focused on masculine values. This goes hand in hand with a focus on the individual. More than a simple "change in fashion" caused by contact with the artistically rich Minoan culture, this signifies a new awareness of the importance of the person, and more specifically of the warrior, who is now glorified. The warrior-hero as individual is visible on the Shaft Grave rings and seals (Figures 2.2; 2.3), which depict highly ritualized and highly personal duels. This emphasis on individuality is also visible in the graves of these early Mycenaeans, and is part of the "warrior package" expressing the identity of the emerging warrior aristocracy. In contrast, the Kolonna depictions of paddlers on a ship subsume the individual to the collective. And although Marinatos (1995, 39–40) has suggested that we can identify the captain of the fleet at Akrotiri, he is nevertheless as inconspicuous as the other members of the fleet.[11] A certain tension is thus visible between the warrior ethos glorifying the individual's prowess on the battlefield and iconography emphasizing the more corporate and cooperative nature of seafaring, where only the collective action of the sailors or rowers has the potential to make (or break) the venture. This difference becomes important in Chapter 6.

[11] One may also note that although the marching warriors on the North Frieze of the West House in Akrotiri carry swords as well as long lances (the tasseled scabbards are visible behind them), the swords are de-emphasized and the warriors march in a file and are as individuals distinguished only by the varied patterns on their oxhide shields and slight differences in helmet, neither of which singles out a certain individual. Perhaps swords were used only after the spear had been lost or group formations had fallen apart (Molloy 2010, 410); another possibility is that swords were used mainly in staged duels and had a largely ceremonial role (cf. Kilian-Dirlmeier 1993, 41). This is suggested by the "spectator" on the Battle of the Glen ring, by the "bloodletting" design of the sword, excellent for a spectacular display of skill and stamina, and by the decorative design of many swords found in graves, with gold-covered hilts and ivory or amber pommels.

3

THE ROLE OF ELITE NETWORKS
IN THE MYCENAEANIZATION
OF THE PROVINCES

This chapter offers a new perspective, rooted in network theory, on the early Mycenaean (LH I-IIA) settlement landscape in the Euboean Gulf area and on the process of Mycenaeanization outside of the core areas of the Argolid and Messenia. It explains why, despite the preponderance of warrior graves, there are apparently so few early Mycenaean settlements in Central Greece; why in the tholos tomb at Volos-Kapakli gold jewelry and ornaments seem to predate any Mycenaean (i.e. lustrous ware) pottery; and why, although to date no LH I pottery is known from the Volos area, LH I Vapheio Cups were evidently in use in Torone, further to the north (Cambitoglou and Papadopoulos 1991, 161, 165 fig. 22; 166 fig. 23; Cambitoglou and Papadopoulos 1993).

EMERGING CENTERS: EARLY MYCENAEAN NETWORKS

Despite the emergence of regional centers, a comparison of settlement distributions maps for the MH and the LH I-IIA periods in Central Greece leaves one with the impression that habitation plummeted in the early Mycenaean period (Figures 3.1 and 3.2; see also Phialon 2011, maps 2–7): the density of MH sites along the Euboean Gulf is between three and six times higher than that of LH I-IIA sites, and only in LH IIIA do we find a number of sites comparable to that in the Middle Bronze Age. Even accounting for the shorter duration (about two centuries, rather than four) of LH I-II compared to MH, there are far fewer sites in LH I-II than one might expect. These maps suggest that the Euboean coasts and their immediate hinterlands were virtually deserted in the early Mycenaean period. Yet, the evidence for emerging centers seems to argue against a picture of decline or depopulation.

Although a certain amount of centralization might be held responsible for the disappearance of sites, a scenario in which more than 65 percent (and possibly as much as 80 percent) of all sites disappears, only to reappear two centuries later, is unlikely. Thus explanations taking the lack of LH I-II material at face value are unsatisfactory. Already Sackett and his team,

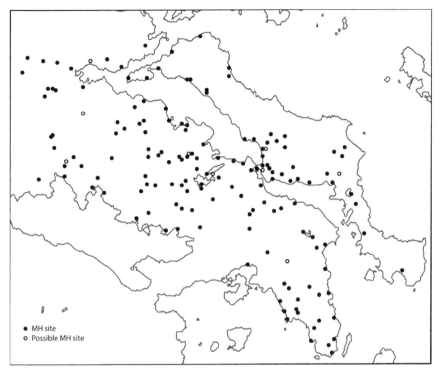

FIGURE 3.1. MH sites in Central Greece. Adapted from Phialon 2011, carte 6.

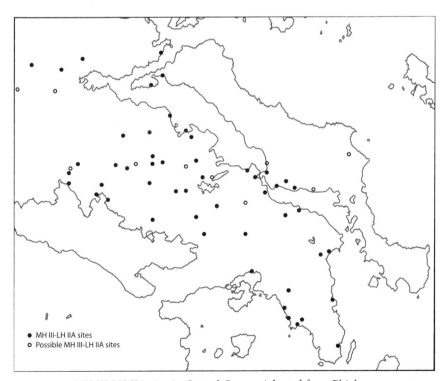

FIGURE 3.2. MH III-LH IIA sites in Central Greece. Adapted from Phialon 2011, carte 7.

noticing the scarcity of LH I-II material on Euboea, assumed continuity for most Euboean sites that have both MH and LH III material (Sackett et al. 1966, 99–102), and they were certainly correct. Most convincing explanations for the scarcity of LH I-II material are rooted in survey mechanics and the limitations of the method. Almost all sites with an apparent habitation gap in LH I-II are sites known only from survey, suggesting that the method of investigation is at least partially to blame. Rutter has pointed out that certain periods – LH I and II among them – tend to be consistently underrepresented in survey material, probably because these sherds do not survive as well as sherds from other periods or are not so easily recognizable or because these periods are very short and therefore produced little material to begin with (Rutter 1983). The discrepancies in recovered evidence from casual (extensive) survey, fine-grained survey, and excavation are clear in the case of Mitrou's LH I phase. Fossey, after casual survey, reported only MH and LH IIIA-C (Fossey 1990a, 50). Intensive survey detected an important LH I phase: the records from the CHELP surface survey show that the LH I pottery there, though forming only a small percentage of the total diagnostic pottery recovered, was distinctive and included a large percentage of Vapheio Cup fragments suggesting the presence of an elite concerned with drinking (Kramer-Hajos and O'Neill 2008, 198–204). But excavation was necessary to get a clear indication of the importance of the LH I phase at Mitrou, with emerging elites importing exotic goods as well as ideas from the wider Aegean and erecting monumental structures (Van de Moortel 2007, 247–248). Bintliff and his colleagues went as far as to suggest, based on their survey data from Boeotia, that entire periods remain "hidden" from us; they coined the "hidden landscape" phrase (Bintliff et al. 1999). Their explanation for this was twofold: first certain periods produce sherds that disintegrate easily or, even if they do not disintegrate, are barely recognizable as sherds; second, settlement patterns differed in different periods so that periods in which settlement was nucleated tend to be more easily recognizable, producing a clear "on" or "off" pattern, whereas periods in which settlement was dispersed are less recognizable in the survey record, producing varying shades of gray on the survey map.

The combination of Rutter's and Bintliff's factors goes a long way to explain the ubiquity of MH sites on the maps: MH Gray Minyan Ware is hard fired and virtually indestructible, immediately recognizable, and represents the preferred fine ware for about four centuries. In the early Mycenaean period, on the other hand, most vessels continued to be made in the MH traditions: in excavated assemblages from Central Greece, quantities of Gray Minyan, Matt-painted and Polychrome Matt-painted, and burnished, pale unpainted pottery greatly outnumber lustrous painted pottery (Mountjoy 1993, 33). It is, however, the lustrous pottery that is most easily recognizable as certainly LH I-IIA (as opposed to possibly MH), even from small, featureless sherds; small body sherds, as one is apt to encounter in surface surveys, of vessels that are rooted in MH traditions can easily be misattributed to the MH period. Only recently has it become possible to distinguish MH unpainted fine and coarse wares from LH ones, resulting in a gross under-estimation of LH I-II sites on maps that are based on older surface survey results.

The problem of difficult-to-attribute sherds has been taken up more recently by Schon. Analyzing the numbers of ceramics collected in the Eastern Korinthia Archaeological Survey, Schon concludes that if only those sherds that are securely datable are taken into account, LH I-IIA shows a pronounced "dip" in numbers, consistent with the observed scarcity of this period in Central Greece. However, if sherds that *may* date to this period are included, there is, in contrast, a great increase from MH numbers, almost equal to the LH III peak (Schon 2011, 235–236, figs. 2 and 3): although *certain* evidence for LH I-IIA suggests scarce settlement, the *possible* evidence suggests instead dense settlement. When Schon corrects for, respectively, duration of each period and relative proportions of securely dated finds, the LH I-IIA numbers are not as impressive as in the uncorrected method, but still surpass those for the MH (Schon 2011, 238, figs. 6 and 7).

A real scarcity of sherds thus underlies the virtual absence of sites from the early Mycenaean period; however, this is not a scarcity of sherds belonging to the time period but a scarcity of sherds of a certain ware that are immediately recognizable as belonging to the time period. If the picture is extended to include a proportion of all those unpainted sherds that *might* be LH I-IIA, the number of LH I-IIA sites is more in accordance with our expectations. This suggests that in the LH I-II period there is a divergence of sites, in which some sites gain prominence and are visible by characteristic early Mycenaean assemblages, whereas the vast majority of sites retain an essentially MH character and are therefore "missed" in surface surveys: dramatically new lustrous painted fine ware was limited to a mere handful of sites. An example from Euboea is Aidepsos-Koumbi, where an LH I phase was recognized by "at least one pot that resembles matt painted ware" (Whitley 2002–2003, 48). Had but a fragment of this vessel been found in a surface survey, it might easily have been attributed to the MH phase. This site, therefore, on present evidence (which is, admittedly, preliminary), was inhabited in LH I without producing or importing that marker of early Mycenaean culture, lustrous ware. In addition, Hankey notes that some pots from the tombs at Chalkis-Trypa "look and feel like Minyan," and that the fabric of many LH I-II vessels is "in the Minyan technique": even at sites where lustrous ware is attested, much of the pottery retains its MH character (Hankey 1952, 54; see also Mountjoy 1993, 33). The same is true for Mitrou (Kramer-Hajos and O'Neill 2008, 198), and in Attica, too, with the exception of coastal Thorikos, most sites retained a strong MH character well into the LH period

(Papadimitriou 2010).[1] Contrary to what our maps suggest, we should thus not imagine an empty countryside in the early Mycenaean period, but a densely populated one, where most sites however continued to look like they had done for centuries.

Why and how did this happen? The competition between emerging early Mycenaean elites grew organically out of the MH societies when the mainlanders increased contact with Crete. This contact privileged coastal sites: Thorikos, Lefkandi, Dramesi, Chalkis, and Mitrou are all coastal sites near or on the Euboean Gulf where early Mycenaean elites emerged; a maritime network connected these sites to the southern mainland, Aegina, Keos, and Crete. The situation in Attica serves as a useful comparison: whereas west of Mt. Hymettus only "Athens and Eleusis appear as large settlements, situated within seemingly 'empty' plains" in the early LBA, in eastern Attica "several fortified citadels hint at a high level of competition between peer polities" (Privitera 2013, 173).

The Cretan ties of Chalkis in LH I-II are visible in the pottery from these tombs, which includes an alabastron that seems to be an imitation of an alabaster vase; a bridge-spouted jug (a Cretan shape); an LH IIA stirrup jar in palatial style and of a fabric suggesting it may have been imported from Laconia or Kythera (Figure 3.3); an LH IIA deep cup decorated with scale

5 cm

FIGURE 3.3. Chalkis-Trypa, LH IIA stirrup jar with three handles and figure-8 shield decoration, import from Laconia/Kythera or local fabric. H. 0.155, D. 0.165 m. After Hankey 1952, 79 fig. 4.

---

[1] The same was argued by Pavúk in a paper given at the 4th Archaeological Meeting of Thessaly and Central Greece, 2009–2011, in Volos, March 2012.

pattern and a monochrome interior, in Minoan fashion, suggesting Minoan influence; and an LH IIA squat jug of Minoan shape, a type which is equally rare in Boeotia and Euboea, but common in the Peloponnese.[2] This suggests that LH I-IIA Chalkis was part of a network with links to the south, and given the lack of strong parallels with contemporary pottery from Thebes, it is reasonable to assume that the network's links used the maritime route of the Euboean Gulf. LH I and IIA pottery from Mitrou suggests it was part of the same network: an LM I cup found at Mitrou suggests that this network was in place already in the LH I period, and an LH IIA sherd from a piriform jar with a clearly Minoanizing octopus or Argonaut shows its continued importance (Kramer-Hajos and O'Neill 2008, 201; Kramer-Hajos 2008, 77). Given Chalkis' location on the Euripos it is likely that Chalkis was a node with ties both to the southeast and the northwest.

Like these Cretan influences, lustrous ware – essentially a Minoan–Mycenaean hybrid – too, is limited to a select number of centers. Inspired by Minoan pottery, the lustrous LH I and II wares are of Mycenaean manufacture and characterized by lustrous dark motifs on a light-slipped background. The distribution of Mycenaean lustrous ware allows us to begin to model the sort of networks and their transformation in the early Mycenaean period. The lustrous LH I-II ware represents the early Mycenaean ware *par excellence*.[3] Almost all lustrous LH I pottery belongs to cups or other shapes associated with drinking, an elite activity allowing for cementation of social bonds as well as emphasizing social differences (see Chapter 2). This new Mycenaean style, influenced by Minoan pottery, traveled via Kythera to Laconia and the Argolid on the mainland (Dickinson 1977, 108, note 2; Mountjoy 1993, 5). By the end of the LH I phase it is found everywhere in the Peloponnese, apart from Arcadia and Achaea, and more sporadically in south-central Greece in Attica, Boeotia, Phokis, and Euboea (Mountjoy 1993, 5). On Euboea, the earliest lustrous ware is dated to LH I-II at Lefkandi.[4] LH IIA lustrous ware is known from Amarynthos, Chalkis, Manika, and Aidepsos-Koumbi, where sherds decorated with figure-of-eight shields were recovered.[5] Mitrou has significant amounts of it (Kramer-Hajos and O'Neill 2008, 200), but it did not reach Volos until LH IIB (Mountjoy 1999, 24; 823, no. 103). However, at Torone in the Chalkidike, LH I Vapheio Cups were used.[6] It has

[2] See, respectively, Hankey 1952, 54, no. 402A; Hankey 1952, 55, no. 539; Mountjoy 1999, 695, 698; Hankey 1952, no. 544, pl. 20; and Hankey 1952, no. 539, pl. 24.

[3] Other, much more common, fine wares in the early Mycenaean period (burnished unpainted wares, Mainland Polychrome Matt Painted) are rooted in MH traditions.

[4] Evely 2006, 91; Sackett et al 1966, 100 fig. 25, nos. 2, 5, 6, and 7.

[5] Amarynthos: Sackett et al. 1966, 100 fig. 25, no. 4. Chalkis: Hankey 1952. Manika: Sackett et al. 1966, pl. 13d (a shallow cup with hatched loop). Aidepsos-Koumbi: Whitley 2002–2003, 48.

[6] Cambitoglou and Papadopoulos 1991, 161, 165 fig. 22; 166 fig. 23; Cambitoglou and Papadopoulos 1993; see also Jung 2010).

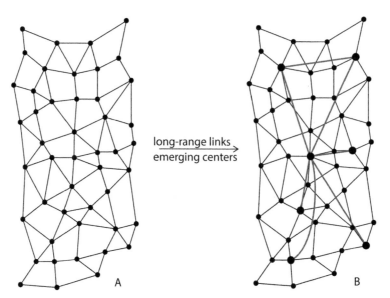

long-range links
emerging centers

A   B

FIGURE 3.4. Schematic representation of MH and LH I sociopolitical network dynamics along the Euboean Gulf. A: distributed (mesh-like) MH network. B: the elite network (overlaid in gray) between emerging centers exists separately from the mesh-like network in LH I. Depiction of network types adapted from Baran 1964, 2, fig.1.

been suggested that Torone functioned as an "emporion," a gateway to the north (Morris 2009–2010). Because of its "betweenness" – its crucial role in connecting the Aegean to an overland network in the Balkans (see p. 63) – it connected to the network of lustrous ware and received lustrous pottery earlier than Volos.

Despite its wide spread from south to north, LH I distribution coverage was thus far from complete: Mountjoy notes that "even in the Argolid [LH I lustrous pottery] was not common outside the main centers" (Mountjoy 1999, 20). This suggests that LH I lustrous ware traveled from hub to hub, bypassing most nodes (sites) in the network.[7] This implies an emerging network of scale-free (decentralized) type (Figure 3.4b). The elite character of this network is borne out by the prevalent LH I lustrous pottery shapes: Vapheio Cups are the most common.

The distribution of these early Mycenaean wares indicates that they spread via maritime routes, among them the Euboean Gulf system. The Euboean Gulf had functioned already in the Middle Bronze Age as a sailing route between the southern Aegean and Central Greece, as attested by fragments of Minoan Kamares pottery at Pevkakia Magoula near Volos (Rutter and Zerner 1984, 82, nos. 6 and 9) and at Mitrou (*AR* 2006–2007, 43), suggesting

---

[7] A similar pattern is visible in the distribution of tomb types: at rural, isolated Loukisia, cist tombs (a MH form) were used as late as LH IIB when at coastal Chalkis, Mitrou, and Kynos, chamber tombs were already in use.

the existence of a Minoan maritime trade route of the Old Palace period between Euboea and the Central Greek mainland to Thessaly. This route may have been disturbed during the turmoil of the MH-LH transition, given the complete absence of LH I pottery around the Gulf of Volos. This complete absence and the rare LH IIA vessels there, all imports, suggest that the Mycenaean culture did not spread this far north during LH I-IIA. Even at Glypha-Phanos, on the Strait of Oreoi, the LH IIA phase is represented by a single imported squat jug decorated with hatched loop; all other pottery is non-Mycenaean (Papakonstantinou 1999, 175 fig. 8). LH I and IIA pottery from coastal Mitrou, on the other hand, is uncommon but not unique, and similar to contemporary pottery from Boeotia and southern Greece.

Yet, at Volos-Kapakli a gold leaf ornament depicting a tripartite shrine is likely to date to LH I, based on parallels in Shaft Graves III and IV, and a cloisonné piece with a griffin may be of LH I date as well (Avila 1983, 51; Laffineur 2003, 83). This suggests that the consumption of elite Minoanizing objects precedes the consumption of Mycenaean pottery, possibly because emerging elites in the Volos area connected to elite networks in order to enhance their status at home, acquiring only small high-prestige items. This also suggests that the network of early Mycenaean lustrous pottery was not the same as that of (metal) prestige goods, even if both were limited to elites. Finally, it suggest that whereas Torone received lustrous pottery because of its betweenness centrality, the Volos area had a rather different function in the network: rather than functioning as a bridge or a gateway community, it may have connected to an elite network of prestige goods in order to enhance the status of local emerging elites. Simplified, one might say that Torone shows up on the LH I map because of its location in the network, whereas Volos owes its participation in the network to the emergence of local elites.

Pottery suggests that the ties with the southern Aegean become stronger at Mitrou in LH IIA, and this comes at the expense of the local, non-Mycenaean tradition. Mycenaean pottery from Mitrou is being studied by Salvatore Vitale, who has produced several preliminary accounts (Vitale 2011, 2013a, 2013b). For the LH IIA period, he distinguishes five classes: local fine pale unpainted, Mainland Polychrome Matt-painted, Mycenaean lustrous painted (local and imported), imported Aeginetan pottery, and local (hand-made and wheel made) cooking pottery. The local classes are the most common, as one would expect. Aeginetan ware is only occasionally attested in LH I but much more common in LH IIA, suggesting that the ties (links) with Aegina became stronger (more intensive) in the LH IIA period. Of the decorated wares, Mainland Polychrome Matt-painted is the most common in LH I, but hardly existent in LH IIA when it is supplanted by lustrous ware. The Mainland Polychrome Matt-painted has its roots in the matt-painted vessels of the MH regional tradition; the lustrous LH IIA in the Minoan-inspired southern tradition. Thus local wares start declining in LH IIA, indicative of an element of discontinuity with pre-Mycenaean traditions, when influence from the south (the Argolid?) becomes more prominent. Ties with the south thus change the style of pottery until it becomes stylistically indistinguishable from southern Mycenaean pottery.

Not only is LH I pottery not distributed equally over all sites, in addition it is very rare even at sites where it does occur. The vast majority of the early Late Bronze Age ceramics at any site is of the MH tradition. We need to remember here that the nodes in the network are not, strictly speaking, the settlements but the human actors within a settlement. It is likely that only some people in any given settlement would create, maintain, and exploit long links (weak ties): in other words, new and "exotic" material is going to be limited in distribution even within settlements where it does show up. If we assume continuity of habitation, it follows that LH I ware (or the knowledge of creating it) traveled from hub to hub, bypassing most nodes (sites) in the network and creating a decentralized network. The formation of a decentralized network tends to correspond to the emergence of a small-world network, defined as a system in which most nodes are not neighbors of one another, but most nodes can be reached from every other node by a small number of steps, enabling new fashions to spread rapidly. However, it appears that in this transitional LH I period, the innovations brought in via the "weak ties," though spreading reasonably rapidly between hubs through the southern and central Greek mainland, were not shared with most local sites. This suggests that the network was actively exclusionary, which can be explained if it was an essentially elite network of peer-polity interactions: the emerging elites had a vested interest in circulating prestige goods, including Minoanizing pottery, only among themselves during this early stage of status creation (Voutsaki 1995, 1997).

Like Minoanizing pottery, burial customs, too, spread irregularly rather than gradually. The LH I-IIA chamber tombs at Chalkis-Trypa are contemporary with similar tombs at Thebes. The earliest rock-cut chamber tombs on the coasts north of Chalkis date to LH IIB and are found at Agia Triada (associated with the settlement at Mitrou) and Kokkinonyzes, near Kynos. The northern part of the Euboean Gulf area thus lagged behind the southern part by very roughly a century. More significantly, while the people at Mitrou and Kynos started carving out chamber tombs at Agia Triada and Kokkinonyzes, at Loukisia, as at Glypha, the deceased were still buried in cist tombs. This suggests that the spread in customs northward affected first the major coastal hubs, which are characterized by excellent locations and high connectivity; from there the new customs then trickled more slowly into these sites' hinterland, to the less well-connected smaller sites, and spread throughout the region. A hierarchy of sites can thus be established, distinguishing minor and less connected sites from better connected, major sites such as

Chalkis and Mitrou. In the LH I-II phases, not all sites share in the innovations visible at the coastal centers.

I ascribe this, as well as the sparse distribution of lustrous ware, to the exclusionary character of the early Mycenaean elite networks. Lustrous ware, and other innovations, may have traveled only between peer-polities of emerging elites. The peer-polity interaction between the emerging elites created a small world, in which geographically remote sites were in contact with each other directly or via very few intermediaries that functioned as hubs in the network (Figure 3.4b). These long-distance contacts allowed the introduction of new forms of material culture to spread quickly over large distances.[8] These elite indicators did however not spread to neighboring sites, because the elite network was closed and actively exclusionary: the long-distance ties were not shared with local sites but limited to elite centers. Thus in the early Mycenaean period there was the potential to create a small-world network, but this potential was not immediately realized. Instead, there were several different networks, which overlapped spatially but were otherwise separate: an elite network through which, for example, Minoanizing pottery flowed, another elite network of (metal) prestige goods, and a non-elite network.

Since most sites were completely unaffected by the elite exchanges taking place between the hubs, they are, as far as the material record is concerned, barely distinguishable from MH sites. These sites were far from isolated: in fact, the similarity of Gray Minyan shapes, for example, suggests that they were connected with each other in a dense mesh, influenced by their nearest neighbors, but not forming part of the elite network. These non-elite networks must have been already in place in the MH and can be visualized as of a distributed (mesh-like) type (Figure 3.4a). They are characterized by many strong ties, providing a relatively stable, consolidated common culture with similar types of pottery, burial customs, and architecture in large regions and over a large period of time; changes travel slowly in such distributed networks. As there are no large differences between settlements in terms of status, so, too, is there an absence of status differentiation within the settlement (cf. Voutsaki 2010a, 88–91): networks tend to repeat themselves on different scales (so-called pattern propagation, well-known from fractals: see Malkin 2011, 45). The graphs in Figure 3.4 visualize the social networks in MH and LH I-II; the LH I-II situation is here visualized by overlaying an elite network, characterized by long-distance links, over the preexisting dense mesh. I should emphasize again that this is

---

[8] Such long-distance contacts were almost certainly less frequent (less intense, or strong) as contacts with nodes nearby. In network jargon such infrequent long-distance links are known as "weak ties" (Granovetter 1973). In this book, I refrain from adding weight to links in my models since datasets are too incomplete to quantify this; I do, however, recognize the utility of the theoretical concept of the strength of weak ties, and early Mycenaean elite networks are an instance in which their strength is clear.

a schematic representation of reality: the geometric position of the dots repre-senting nodes, as well as the length and shape of lines graphically representing links, carry no information.

Although the two were spatially related, both networks seem to have existed separately from each other. This then provides not only an explana-tion for the virtual discrepancy between the density of MH and LH IIIA sites, on the one hand, and the scarcity of LH I-II sites on the other, it also explains why traditional MH wares continued to be so common throughout the early Mycenaean period. Only at a small minority of settlements would we notice the winds of change, with emerging elites engaging in displays of status by using new forms of pottery and "exotic" goods such as seal stones, jewelry, and warrior implements, representative of their far-flung contacts with the southern mainland, the Cyclades, and Crete. These are the cultural forms that we recognize as Mycenaean: initially, Mycenaean culture was limited to elites (so, too, Feuer 2011, 515), who managed to assimilate the new culture by engaging in exchange with their peers. In other words, it was the exploitation of networks that allowed for the creation of Mycenaean culture; as Parkinson and Galaty suggested (2007, 123), an increase in trade (in other words, intensification in long-distance relations, or an increase in weak ties) allowed for the emergence of Mycenaean society, rather than the other way around. One could argue that there was thus no "Mycenaean identity" common to all inhabitants of a site; what we recognize as Mycenaean was limited to elites, who managed to assimilate the new culture by engaging in exchange with their peers. The active manipulation of networks was absolutely essential in the elite Mycenaean identity-forming process, as it would be much later, in LH IIIB, for the palatial elites at Thebes (see Chapters 5 and 6).

The prepalatial network was not one-directional: evidence from Mitrou and Antron, among other places, suggests that the same route served to disseminate material culture from north to south. The horse-bridle piece from Mitrou with parallels with the Carpathian Basin, already mentioned in Chapter 2, is one of a number of wave-band decorated objects that have been found in the eastern regions of southern and Central Greece. Their distribu-tion suggests a sailing route through the Euboean Gulf and north to Torone and Agios Mamas before turning into an overland route to the Balkans and Central Europe (Maran and Van de Moortel 2014, 541–543). Amber beads, gold, and disk and rod toggles may have reached the early Mycenaean elites via the same route. Since Balkan imports are rare in the Aegean, it is probable that this piece was acquired by Mitrou's elites without Aegean intermedi-aries. The bridle piece is one of only a highly select assemblage of extra-Aegean imports on the Greek mainland in LH I-II contexts, and suggests that the elites at Mitrou made the most of their northern location.[9] In addition, an

[9] Cline (1994) lists fewer than 50 extra-Aegean imports to LH I-II Greece.

LH I bronze wheel-headed pin from Grave 46 of the grave circle at Antron (Glypha) belongs to a type originating in eastern-central Europe (Papakonstantinou 1999, 178 fig. 16; Ruppenstein 2010). Such pins are heavily concentrated in southern Germany and Central Europe (Ruppenstein 2010, 644 fig. 2). A similar pin was found in Mycenae's Shaft Grave Ypsilon in Grave Circle B, and since Grave Circle B also included at least two imported vessels of a reddish-yellow burnished ware that is typical in the Magnesia peninsula, the Spercheios Valley, and Phthiotis, it is likely that Euboean Gulf sites like Mitrou owed their prominence in the early Mycenaean period at least partially to their participation in the maritime network and their function as gateway communities between the central European and the southern Aegean cultures. The existence of such a route is also suggested by the early presence of LH I ware, exclusively Vapheio cups, at Torone.

The increasing visibility of important individuals – the emerging elites – corresponds to the increasing hierarchical differences between sites. As strong leaders emerged on the intra-site level, so hubs emerged on the regional level: on different scales, networks played out the same way (pattern propagation). Similarly, the scarcity of LH I lustrous ware on a regional scale is repeated on the intra-site level: the vast majority of the ceramics from the early Mycenaean period at any Central Greek site is of the MH tradition. Both phenomena are fueled by the greater access to prestige goods; underlying them is an increasing emphasis on the individual at the expense of corporate identities and strategies.

Rather than nucleation or even depopulation, we should thus assume a situation of increasing differentiation between few hubs and many less well-connected nodes – in network terms, scale-free network growth or "the rich get richer" phenomenon: once a site is a center, or a hub, other nodes are more likely to connect to it (a process known as preferential attachment). This leads to a process of increasingly prominent hubs: with each site centering on an existing hub, that hub becomes more attractive as a hub to link to for other sites, in turn increasing its attractiveness further. This process can be seen during the later MH and the early LH periods, when a distributed network consisting of nodes of the same size and importance starts changing into a decentralized network: certain sites (e.g., Orchomenos, Thebes, and, on a smaller scale, Lefkandi or Mitrou) become centers that grow out into major hubs in a relatively short period of time. This mechanism also describes the "sudden" prominence of Mycenae: its connections increased dramatically, resulting in higher status, which in turn led to an even greater number of connections.

THE MICROSCALE: POTTERY PRODUCTION AT MITROU

How did early Mycenaean potters learn to produce the standard Mycenaean lustrous ware? The large range of wares from early Mycenaean Mitrou suggests a potter community learning by experimenting. The varieties of pottery characterizing early Mycenaean Mitrou suggest intensive proximal contacts between potters or at least materials, as modeled in simplified terms for Minoan Prepalatial-Palatial Crete by Knappett (2011, 74–82). The occurrence of Mycenaean shapes in Gray Minyan fabric (Kramer-Hajos and O'Neill 2008, 198–199), or in local fine orange fabric (Vitale 2009), for example, suggests local potters interacting with and consciously imitating new forms while using their traditional medium. Since most lustrous ware was used for drinking cups, it may have been an obvious adoption for the wheel-throwing, goblet-producing Gray Minyan potters. The occurrence of handmade lustrous ware (Vitale 2009) is odd and suggestive of local potters who specialized in hand-building their vessels (typically reserved for household pottery, larger storage vessels, and jugs and jars) and now tried their hand at a new decorative tradition. It is possible that potters of the Mainland Polychrome Matt-painted tradition, who typically hand-built their vessels, thought that decorated pottery ought to be their domain and learned the specialized lustrous painting technique from lustrous ware potters. Slipping of lustrous ware (Vitale 2009) could be due to local potters trying to imitate lustrous prototypes faithfully, but it could also suggest "foreign" artisans doing the best they could with local clays. It should be noted that the first two examples (Gray Minyan and orange unpainted imitations of new Mycenaean shapes) constitute a different manner of interaction with the new Mycenaean material than the latter two (hand building and slipping of lustrous ware): the latter suggest attempts to recreate as faithfully as possible the desired original, using different methods (a different process with a similar end result), while the former represent new, hybrid forms that are inspired by the new Mycenaean wares without aiming for a faithful reproduction.

The amount of experimentation and crossover taking place in the early Mycenaean period suggests interaction between different groups of potters: the networks represented by LH I-II wares within Mitrou are rather fluid. Some may be the result of face-to-face interaction with potters skilled in producing early Mycenaean lustrous ware; others represent reactions of potters to *material*. Vapheio Cups, and lustrous ware in general, were entangled in a web of feasting, drinking, and elite associations, and since these entanglements were with Gray Minyan ware earlier, Vapheio Cups and Gray Minyan ware hybridized occasionally: they were used for the same functions and perhaps made by the same potters, and therefore combine features.

CONCLUSIONS

By providing an explanatory framework for the general absence of clearly identifiable lustrous Mycenaean LH I ware, the virtual discrepancy between the density of MH and LH IIIA sites, on the one hand, and the scarcity of LH I-II sites, on the other, is explained. The proposed mechanism suggests that the active manipulation of networks was absolutely essential in the Mycenaean identity-forming process. I suggest that the spread, as well as the limited distribution, of cultural assemblages that are recognizably Mycenaean in the LH I-II periods is largely due to the exploitation of weak ties (sporadic long-distance contacts).

It seems that at least two network types coexisted in the early Mycenaean period: an elite network of an emerging decentralized type, creating a small world of peer polities held together by weak ties, in which prestige goods were circulating, versus a non-elite network. The weak ties exploited by the elite networks had little to no effect on the culture of the surrounding area, since the actors of the two networks moved in different social circles. Thus the networks of circulating materials did not interact and the goods, knowledge, and customs acquired by the superregional contacts did not trickle down into the regional network of smaller sites. The exploitation of weak ties resulted in a change in elite *habitus*, and allowed the emergence of an elite class. The exotica acquired via the long-distance weak ties legitimized the elevated status of the emerging elites.

4

SEALS AND SWORDS AND CHANGING IDEOLOGIES

The LH IIIA period is a transitional one, in which the chiefdoms that were formed in the early Mycenaean period underwent, in some regions, the transition to states: social–political organizations with a centralized and internally specialized administration. This resulted in a greater differentiation between chiefdoms that made this transition to state versus those that did not; in regional, rather than intra-settlement competition and instability; in a restriction of warrior display; and in increased differentiation between second- and third-tier settlements as prominent chiefs vied with competitors for loyalty of regional elites. In the provincial area of the Euboean Gulf coasts and their hinterland all these are visible.

THE CREATION OF A SMALL-WORLD NETWORK IN LH IIIA1

Evidence from settlements and cemeteries alike points to a change in network structure taking place between the early Mycenaean prepalatial period (LH I-II) and the LH IIIA1 period. Mycenaean cultural markers – especially pottery, but also tombs – are found throughout the region in LH IIIA. This spread suggests that the early elite centers now functioned as hubs in the local networks as well (Figure 4.1b). The smaller sites realigned their ties to these hubs (via preferential attachment) and characteristic traits of the Mycenaean culture now dispersed quickly throughout the hinterland. Thus in LH IIIA a "Mycenaean identity" encompassed not just a few elites but most or all inhabitants of most or all sites.

This change in network structure is not limited to the Euboean Gulf area; it happens elsewhere on the mainland as well. The dispersal of amber gives a good idea of what is happening. Although the compilation of the evidence for amber in the Mycenaean world by Harding et al. (1974) is now outdated, especially for the region of Central Greece, their general findings continue to hold up. They show how amber beads in Mycenaean burial assemblages steadily decline in number through the LH IIIA period: a staggering amount

TABLE 4.1. *Numbers of amber beads (after Harding et al. 1974)*

Late Helladic	I	II	IIIA	IIIB	IIIC	Submycenaean
Find-places	9	19	16	11	26	4
Sites	3	12	13	8	14	3
Pieces	c. 1560	c. 820	c. 182	c. 40	60+ ?	8?

of 1560 pieces in LH I (mostly from the Shaft Graves) decreases to 630 in LH IIA, 190 in LH IIB, and 160 in LH IIIA1 contexts, before reaching an all-time low at 22 LH IIIA2 pieces (Harding et al. 1974, 151). However, as the amount of amber decreases, the number of sites with amber does not, due to a shift from deposition of complete necklaces in LH I to individual beads (Table 4.1). Additionally, whereas amber was in the LH I period limited to Mycenae and Pylos, it started spreading as early as LH II, when it is found in the Argolid and the Pylos area, with a few pieces in Thebes. In LH IIIA, the distribution widens further, with finds in Kos, Crete, Cyprus, and Syria in the east; Zakynthos, Sicily, and the Aeolian Islands in the west; and in Central Greece, Euboea, and Thessaly to the north. In LH IIIA1 and 2 combined, the number of amber pieces is only about a tenth of what it was originally; yet the number of sites increases more than fourfold. What is more, hardly any amber from these periods is found in the original centers of amber concentration, Mycenae and Pylos. Harding et al. explain this pattern by assuming that after the initial large amounts of LH I amber, in subsequent periods individual beads were handed down to lower, and local, elites. These newly enfranchised elites would, it seems, at least occasionally be buried with their single amber bead.

In network terms, the Mycenaean amber network barely existed in LH I: two places had weak ties allowing them to acquire large concentrations of amber, but they did not share this resource with other sites. Two regional networks started being built out in LH II, when amber was distributed to other sites in, respectively, the Argolid and Messenia, and a long-distance link was created with Thebes. It is notable that in Messenia, hundreds of amber pieces find their way to Kakovatos and Peristeria, while in the Argolid, only single beads show up. In LH IIIA the networks are extended further and include relatively minor sites.

Since 1974, new evidence has come to light from Central Greece suggesting that Thebes, Chalkis, and Mitrou were among the first places to benefit from the initial distribution of amber beads to places outside Mycenae and Pylos. One amber bead was found in Agia Anna Tomb 2 at Thebes as early as LH I-II (Harding et al. 1974, 148); four beads come from LH I or IIA to IIIA1 at Chalkis (*ibidem*). Amber is also reported for Mitrou's grave in Building D late in LH I (Van de Moortel 2013). Despite Mitrou's contacts with the Balkans, it is likely that the early amber at Mitrou reached it from the original consignment to Mycenae, whether directly or via Thebes or Chalkis: one might expect to find higher amounts of amber if the Mitrou elites somehow had independent access to it via a northern source. Elsewhere in the region, an amber bead is found at Livanates-Kokkinonyzes, near Kynos (LH IIB-IIIA1), Kalapodi-Kokkalia (LH II-IIIA), Zeli-Golemi (LH IIB and IIIA2-IIIC), and Atalanti-Spartia (LH IIIA2 late-IIIC Early). The chronological uncertainties – were the beads at Chalkis and Kokkalia later than those at Mitrou and Thebes, or contemporary? – do not allow for many firm conclusions; a distribution via the Euboean Gulf is as likely as an overland network via Thebes. The number of beads from Chalkis (four) might suggest an early or long-term participation in the amber distribution network.

Unsurprisingly, the major sites in the region – Thebes, Mitrou, and Chalkis – are among the first sites to acquire amber beads. Perhaps surprisingly, though, Thebes is, on current evidence, neither earlier nor more benefiting than the other two sites, suggesting the possibility that the three sites were of roughly equal status and importance in the early prepalatial period, consistent with the picture of early thriving of the Euboean Gulf coasts. Since the quantities are small, however, it may be wisest to suspend judgment. After these three sites, amber spreads to smaller sites as well. Thus Thebes, Mitrou, and possibly Chalkis and Kokkalia were part of the early network of elite peer-polities; the spread to somewhat smaller sites a bit later (Golemi, possibly Spartia) is consistent with the change to a true small-world network, incorporating smaller sites (Figure 4.1). The reasons for dissemination may well have been political: gift-giving mechanisms were employed by

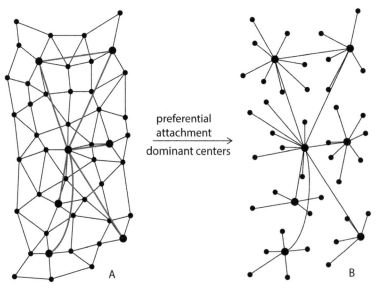

FIGURE 4.1. Schematic representation of changes in sociopolitical network structure between LH I-II and LH IIIA. Depiction of network types adapted from Baran 1964, 2, fig.1.

major centers and the higher elites in order to build alliances with (and buy the loyalty of) lower elites to gain the upper hand over competing centers and elites.

Tombs themselves reveal similar patterns. In stark contrast to the warrior tomb in Building D at Mitrou stand the nine chamber tombs at Agia Triada (LH IIB-IIIB, with most evidence dating to LH IIIA), overlooking the site. They have a long and wide dromos, a rectangular entrance closed with rubble masonry, and a roughly rectangular or roughly round chamber.[1] The only features that distinguish these tombs from other Mycenaean chamber tombs are their small size and the irregular shape of the chambers, which is attributed to the hardness of the local rock (*ArchDelt* 47, 205–206): the Agia Triada cemetery is located in an area of hard limestone, formed in the Mesozoic period, which is in fact not very suitable for chamber tombs (Kramer-Hajos 2008, 21–23). The same is the case with the relatively early (LH IIIA1) Kolaka-Agios Ioannis cemetery in the Kopais; the LH IIIA1 chamber tomb at Limni, opposite Mitrou on the Euboean coast, was very small as well, with a chamber measuring a mere 1.25 m in diameter.[2] These instances might reflect a lack of awareness of landscape types in which to practice the still relatively new custom of rock-cut chamber tomb cemeteries: in the case of Agia Triada and Kolaka, much better limestone is located nearby. However, the establishment of chamber tomb cemeteries even in locations where carving them out is difficult may also reflect a more conscious decision at a time when the sociopolitical climate was once again rapidly changing.

The shift from tombs in or adjacent to the settlement to a cemetery well outside the boundaries of the settlement has elsewhere been interpreted as a means to "establish and socially mediate ownership over the landscape" (Winter-Livneh et al. 2012). Ethnographic studies suggest the same. Whereas the monumental warrior tomb in the enclosure in the center of the settlement symbolically emphasized the centrality of Mitrou's warrior–elite to the settlement and its population, the spread of chamber tombs in the landscape may constitute a message directed primarily to other settlements. In the case of Mitrou, where settlement as well as cemetery are known, it is moreover clear that from the cemetery, located in the hills above the settlement, one has a view over a far greater territory than from the settlement: the cemetery symbolically claims a great area. It is noteworthy that this happens relatively late along the northern part of the Euboean Gulf: the chamber tomb cemetery at Kalapodi does not predate LH II, and the earliest tombs at Agia Triada are LH IIB or IIIA1. (In contrast, such territorial claims were made as early as

---

[1] See *ArchDelt* 47 (1992) B1, 205–206, pl. 62; *ArchDelt* 48 (1993) B1, 209–210, pl. 68; *ArchDelt* 52 (1997) B1, 436–437, pl. 172; *AR* 44, 1997–1998, 74; *AR* 45, 1998–1999, 75; *AR* 49, 2002–2003, 49; Dakoronia 2002a, 39 fig. 17.

[2] See Hankey 1966 for this tomb and its assemblage.

MH-LH I at Thorikos and Marathon, where tumuli dominated the land-scape). This suggests that settlements occupied the landscape in an estab-lished, originally heterarchical, system which did not necessitate statements of ownership over the landscape. That this changes everywhere in the region during LH IIIA1 suggests in turn not only that this Mycenaean custom of burial in chamber tombs is quickly disseminating throughout the region (reaching even the smallest settlements via local hubs) and catching on among the lower layers of society but also that social-political systems are changing, so that now settlements feel it expedient to lay symbolic claim to tracks of land. In the LH IIIA phase, the Euboean Gulf area appears to have been a stage for power struggles and a period of drastic social change. Whereas in the early Mycenaean period we witness intra-settlement compe-tition when rival chiefs struggle to gain a strong foothold, in the LH IIIA period the settlements seem to be internally stabilized, and regional competi-tion takes over.

While the people at Mitrou and Kynos started carving out chamber tombs, at Loukisia the deceased were still buried in cist tombs.[3] This suggests that the spread in customs northward, via Thebes or the Euboean Gulf, affected first the major hubs, which are characterized by excellent locations and high connectivity; from there the new customs then trickled more slowly into these sites' hinterland, to the less well connected smaller sites, and spread throughout the region. This process is only complete by LH IIIA, when chamber tombs become standard and widespread in the Euboean Gulf area. A hierarchy of sites can thus be established, distinguishing minor and less connected sites from better connected, major sites such as Chalkis and Mitrou. In the case of Mitrou, the distinction between (early) LH I cist tombs and the (later) LH I built chamber tomb also points to the emergence of an elite imitating newer, fashionable, and grander burial customs.

After the ostensible dearth of LH I-II settlements, in LH IIIA we see an explosion of sites with recognizable Mycenaean assemblages. Many are cemeteries, consisting of canonical rock-cut chamber tombs containing standard Mycenaean (lustrous) pottery: alabastra, jugs, and kylikes. Although pottery shows some regional idiosyncracies, for example, in inter-ior pockets of Phokis and Thessaly, pottery in the Euboean Gulf area becomes standardized in this period, attesting to a successful Mycenaeanization of this area. Many of these sites were not visible before, suggesting that the early elite centers now functioned as hubs in the local networks as well: this is the period in which the true potential of a small-world network is realized, resulting in a network structure that is

---

[3] The LH IIB cist tombs at Loukisia may well constitute reuse (as is the case at Glypha-Antron on the Strait of Oreoi, in LH IIA: Papakonstantinou 1999, 175). Their late use nevertheless suggests an adherence to earlier customs betraying that these areas had not yet fully embraced the Mycenaean culture.

decentralized and scale-free (Figure 4.1b). This happened through a process of preferential attachment (or cumulative advantage) in which most nodes (smaller sites) connected to nodes that were already well connected (the emerging centers), which allowed flow of goods and technologies to these smaller sites. This resulted in the emergence of a few hubs with a very high node degree. The resulting scale-free network is resilient against the random removal of nodes or links, but vulnerable to the removal of hubs; the previously established long-range links between hubs act as bridges, whose removal would disrupt the network. The result of the creation of this scale-free network was that characteristic traits of the Mycenaean culture now dispersed quickly throughout the hinterland. Thus in LH IIIA a "Mycenaean identity" encompassed not just a few elites but most or all inhabitants of most or all sites. The koine – the common culture – that characterizes LH IIIA and B is thus, in network terms, caused by intensification in contact between hubs and smaller nodes.

One may explain all this by assuming a change in network structure along the lines of Figures 3.4 and 4.1. In the MH, the largely heterarchical settlement structure is typical for a distributed network. This changed, as argued in the previous chapter, in the LH I-II period, when the limited distribution of recognizably Mycenaean goods was limited to a few elite centers, the hubs in an emerging small-world network. The long-distance links[4] with other elites resulted in the accumulation of elite goods at certain centers. These goods were however not yet shared with other local sites and communities, since this is the period in which elites emerged and needed to differentiate themselves from non-elites: local, intra-settlement differentiation took place, resulting automatically in inter-settlement differentiation. In LH IIIA the elite hubs, still connected to each other via long-distance contacts, started sharing their culture with local settlements, which suddenly become visible: a Mycenaean koine emerged, in which similar burial customs, types of pottery, and other material assemblages were found over large areas. The reason for this change is that, after elites had established themselves at various sites and on the local level, the competition changed from the local to the regional level. The elite peer-polities, previously sources of wealth and exotica, now became rivals in a competition for regional (rather than local) supremacy. In this competition, it made sense to forge local alliances, creating a class of sub-elites by controlled gift-giving. Thus small prestige items,

---

[4] With "long distance" I mean here nothing more than "more distant than an immediate neighbor." In other words, the term is to be understood as relative to a regional scale: Thebes and Chalkis, for example, could share a long-distance link. On a larger scale, these long-distance contacts allowed for Minoan–Mycenaean contact, for example, and on an even larger scale, long-distance contacts resulted in extra-Aegean (Egyptian and Baltic, for example) contacts with Mycenae.

such as beads and seals, now have a wider distribution: they are no longer limited to a few centers but appear in graves throughout the region.

The hubs in the simplified model in Figure 4.1b monopolize the links to local settlements; that is, these local settlements are in the model no longer connected to each other. Although in reality they must have maintained intensive contact with each other, the distribution of lower-level elite goods such as beads or seals was probably controlled by the hubs. This is important since it suggests an increasing dependence of smaller sites (and sub-elites) on larger centers (and the higher elites).

The shift from individual strife for power to strife between regional elites is reflected, I argue, in a change in ideology that takes place. This change of ideology is visible most clearly in an altered perception of the sword.

CHANGING IDEOLOGIES

On a Mycenaean krater from Ugarit dated to the late fourteenth century BCE (LH IIIA2), three men carrying swords in scabbards with tassels across their chests are juxtaposed with a chariot occupied by three men, followed by another standing figure with sword (Figure 4.2). All figures wear the same long, dotted robes with a double border and barred hem at the bottom: an outfit uniquely unfit for battle. Their formal, stiff arrangement is likewise suggestive of a ceremonial, rather than a martial, function: the swords are worn here as a marker of official status.

This change in sword iconography continues during the LH IIIB period, when on a krater, possibly from Cyprus, a groom with a sword follows three men in a chariot preceded by a rider (Vermeule and Karageorghis 1982, V.17). Although in this case the sword bearer wears no restrictive clothing, he does not actively use his weapon any more than the men on the Ugarit krater; he meekly follows along in a stately procession. And in the Cult Center at Mycenae a LH IIIB fresco adorning the east wall of the so-called Room with the Fresco shows a figure at left, recognizable as female by the white color of her feet, dressed in a long shaggy robe, holding a long sword in front

FIGURE 4.2. Krater from Ugarit, LH IIIA2 (late fourteenth century BCE). After Vermeule and Karageorghis 1982, IV.50.

of her, point down (Immerwahr 1990, pl. 59, 60). She may be a priestess or a goddess (Rehak 1984). Opposite her stands another female figure, this one dressed in Minoan fashion (long, tiered skirt, open blouse) and holding a staff or possibly a spear in front of her. In between "float" two small, naked (and therefore male) figures, one black and one red, their arms stretched out toward the first figure.

The contrast between these depictions and the seals from Chapter 2 is striking: long swords are now shown in a completely different, ceremonial, cultic, or processional context (Molloy 2010, 411). Although "ceremonial" (gold covered) swords were buried in high-status burials before, now swords lose any pretense of being primarily weapons of attack. They are no longer associated only or even primarily with warriors. In this chapter I argue that such depictions attest to a "domestication" of the warrior in palatial times, and that this is part of a set of broader ideological changes.

THE DISAPPEARANCE OF CHARIOTS ON SEALS

Seals are artifacts with multiple meanings that can at times seem contradictory. On the one hand, they can fulfill a utilitarian function in administration, when they are used to seal goods or to document and approve transactions. On the other hand, since they are often made of colorful, semiprecious stone or of precious metals; are intricately carved; and can be worn as jewelry by a string on the wrist (see Rehak 1994), they are also highly personal items of adornment. Their practical function is visible in sealings, seal impressions on clay that form evidence for the use of seals in transactions and documentation, whereas their use as personal possessions is emphasized when they are deposited in graves. Even seals that were actually used for sphragistic purposes, visible by their worn surface, can be deposited with their owner in a tomb, suggesting that at the time of deposition they were used to identify and represent primarily the individual, rather than the (more abstract or generic) office that the person held. Thus seals may be vehicles for the expression of different ideologies, and since their primary function was use in official administration, and since they were made in specialized workshops, they can be assumed to depict generally acceptable themes. Although it may not always be possible to link certain seal imagery with supposed administrative duties or the nature of an office (Petrakis 2011, 199, no. 78), analysis of their contexts of deposition in combination with their subjects of depiction and usage more broadly suggests that seals shifted in meaning during the Mycenaean period, and that this shift reflects changes in ideology.

The inclusion of seal stones or seal rings in tombs dates back to the very beginnings of Mycenaean culture: Shaft Graves Gamma, Mu, and Omikron in Grave Circle B contained a stone seal each (CMS I 5–7); Shaft Grave III included no fewer than six seals associated with three burials (CMS I 9–14 and Figures 2.2; 2.4); and Shaft Grave IV contained two gold seal rings with depictions of hunt and battle (CMS I 15, 16 and Figure 2.3). Since the first seals from the Mycenaean culture are associated with contexts rich in Minoan goods, it is reasonable to assume that the practice of wearing seals was taken over together with other Minoan goods and craft forms. Many seals found on the Mycenaean mainland unsurprisingly conform to standard Minoan iconography, in use since the Middle Bronze Age, and they cannot easily be taken to reflect Mycenaean concerns and ideologies; seals with depictions of ships are among these.[5] However, chariot scenes and horses occur first in LM I (Krzyszkowska 2005a, 141): they are thus contemporary with the inception of the warrior culture.

Chariot scenes on seals found in Minoan contexts can be counted on the fingers of one hand (Table 4.2): one seal in the British Museum was said to have come from Knossos (CMS VII 87), an impression from Knossos shows a griffin-drawn chariot (CMS II 8 193), a seal from a tomb near Lyttos depicts a goat-drawn chariot (CMS VI 285), and a large gold ring impressed sealings with a chariot at Agia Triada, Sklavokambos, and Akrotiri (Table 4.2; Krzyszkowska 2005a, 190).[6] Thus no more than four seals with chariots are known from Minoan Crete (of a total of about 1800 Neopalatial seals: Krzyszkowska 2005a, 120), and the motif is likely to be emblematic of Knossian power (Weingarten 2010a, 411–412 and cf. Hallager and Hallager 1995 about bull leaping rings). From the Mycenaean mainland six chariot seals and a sealing are known (Table 4.2). Since the number of Minoan seals and sealings *in toto* far exceeds that of Mycenaean seals, this suggests that the chariot motif resonated with Mycenaean patrons.[7] Yet, compared to the host of other seal depictions, chariot scenes remain very rare and must therefore have had a powerful impact. Their material (gold in four out of seven cases) and find contexts (rich warrior tombs in four cases, a palatial sealing in one case) suggest that chariot seals were restricted to the highest elites: the chariot served as emblem of highest power. This is unsurprising, as chariots formed a part of the pan-European warrior package in the early Mycenaean period; the grave stelae at the Shaft Graves, "status indicators of the utmost

---

[5] Five or six seals or sealings depicting a ship have a mainland provenance (Wedde 2000, nos. 906, 910, 911, 925, 941, and 976). Wedde expresses his doubt as to whether no. 976 represents a ship (Wedde 2000, 242). Nos. 910 and 925 (possibly found at Eretria), and 941 belong to the so-called talismanic style and are likely to be of Cretan manufacture (LM I); 906 and 976 are sealings from Pylos, dated by context to LH IIIB, but impressed with seals of LB (Late Bronze Age) II-IIIA and LB I-II date. No. 911, a gold ring from Tiryns, is of LH II date.

[6] In addition, a now lost sealing from Knossos was found in a LH IIIA context in the Room with the Chariot tablets (Crouwel 1981, G9).

[7] Compare these numbers with the numbers of seals depicting a ship: of 81 seals and sealings in Wedde's catalog (Wedde 2000, 339–349), only 7 are certainly or possibly found on the mainland (at Pylos, region of Thebes(?), Tiryns, Eretria(?), Brauron).

TABLE 4.2. *Minoan and Mycenaean chariot seals*

Site	Context	Material	Shape	Iconography	Reference
		Minoan			
Knossos?		Carnelian	Amygdaloid	Horse-drawn	CMS VII 87
Knossos		Sealing		Griffin-drawn	CMS II 8 193
Lyttos	Tomb	Agate	Ring	Goat (agrimi)-drawn	CMS VI 285
Agia Triada, Sklavokambos; Akrotiri		Sealings made by a metal ring	Ring	Horse-drawn	CMS II 6 19 (AT); II 6 260 (Sk), V Suppl. 3 391 (Ak)
		Mycenaean			
Mycenae	Shaft Grave IV (LH I)	Gold	Ring	Horse-drawn; hunting scene	CMS I 15
Vapheio	Tholos tomb (LH IIA)	Agate	Lentoid	Horse-drawn	CMS I 229
Vapheio	Tholos tomb, cist (LH IIA)	Carnelian	Amygdaloid	Horse-drawn	CMS I 230
Kazarma	Tholos tomb (LH I-II)	Amethyst	Cylinder seal	Lion-drawn	CMS V 585
Anthia	Tholos tomb (LH IIA-B)	Gold	Ring	Griffin-drawn	CMS V Suppl. 1B 137
Aidonia?		Gold	Ring	Horse-drawn	CMS V Suppl. 3 244
Pylos		Sealing	Ring	Horse-drawn, with duel	CMS I 302

importance" (Graziadio 1991, 411), are overwhelmingly decorated with chariot scenes (on eight of 12 stelae; Younger 1997).

Depictions of a man in a chariot on seals found on the mainland occur at Mycenae (CMS I 15, from Shaft Grave IV), twice at Vapheio (CMS I 229 and 230), Kazarma (CMS V 585, a lion-drawn chariot), the tholos tomb at Anthia in Messenia (CMS V Suppl. 1B 137 [VS1B 137], a griffin-drawn chariot), and possibly at the Aidonia cemetery, though provenance is uncertain (a gold ring similar to the Cretan sealings: Krzyszkowska 2005a, 141). In addition, a sealing from Pylos (CMS I 302) depicts a man in a chariot next to a man fighting a lion, a depiction that seems to foreshadow the Homeric use of the chariot as "taxi" for transporting warriors to the battlefield. The realistic, horse-drawn chariots are most popular among the Mycenaeans, possibly because they reflect the warrior ideology prominent in the early Mycenaean period. In addition, lions may be recruited to draw a chariot because of the special status of the lion among the early Mycenaeans. Goats find unsurprisingly no favor among the Mycenaeans: on Crete, agrimia (wild goats) were prominent both as real animals dwelling in the mountains, and in Middle Bronze Age art (Burke

2005, 415), but since agrimia are not found on the mainland, it is likely that the Mycenaeans thought of goats only as livestock, lacking special connotations.

The contexts in which the Mycenaean chariot seals were found corroborate their rare status and their links with warrior ideology: the tholos at Vapheio contained an extraordinarily rich warrior burial (Kilian-Dirlmeier 1987), and the tholos at Kazarma contained plenty of weapons as well: a sword, two daggers, a knife, arrow heads, and a boar's tusk helmet. The ring from Shaft Grave IV at Mycenae (CMS I 15) seems to have belonged to a female burial (Laffineur 1990, 123), but many weapons belonging to three male burials designate the grave as a whole as a warrior tomb as well.

Thus all chariot seals date to LB I-II and they are disproportionally found in Mycenaean contexts. The chariot symbol is rare, denoting high status, and restricted to the earliest Mycenaean period; on present evidence, beginning with LH IIIA, chariots are no longer used as a motif on seals (Krzyszkowska 2005a, 252). This is not because of a demise in status of the chariot motif: chariots are popular on frescoes decorating the palaces in LH IIIA-B, suggesting that they retain their associations with royalty. Instead, the reason must be sought in changes in use, status, and associations of seals.

In the early Mycenaean period seals can perhaps best be understood as expressions of personal adornment, in line with the ideology of the emerging warrior aristocracy, deriving their status predominantly or even exclusively from the preciousness of their material (gold or semiprecious stone) in conjunction with their carved depictions. This is visible by the inclusion of these precious objects in elite burials at a time when no sealings are known from the Greek mainland. Although they do not in all instances occur with male burials (Laffineur 1990, 122–123), they depict overwhelmingly "masculine" themes befitting a warrior culture: the hunt, battle, or lions mauling prey.[8] The many seals from the LH IIA tholos tombs in Vapheio are accompanied by an abundance of weapons. Interestingly, female status seems to be expressed in these masculine terms as well. Of ten seals from Grave Circles A and B only one was associated with a male burial, and the five gold and two stone seals from Shaft Graves III and IV are all associated with female burials (Laffineur 1990, 122–123). Yet seven of these eight seals bear masculine scenes of hunt and battle. Status is, for these warrior elites, by definition based in

---

[8] It should be noted that in general, martial iconography is not exclusively male in the Bronze Age Aegean: e.g., fragments from a boar hunt fresco in Tiryns depict female hands holding spears (Anderson 1985), the wall painting from the Room with the Fresco in the Cult Center of Mycenae and the plaque from the Tsountas House at Mycenae show, respectively, a female figure with a sword and one with sword and shield (see Rehak 1998), and there are a female archer on a fresco fragment from Pylos (Brecoulaki et al. 2008) and a female with a sword on a seal from Knossos (CMS II 3 16). This suggests, in line with the Shaft Grave evidence, that status can be expressed in masculine terms for males and females alike.

masculine pursuits and masculine excellence and can only be expressed in masculine terms.

After the early Mycenaean period, however, seals at Mycenae became increasingly associated with minor elites. In the chamber tombs at Mycenae, seals are abundant and can, judging from associated grave goods, be associated with men as well as with women, and occasionally with warriors. It is striking, however, that they rarely seem to be associated with first-rank warriors. Instead, judging by the absence of a sword (the early Mycenaean warrior attribute *par excellence*), they are overwhelmingly found in the tombs of warriors of lower rank (Laffineur 1990, 128–129). Although it is likely that the robbed Mycenae tholos tombs would have held the remains of the highest elites, and it cannot be excluded that many seals would have been buried with them, there is no existing evidence to support this notion. In fact, one might reasonably expect more seals to have escaped the robbers' attention and come to light than the single LH IIIA2-B steatite Mainland Popular Group seal from the Cyclopean Tomb.[9] Laffineur's tentative conclusions, based on analysis of the association between offensive weapons, jewelry, and seals, is that seals seem to represent a slightly lower class of elites: the warrior graves with the most weapons lack seals, while large quantities of seals can be found in graves with spearheads and arrowheads, but lacking swords (Laffineur 1990, 129). The only instance of a chamber tomb with seals and swords is the LH II-IIIA1 Tomb 91, in which two bronze swords were found associated with four gold seal rings, two of which bore a depiction of a cult scene, one of a sphinx, and one of a seated man and a griffin. Together with two bronze mirrors and plenty of gold beads, rings, and other ornaments, these finds were all associated with three burials (Laffineur 1990, 129). The lack of accompanying weapons may reinforce the idea that swords started losing their purely martial connotations in favor of associations with the cultic sphere; the depictions on the seals seem to support this notion.

If we would only notice that in LH II-IIIA1 minor elites get seals, we might suggest that seals are now more widely distributed, like amber beads, and suggest a gift-giving mechanism at work by which seals were distributed "down" to lower-level elites in an attempt by the palatial elites to bind lower elites to them. However, they do not appear in lower-ranking tombs *in addition to* the richest warrior tombs, but apparently *instead of*. If this observation is correct, we seem to witness a divorce between the warrior ideology and seal wearing well under way in LH IIIA. We see here the creation of two different ideological spheres: the sphere of the high-ranking warrior versus the sphere represented by seals and taken up by minor warriors and non-military officials. Initially seals,

---

[9] Laffineur suggests that the dearth of seals from these tholoi may reinforce his suggestion that high elites were not given seals (1990, 129). It should be noted that the tholoi at Mycenae were all already robbed when excavated.

as prestigious jewelry, were associated with the highest warrior–elites and at least at Mycenae especially with the female members of these elites, who may have worn seals as jewelry. In the later burials seals become divorced from elite weapons, suggesting that they represent a slightly lower elite (Laffineur 1990, 128–129), or not a military elite. Weapons (especially swords), it is thought, are reserved for the few at the very top; seals (sometimes with spearheads and arrowheads, indicative of warriors of a lower rank) are more widely distributed.

This change coincides chronologically with the period for which the beginning of Mycenaean administration at Knossos has been proposed (Driessen 2008, 70–72): Mycenaean administration (and therefore sealing practices) was in use by LH II at Knossos (visible in the use of Linear B tablets in the Room with the Chariot Tablets), and the large proportion of Greek personal names (Driessen 2000, 191) suggests that at least some Mycenaeans were not just aware of the practice but also intimately familiar with it. Although there is currently no evidence that seals were actually used on the mainland for documenting transactions as early as LH IIIA (all sealings date to LH IIIB: Krzyszkowska 2005a, 279), the knowledge of the sphragistic use of seals may well have spread rapidly among the elites. One may imagine that this knowledge gradually changed the perception of seals, from sheer status items to practical administrative tools: seals were no longer entangled in a web of associations with elite warriors, but became instead associated with administrative power. This change also coincides with the period of cementation of the *wanax* ideology: at several sites (Tiryns is a prominent example) the standard elements of palatial architecture, aimed at proclaiming the might of the *wanax*, were in place by LH IIIA1, which suggests at least the possibility that other practices may have been in place as well (Kilian 1988). The inclusion of seals in warrior tombs from the LH IIIA period outside Mycenae (at e.g., Dendra, where a LH IIIA1 warrior tomb contained a full set of weapons as well as six seals) suggests a gradual rather than a sudden change, as expected when change is due to changing value perceptions; this also corresponds to how ideas travel through a scale-free network.

The most judicious stance is to cite the lack of evidence for sealing and administration from the mainland as suggestive of its actual absence. Even then, the brief floruit and then disappearance of chariot imagery on seals does suggest a manipulation of images by those who controlled the workshops or commissioned the seals, and an emerging palatial power is the most likely candidate for this role, since palatial workshops increasingly monopolized stone and metal working (see Chapter 6). This combination of distribution (of seals) and restriction (of the "royal" chariot motif) serves as an example of the mechanisms employed by the palatial elites to control their subordinates.

Interestingly, on pictorial pottery the chariot appears first in LH IIIA2, almost exclusively on kraters. Corresponding to the trends we have identified earlier, however, they are rare until the transitional LH IIIB-C period and reach their greatest popularity in LH IIIC, after the fall of the palaces: Vermeule and Karageorghis (1982) list five examples of kraters with chariots, all from the Argolid (Berbati, Nauplion, Mycenae), for LH IIIA2; six to ten examples, from Mycenae, Corinth, and Attica for LH IIIB; 15–28 examples, all but one (Athens) from Tiryns and Mycenae for the transitional period of LH IIIB-C; and no fewer than 31–41 examples, mostly from Mycenae and Tiryns, but also from Athens, Salamis, Perati, and Lefkandi, for LH IIIC.[10] Partially these numbers are a function of the increasing popularity of pictorial pottery as a genre as time goes on, but when looking at these numbers as a fraction of the total amounts of mainland pictorial pottery, a clear trend emerges. Using once again the data compiled by Vermeule and Karageorghis (1982), in LH IIIA2 chariot depictions make up approximately 15 percent of all pictorial pottery, in LH IIIB this diminishes to around 5 percent; it picks up again in the LH IIIB-C transitional period (about 13 percent), and culminates with an approximate 20 percent in LH IIIC Middle.[11] It is thus in the period of strictest palatial control that chariot depictions occur least frequently on pictorial pottery.

Chariots as a pictorial theme on pottery seem to originate in the heartland of the Mycenaean palatial culture. This is what we would expect if palatial elites appropriated the chariot after the early Mycenaean period. The road system emanating from Mycenae extended to Berbati, which seems to have been a production center for chariot kraters made for export to Cyprus and the Near East (Schallin 2002) and was under Mycenaean control (Schallin 1996, 124): potters and pictorial painters from Berbati may have seen actual chariots from Mycenae on these roads on occasion, or they may have seen the frescoes adorning palace walls and used those as inspiration. This might be seen as an imitation and translation of popular palatial themes into a more humble medium: although probably somewhat more costly than ordinary Mycenaean decorated fine ware, many pictorial vessels have nevertheless been found in quite ordinary houses and tombs (Vermeule and Karageorghis 1982, 2), suggesting they functioned differently from frescoes (limited to the

---

[10] The range in numbers for the LH IIIB-C periods is because of a corresponding uncertainty in identifying chariot scenes on fragments where no chariot is preserved. After LH IIIA2, Vermeule and Karageorghis lump chariot scenes and horse depictions together. In some cases the placement of a human figure or the harness of the horse make clear that we are dealing with a chariot scene; in other cases it is uncertain whether the original picture showed merely a horse, or a horse-and-chariot. LH IIIA2: Vermeule and Karageorghis 1982, VIII.1–5; LH IIIB: *ibidem* IX.1–10; LH IIIB-C Transitional: *ibidem* X.1–28; LH IIIC: *ibidem* XI.1–41. Clay models (which would have been made by the same people who created utilitarian pottery) of chariots or horses and riders were common as well: Crouwel lists 14 examples most likely predating LH IIIC (Crouwel 1981, 161–162).

[11] These percentages exclude the doubtful chariot scenes. Including them results in 8% for LH IIIB, 24% for LH IIIB-C Transitional, and 27% for LH IIIC. The broad trend, of minimal popularity in LH IIIB versus maximum popularity in LH IIIC, persists in both cases.

palatial elites) and seals (limited to subelites). They reflect the tastes of "ordinary" Mycenaeans, and functioned outside the contested spheres of warrior–elites and palatial officials in a segment of society that the palace was arguably less concerned with.[12]

In addition to changes in popularity, there seem to be shifts in meaning through time: whereas pictorial kraters in the LH IIIB period show chariots with robed figures of high but not military status (Figure 4.2), in LH IIIC the chariot becomes again – as it was in the early Mycenaean period – associated with warriors and warfare (e.g., Vermeule and Karageorghis 1982, XI.16, XI. 18, and XI.28, all from Tiryns). This is part of a broader shift in ideology occurring in LH IIIC, as I will argue in Chapter 7.

The distribution of chariot depictions on pottery shifts over time from the Argolid, where their production centers – one was excavated at Berbati – produced for the local market as well as for Cypriot customers, to the Euboean Gulf area, where chariot kraters start showing up in LH IIIC. A similar shift occurs with imports (Chapter 8), and both seem to reflect shifts in power from the palatial Argolid to the Euboean Gulf coasts.

SYMBOLS OF POWER OUTSIDE THE PELOPONNESE

So far we have taken a chronological perspective. However, spatial analysis of the distribution of seals with certain themes is revealing as well. Chariot depictions on seals are restricted to the Peloponnese and are heavily concentrated in Shaft Graves (Mycenae) and tholos tombs (Kazarma, Vapheio, Anthia); their association with high-status individuals is borne out also by the presence, in the cases of Mycenae and Vapheio, of weapons and other high-status goods in the same tomb. Other examples of "ruler iconography" are duels (see Chapter 2), popular on Crete as well as on the mainland, where the theme is limited to Mycenae, Gouvalari, and Tragana in the Peloponnese.[13] Somewhat more widespread are images of men holding, fighting, leaping, taming, or hunting lions, bulls, boars, or horses: these are found at Mycenae, Prosymna, Asine, Vapheio, Pylos, Routsi, Kakovatos, Varkiza, and Dimini.[14]

However, although such straightforward "ruler iconography" is largely limited to the Peloponnese, indirect and symbolic indications of rulership are created by such themes as lions attacking other animals. In these cases the

---

[12] There is in addition a pictorial larnax fragment with a chariot from Mycenae (Vermeule and Karageorghis 1982, VIII.5.1). Larnakes are objects fixed in place rather than mobile pottery (or seals): this larnax is as palatial as the frescoes.

[13] CMS I 11, 16; V2 643; I 273.

[14] Mycenae: CMS I 79, 82, 89, 95, 112, 133, 137; Prosymna: CMS I Suppl. (IS) 27; Asine: CMS I 200; Vapheio: CMS I 224, 227, 228; Pylos: CMS I 290, 294; Routsi: CMS I 280; Kakovatos: CMS XI 208; Varkiza: Laffineur 1990, 147; Dimini: CMS I 408.

heroes are replaced by lions. Lions are frequently juxtaposed with heroes in early Mycenaean art as well as in Homeric similes; for example, one side of a dagger from Shaft Grave IV depicts a lion pursuing deer, while the other side shows men hunting a deer (Vermeule 1964, 41–42, 65). In the *Iliad*, Menelaos, the first warrior to be introduced with a simile, is compared to a lion (*Iliad* 3.21–26; Morris 1989, 517 no. 37).[15] This suggests that a long association between lions and heroes existed, which in turn allows us to identify seal images with attacking lions as symbolically similar to such images with human attackers (Morgan 1995). In addition, the lions on these seals may play similar roles as human heroes, such as attacking bulls. These images are, like chariot depictions, "power images," which symbolize high status, whether social, political, ritual, or military (or any combination of these).

The high status ascribed to the theme of lion-attacking-a-bull is suggested by the gold mounting of an agate seal with this theme from Orchomenos (CMS V 688). The theme is common in the Peloponnese but occurs also in Attica and Boeotia (see Table 4.3). The following observations can be made: first of all, seals with a lion attacking a bull are relatively rare (17 examples: a small subset of more than 80 known lion seals) and concentrated in the Argolid (six examples) and the southern Peloponnese (five); second, they are concentrated in elite contexts: tholos tombs, warrior graves, and tombs with gold jewelry; third, in a third of all cases, which constitutes all tholos tombs where they occur, they are found in pairs or triplets; fourth, they are found mostly with at least one other seal; fifth, in the southern Peloponnese they are most likely to be part of large collections, whereas in Boeotia they are one of a mere two seals. All this suggests that these are "power depictions" of which individual examples "trickled down" to lower-ranking elites in the Argolid and to Boeotian elites.

Griffins, too, seem to have been symbolic of high status. Hybrid animals with the head of an eagle and the body of a lion and as such merging the most powerful land animal with the most powerful animal of the skies, they were among the palatial symbols of power and are found on (palatial) frescoes, for example flanking the throne at Knossos and on the walls of the megaron at Pylos, on seals,[16] and on a Syro-Palestine ivory scepter head from Thebes (Aravantinos 2010, 88). Of the 23 seals with griffins in Laffineur's catalog (Laffineur 1990), no fewer than four (I 102; 128; 129, 218) are gold signet rings;

---

[15] The hero association of lions may also be the reason that early Mycenaean heroic hunters carry shields when hunting lions.

[16] E.g., Single griffins: CMS I 85; 128 (with seated female figure); 223 (with priest); 269 and 271 (lactating); 285 (with male ?hunter); 383; 389; V 437; 438; 584 (with male figure and lion); 590; 642 (carrying a dead deer); 672; 684. Two griffins: CMS I 73 (with altar); 98 (facing a column); 102; 206; 218 (facing a column); 282; 304 (with two baby griffins); V 654 (flanking a female figure).

TABLE 4.3. *Seals with lions attacking bulls*

Site	Tomb	Number	Number of other seals	Notes	Reference
Mycenae	Chamber tomb 28	1	0		CMS I 70
Mycenae	Chamber tomb 83	1	0		CMS I 116
Dendra	Tholos	2	4 associated with the same burial; another 3 with other burials	Warrior tomb	CMS I 185, 186
Dendra	Chamber tomb 8	1	0	Warrior tomb	CMS I 190
Argos	Chamber tomb 7	1	1	Gold and glass paste jewelry	CMS I 204
Nichoria	Tholos, pit 4	2	4 in pit 4; 6 elsewhere in tholos	Gold, glass paste, faience, amber, and stone beads; parts of alabaster vase	CMS V 435–436
Vapheio	Tholos, pit	3	28 in pit; 12 in chamber	Warrior tomb	CMS I 251, 252, and 253
Menidi	Tholos	2	4		CMS I 384 and 388
Salamis	Chamber tomb Θ	1	0		CMS V 660
Thebes	Chamber tomb 17 (Kolonaki)	1	1		CMS V 678
Orchomenos	Settlement	1	1	Gold mounted	CMS V 688
Kalapodi	Chamber tomb 1	1	1		CMS VS3 63
Routsi	Tholos floor	2	10 on floor; 6 in shaft 2	Calf and ox instead of bull. Warrior tomb.	CMS I 286 and 278
Asine		1	5	Calf instead of bull	Laffineur 1990, 134
Prosymna	Chamber tomb XLI	1	2	Ox instead of bull. Ivory comb; gold beads; javelin point	CMS I 214

I 304 is a metal signet ring; and four (I 206; 285; V 584; 672) are hard stone cylinder seals, which are rare in the Aegean (Krzyszkowska 2005a, 13, 30).[17] All other seals with griffins are made of hard stone (agate, jasper, carnelian), except for I 269 (a soft stone cushion seal). Additionally, five griffin images from Thessaly include a griffin in cloisonné enamel on a decorated finger ring from Volos-Kapakli and a gold ring with two griffins attacking a bovid from Georgiko in Western Thessaly (Intzesiloglou 2010).

Table 4.4 shows the frequencies with which several other "high power" scenes occur on different types of seals. Based on frequency of occurrence and material of the seal, griffins seem to take a position between sphinxes

[17] Laffineur includes CMS I 129 (Laffineur 1990, 126) among griffin depictions. The face of the creature is however human: this is a winged sphinx.

TABLE 4.4. *Numbers of selected "power depictions" on various types of seals (after Laffineur 1990)*

	Gold ring	Metal (probably gold) ring	Hard stone cylinder seal	Other seal	Kalapodi
Cult scene	10				yes
Sphinx	3				no
Griffin	3	1	4	15	yes
Lion	4		2	80	yes
Chariot	3	1	3		no
Duel	1			3	no

(occurring but three times on seals, but exclusively on gold signet rings) and lions (occurring four times on gold rings, twice on a cylinder seal, and no fewer than 80 times on other seals). Although griffins are occasionally portrayed with their young on these seals (and CMS I 269 and 271 each show a lactating female griffin), suggesting that they were thought of as actual animals,[18] their rarity and the precious material or rare, eastern shape of the seals on which they occur suggest that they were nevertheless emblems of authority or possibly even divine status: the griffin accompanying the "Goddess" in Xeste 3 or that carried by the helmeted female figure on the plaque from Mycenae have been taken to argue for the divine status of the female figures with which they are associated (Rehak 1984, 1998). The griffins' importance is further suggested by their frequent portrayal in heraldic positions.

With this in mind, let us turn to the Euboean Gulf area. Altogether 16 seals from Late Bronze Age (LBA) I-IIIA1 contexts are known from the area; seven of these (two gold rings and five seal stones) were found in three LH II-IIIA1 tombs (Tombs I, III, and IV) at the location of Kokkalia in Kalapodi (a lentoid seal of the Island Sanctuaries Group, dating to LH IIIA2 at the earliest, was found in a Mycenaean stratum at the nearby temple of Kalapodi: *AR* 2008–2009, 45).

Tombs I and III at Kalapodi are each marked by the presence of a side chamber, an unusual feature in chamber tombs of the Euboean Gulf area and possibly suggestive of an attempt at monumentalization. Since side chambers in chamber tombs are common in the Peloponnese, it is also possible that the shape of the tomb reflects influence from there. Both tombs were extraordinarily rich in grave goods (pp. 42–43), as was Tomb IV: it produced a set of tinned vases (a two-handled stirrup jug and four kylikes), jewelry, and an ivory buckler.

The seals deposited in these tombs (Table 4.5) reinforce the high status of the deceased. The two gold LBA I-II signet rings from Tombs III and IV are unique

[18] Rehak (1994, 83, note 31) proposes that imported ostrich eggs may have served as "proof" of the existence of griffins. One may well wonder if this characteristic – not "real" like the lion, yet not completely imaginary like sphinxes – is reflected in their status between the two.

TABLE 4.5. *Seals at Kalapodi-Kokkalia*

Tomb	Grave	Material	Shape	Iconography	Date	Reference
I (LH IIB-IIIA1)		Carnelian	Lentoid	Griffin	LB I–II	CMS VS3 64
		Carnelian	Lentoid	Lion attacking bull	LB II–IIIA1	CMS VS3 63
III (LH IIIA1)	Pit A	Gold	Ring	Bull	LB I–II	CMS VS3 66
	Pit A	Agate	Lentoid	Griffin	LB I–II	CMS VS3 67
	Pit A	Agate	Lentoid	Goat(?) with 2 animal heads	LB II–IIIA1	CMS VS3 65
IV	Pit B	Gold	Ring	Cult scene	LM I	CMS VS3 68
IV	Floor	Crystal	Lentoid	Quadruped	LB I–II	CMS VS3 69

for the area. Gold seals (whether rings or cushions) are heavily concentrated at Mycenae: five in the Shaft Graves, 16 in the chamber tombs, one from the Ramp House; there are only three elsewhere in the Argolid, four in Messenia, one from Vapheio in Laconia, four in Attica, and one each in Elateia, Medeon, Dimini (Tholos A), and Mega Monastiri (northwest of Dimini).[19] Their rarity is an indication that their use was restricted to the highest echelons of society. The Kalapodi cult ring is dated to LM I, based on stylistic criteria: although it is impossible to know when it was acquired, it was an antique by the time it was deposited at Kokkalia. There are only three definite LM I rings on the mainland (Vapheio, Elateia, Kalapodi; Krzyszkowska 2005a, 305) and it is interesting that two of them ended up relatively close to each other in Central Greece. The second ring, with a bull in flying gallop, has no parallels among the known Cretan or mainland repertoire, and the workmanship is mediocre; Pini sees it as "eine lokale Arbeit" (CMS VS3, page 28). The occurrence of these gold signet rings at Kokkalia places the elites here in a highly select company of Mycenaean elites outside the Peloponnese.

The stone seals, too, reinforce the high status of these tombs by the carved depictions and possibly by the material from which the seals are made: the vivid, translucent red carnelian may have been imported, although Hruby (2012) expresses her doubts and suggests an origin in the Argolid; the banded agate may have originated in Central Europe (Younger 1979; Rehak and Younger 2000, 260). Tomb I contained two carnelian seals, one dated to LBA I-II (CMS VS3 64) and one to LBA II-IIIA1 (CMS VS3 63). Both were associated with the warrior burial (Dakoronia 2007, 59): at this provincial place, far from Mycenae, seals are apparently still associated with personal (warrior) prowess and regarded as personal status ornaments. One of the seals from Tomb I (CMS VS3 63) shows a lion attacking a bull, a symbolic reference to power and a masculine theme suitable for the warrior ideology (Figure 4.3).

[19] CMS I 10–12, 15–17, 58–59, 86–87, 90–91, 101–102, 108, 119, 125–129, 155, 189, 191, 218–219, 274, 283, 292–293, 390–391, 407; CMS V 173, 336, 728; CMS VS2 106; Laffineur 1990, 147.

VS3-063-1

FIGURE 4.3. Carnelian seal from Kalapodi-Kokkalia Tomb I. Drawing of impression showing a lion attacking a bull. CMS VS3 63. Courtesy CMS.

The distribution of seals in the Kalapodi tombs suggests conscious manipulation by those making the interments: the warrior in Tomb I received two lentoids of carnelian, one antique by the time he lived, the other contemporary, both with power depictions. The interment in Pit A of Tomb III likewise possessed two lentoids, one heirloom and one contemporary, both made of agate. The two gold rings attest to links between Tombs III and IV; even stronger links are suggested between Tombs I and III, both of which have a lentoid seal with a depiction of an eyeless griffin (Figures 4.4a and b). Of the Cut Style, the two griffins, with wings coming out of their backs and looking back over their shoulders, are virtual mirror images of each other; although the griffins are executed in mirror image on the two seals, and the two are of different material, the similarities are too great to be dismissed and are likely to be intentional.[20] That this is not the only or "obvious" way to carve a griffin is shown by many other seals that depict drastically different looking griffins (Figures 4.5a and b). Look-alikes do sometimes reverse the basic motif (Krzyszkowska 2005a, 182); given some differences in the beak and wings of the two griffins, and their mirror-image, one wonders if the second seal was

---

[20] There is some dissension among scholars whether "look-alikes" are merely products of the same workshop or even just representing the same style (Krzyszkowska 2005a, 182), or whether they are intentionally carved in order to create an impression similar enough to function in the same way (e.g., Weingarten 2010a; 2010b, 324). Given the close similarities between many of these look-alikes, I am inclined to follow the latter. Look-alikes make sense especially in an administrative context (Weingarten 2010a).

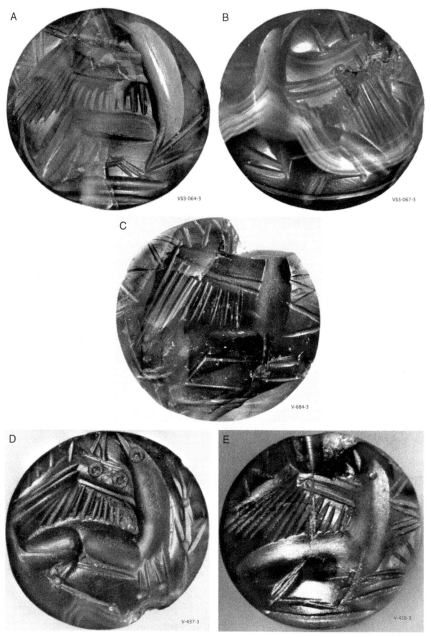

FIGURE 4.4. Look-alike lentoid seals from Kalapodi, Tanagra, and Nichoria showing griffins.
a and b: Kalapodi, CMS VS3 64 (carnelian) and 67 (agate); c: Tanagra, Dendron Tomb 16, CMS
V 684 (carnelian); d and e: Nichoria, CMS V 437 (agate) and 438 (carnelian). Courtesy CMS.

commissioned on the basis of an impression (or even a sealing). Regardless of
the exact process, the two look-alikes underscore the other similarities
between the assemblages of the two tombs (weapons, rare grooming or
possible medical equipment) and may suggest members of the same lineage.

FIGURE 4.5. A pair of griffin cushion seals from Routsi. CMS I 269 (soft stone) and 271 (agate). Courtesy CMS.

Rehak and Younger (2000) have noted that such pairs (and occasionally triplets) of seals that are linked by shape or decoration (e.g., a lion attacking a bull; two resting bovines) or both occur with some frequency in tombs in the Peloponnese: they occur at Mycenae's Grave Circle A (two triplets, one pair),[21] Kazarma (CMS VS2 577–585: three pairs, one triplet), Tragana

---

[21] CMS I 9–16. The six seals from Grave III (CMS I 9–14), associated with three burials, can be viewed as two triplets (three gold cushions and three stone seals). It is also possible to divide them into three pairs, based on iconography and shape: two gold cushions with a defeated lion; one gold cushion and one stone amygdaloid with a duel; and two stone lentoids with apparently unrelated themes. It should be noted, however, that the association with individual burials supports neither grouping.

Tholos 1 (CMS I 263–268: one pair, one triplet; a seal from a different grave within the tholos may belong to the pair based on its shape or have formed a pair with a seal from Gouvalari based on its iconography), Routsi (CMS I 269–286: two pairs, one of them illustrated in Figure 4.5a-b, and one triplet in Pit 2; four pairs and two others on the floor, although one of the unmatched seals forms a pair with one of the triplet seals from Pit 2), Nichoria (CMS VS2 430–441: five pairs), and Gouvalari (CMS VS2 639–646: two pairs, one triplet, and one seal not matching any others). At Gouvalari, the two seals that are look-alikes (CMS V 645 and 646) were buried in two separate tholoi, similar to the situation at Kalapodi. Finally, they note a pair at Vapheio, where two lentoids show "similar depictions of scratching dogs in mirror-image poses"; one of the seals is, however, made of lapis lazuli (Rehak and Younger 2000, 260), while the other is "pseudo-jaspis." Its mirror-image is reminiscent of the Kalapodi agate griffin seal. Based on the frequent occurrence of matching seals (these are not in all cases "look-alikes"), Rehak and Younger proposed that they served in a simple system of administration, in which an aristocrat would have another seal or two for use by one or two "lieutenants"; when the aristocrat died, the lieutenant gave his seal back to be buried with its owner. This idea is similar to that of Harrell's in the context of Shaft Grave swords, although in the latter case it is the remarkable individuality, rather than the similarity, of the Shaft Grave swords that has prompted Harrell to suggest that they functioned in a gift-giving system (or perhaps rather a lending system, since they were, in her reconstruction of the events, returned to the original owner upon his death) between elite individuals of different ranks (Harrell 2014). Although both Harrell's and Rehak and Younger's scenarios are speculative, they correspond well to the mechanisms for status enhancement and alliance building sought by, respectively, lower and higher elites, as proposed by, e.g., Wright and Voutsaki for the early Mycenaean period (Voutsaki 2001; Wright 2001, 2004c). At a time when the social fabric was changing, such strategies were, they argue, widely employed by individuals and groups wishing to advance their status in society. Alternatively, the pairs and triplets of seals may represent deliberate "collections."

Curiously, three other look-alikes to the Kalapodi griffins are known from the mainland. Facing left on the original seal, they resemble VS3 64 (Figure 4.4a). One was found in Tanagra, Dendron Tomb 16 (Figure 4.4c), the other two in Nichoria (Figure 4.4d–e). The Nichoria seals differ slightly: their griffins have eyes and their bodies are less angular and do not curve down abruptly at the hind legs. V 437, although in the Cut Style like the others, has some stylistic idiosyncrasies: its griffin has ringed eyes (repeated on the wing) and dotted joints. The carving on the Tanagra seal is more similar to the Kalapodi examples although, since the head is broken off, the presence or absence of an eye cannot be verified. The two seals from

Kalapodi are most similar, except for the material and the mirroring of the image.[22]

Contact between Kalapodi and Tanagra would not surprise: about 50 km apart as the crow flies, both were important centers, although most evidence at Tanagra dates to LH IIIA-B. Yet, even in the case of Nichoria in Messenia, the existence of pairs of look-alikes at Kalapodi and Nichoria suggests contact of some sort between the two places: Nichoria, Kalapodi, and Tanagra functioned in a network of look-alike griffin seals. Since we lack the evidence of sealings, we do not know whether these seals actually functioned as look-alikes in an administrative system. If the seals were carved intentionally similar, the reason would be that they could be used in interchangeable ways, by individuals of similar rank or station (Weingarten 2010a, 407; 2010b, 324–325). Weingarten has argued convincingly that this is how look-alikes functioned on Crete. It should be noted that the subtle differences that are visible on the much enlarged photos or drawings that are available in publications would be barely distinguishable on an actual small clay sealing, barely an inch across, allowing different administrators to seal similar documents. Since the differences between the five seals increase with distance, one might imagine a chain of artists from Crete, via Nichoria, to Central Greece, carving the seals based on an example from each previous locale.

On the other hand, it is often thought that hard stone seals of the Cut Style were carved only in Crete, since they are predominantly found in Crete and since no hard stone seals were engraved after the fall of Knossos (Younger 2010, 329). Working from the assumption that the Cut Style seals were made on Crete, where most of them have been found, and that pairs (or triplets) of seals represent "purposeful collections," Younger has recently proposed that such pairs may have been given to an administrator before his departure for the mainland (Younger 2012). In this scenario, the look-alikes might have been intended to function in an administrative system, as they did on Crete; on the mainland, however, they seem not to have been used as such and simply accompanied Younger's hypothetical administrator to the grave. If Younger's idea is correct, it follows that the Mycenaean palatial administrators on Crete were not only interested in keeping administrative ties with sites in the Argolid and the southwestern Peloponnese, but also with centers in Boeotia. However, this scenario does not explain the presence of five look-alikes at different sites, nor does it explain the presence of pairs and triplets (buried with women, perhaps incorporated in necklaces) as early as the Shaft Graves.

---

[22] In addition, a fragmentary carnelian lentoid with unknown provenance (CMS VIII 88) shows what seems to be a similar griffin, with three "eyes" on its wing. Two lentoids from Crete in the Cut Style (CMS VI 268 [Agia Pelagia?] and 270 [Dictaean Cave?]) are quite different.

Tomb IV, which dates to LH IIIA1, contained two seals that were already heirlooms when they were deposited in the tomb: a gold ring with a cult scene is dated to LM I and was associated with Burial B; a crystal seal, found in the northeast corner of the tomb, is dated to LBA I-II. The amount of jewelry and the absence of weapons may suggest that this was a female burial; one may wonder if the ring with the cult scene is especially appropriate in a female burial. Rock crystal is not much favored in Mycenaean workshops (Krzyszkowska 2005a, 266), suggesting that this seal hails from Crete.

With the exception of an imported Mitanni cylinder seal in Tanagra, Dendron (CMS VS1B 360) and three in or near Chalkis (CMS V 230, 231, and VS1B 359), only five other hard stone seals are known from the coastal areas of the Euboean Gulf. An agate LM I talismanic seal with ship depiction may come from Eretria (CMS VI 205); an LBA IIIA scarab-shaped lapis lazuli seal from Lefkandi shows a lion attack (CMS V 424); a chalcedony seal from Tanagra Dendron Tomb 31 shows a deer (CMS V 686: LB IIIA); an agate LBA I-II seal stone from Agia Triada near Mitrou bears a depiction of a bare-breasted female with raised hands wearing a Minoan-type skirt (CMS VS3 085); and a quartz seal from Kynos shows a bull sacrifice (LB II-IIIA1). The Agia Triada seal, too, was an antique by the time of its deposition (the tombs at Agia Triada have been dated to LH IIB-IIIB, with most evidence dating to LH IIIA1). The seals suggest that Mitrou, Kynos, Tanagra, Lefkandi, and possibly Eretria were major centers in the early Mycenaean period, with access to Minoan crafted seals; on present evidence, however, none of them rivaled Kalapodi. Ruler symbolism is found at Kalapodi and Lefkandi; cult images at Kynos, Agia Triada, and Kalapodi. In addition to the seal with the ship from (possibly) Eretria, another seal with ship depiction (carnelian) was found at Brauron (where it may have been deposited only in Archaic times; CMS V 213). Thus two out of only five find spots of ship-seals on the mainland are along or near the Euboean Gulf area: perhaps unsurprisingly, given their coastal location, the early Mycenaean elites in this area may have been especially interested in the ship theme.

EVIDENCE FOR PROVINCIAL ASPIRATIONS TO ELITE STATUS

The seals discussed so far are all made of hard stone or metal, derived from the Minoan glyptic tradition. Most of these seals may have been made on Crete, since they belong to stylistic groups that are predominantly found on Crete. These seals are found in the earlier (LH II-IIIA1) tombs. All other seals from the Euboean Gulf area belong to the Mainland Popular Group (MPG). These seals are made of soft stone, such as steatite, which is widely available, and usually their carving is poor and highly dependent on stock themes. They date mostly to the end of LH IIIA and LH IIIB (Younger 2010, 332), when with the fall of Knossos hard stone engraving came to an end (administrators at Mycenae, Tiryns, Midea, Thebes, and Pylos used heirloom seals from then on). It is possible that the quantitative and qualitative decline of hard seal stone production represents intentional restriction by Mycenaean elite administrators attempting to increase control over economic activities; such restrictive policies are typical for the palaces (see Chapter 6). The result was increased status of hard seals, which were now only available as heirlooms (Krzyszkowska 2005a, 275).

Elites would, however, have been unable to control production of MPG seals: created with locally available stone, their schematic designs were carved into the soft stone with simple non-specialized tools (Krzyszkowska 2005a, 275). Together with their wide distribution – they are found in non-palatial areas at least as often as in the Mycenaean heartland – this suggests that MPG seals represent to some extent the ideals and aspirations of provincial elites and sub-elites.

Although the development of the MPG postdates the start of seal usage to document transactions in LH IIIA1, evidence for the sphragistic use of MPG seals in the form of sealings is extremely scarce: the only certain MPG sealing is CMS VS3 373 from Thebes (Figure 4.6); although a few of the Pylos sealings were impressed by soft stone seals, they "do not seem typical of the MPG" (Krzyszkowska 2005a, 275). The example from Thebes does suggest, however, that at least in Central Greece MPG seals were not necessarily excluded from dealings with the palatial bureaucracy. Although MPG seals occur in

FIGURE 4.6. Sealing from Thebes, made by an MPG seal. CMS VS3 373. Courtesy CMS.

common graves in the Argolid and in Attica, which has led to the idea that they are indeed "popular" and "deposited in humble tombs" (Younger 1987, 65; 2010, 332), Eder points out that finds of MPG seals at Mycenae, Midea, Tiryns, Thebes, and Pylos suggest that the users of these seals had access to the local palace, suggesting that MPG seals were in fact used in minor local administrative dealings (Eder 2007a; 2007b, 93).

Many MPG seals are found in graves in mint condition, showing they were never actually used or even worn (string holes show no signs of abrasion) but produced specifically for funerary purposes. However, 65 percent of MPG seals found in graves is clearly abraded (Dickers 2001, 76, note 512), suggesting they were actually used in life, probably as identification devices and jewelry. Most seals that were deposited in mint condition are found in the northern and northwestern peripheral areas of Phokis, Magnesia, Thessaly, Aetolia, and Kephallenia (Dickers 2001, 110 note 758).

For the Euboean Gulf area, MPG seals that had actually been used (i.e. worn) were found in graves at Tanagra (Dendron Tomb 18, Tomb 34, and Ledeza Tomb 27: see Table 4.6) and Chalkis (Figure 4.7a–b). The MPG seal from Chalkis-Trypa was found in a relatively rich tomb (Dickers 2001, 110, note 758; cf. Hankey 1952, 52 for the uncertain provenance of the seal stone).[23] This suggests that at Chalkis these MPG seals were associated with a certain status. It is possible, of course, that they were worn merely as jewelry. However, the MPG sealing from Thebes suggests the alternative possibility, that they served to identify individuals involved in minor transactions in the Theban administration. Given the proximity of Tanagra and Chalkis to Thebes, this should not surprise. Linear B texts suggest that Thebes had dealings with the west coast of southern Euboea, and on geographic as well as archaeological grounds it is likely that Chalkis was at least in part under economic control of Thebes (see Chapter 5). At Oxilithos, on the other hand, on the east coast of Euboea, a seal was deposited in mint condition in a tholos tomb (CMS V 227): both the mint condition – not suggestive of pre-funerary usage – and the tholos tomb suggest that Oxilithos was not under Theban control but was rather a small independent polity, proclaiming its independence with a tomb form not used at Thebes or anywhere in the Theban realm.

Two MPG seal stones recently found at Mitrou seem not to have been used, either, judging from the crisp impressions the seals create,[24] and the same seems true for two seals from Megaplatanos-Sventza, near Atalanti

---

[23] Two severely abraded pressed glass seals (CMS VS1A 370–371) were found at Lefkandi, in a Middle Protogeometric grave (Tomb 12B of the Toumba Cemetery) suggesting that either these seals were valued enough to be passed from generation to generation, finally to be deposited in a tomb, or were dug up, recognized as valuable, and redeposited with a single individual.

[24] Unpublished, but photos of both seals and their impressions are shown in newsletters (Van de Moortel 2006 and 2007).

TABLE 4.6. *Condition of MPG seals from the Euboean Gulf coasts*

Site	Date of context	Condition	Context	Reference
Kalapodi	LH IIIA2-B	Lightly worn	Sanctuary	*AR* online database Kalapodi 2010
	LH IIIA2-B	Lightly worn	Sanctuary	*AR* online database Kalapodi 2010
	LH IIIA2-B	Worn	Sanctuary	*AR* online database Kalapodi 2010
	LH IIIA2-B	Worn	Sanctuary	*AR* online database Kalapodi 2010
	LH IIIC-Submycenaean	Worn	Sanctuary	CMS VS1A 382
Kalapodi-Vagia	LH IIIA2-B	Lightly worn	Tomb 1	CMS VS1B 2
Megaplatanos-Sventza	LH IIIB-IIIC1	Mint condition	Tomb 5	CMS VS1B 4
	LH IIIB-IIIC1	Lightly worn	Tomb 6	CMS VS1B 5
Zeli-Agios Georgios	LH IIB-IIIB1	Mint condition	Tomb 23	CMS VS1B 11
	LH IIB-IIIB1	Worn	Tomb 23	CMS VS1B 12
Mitrou		Mint condition?	Surface find	Van de Moortel 2006
		Mint condition?		Van de Moortel 2007
	LH IIIC or PG			*AR* online database Mitrou 2008
Thebes	LH IIIA-B1	Lightly worn	Pelopidou building complex	CMS V 670
		Sealing		CMS VS3 373
Tanagra-Dendron	LH IIIA1-B	Mint condition	Tomb 13	CMS VS1B 683
	LH IIIA1-B	Worn	Tomb 18	CMS V 685
	LH IIIA1-B	Worn	Tomb 34	CMS V 687
Tanagra-Ledeza	LH IIIB-C1	Worn	Tomb 27	CMS V 682
Chalkis-Trypa	LH I-IIIA	Worn	Tomb 8	CMS V 228
Chalkis-Panagitsa	LH IIIA	Worn	Tomb	CMS VS1A 101
Lefkandi		Lightly worn	Surface find	CMS V 425
Lefkandi-Toumba	MidProtoGeo	Abraded	Tomb 12B	CMS VS1A 371
	MidProtoGeo	Abraded	Tomb 12B	CMS VS1A 370
Oxilithos	LH IIIA1-B	Mint condition	Tholos tomb	CMS V 227
Oreoi				Dickers 2001, no. 307

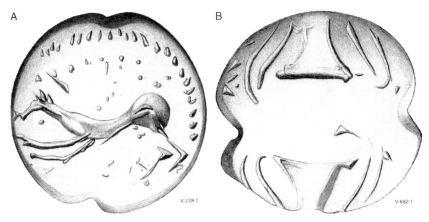

FIGURE 4.7. Worn MPG seals from Chalkis and Tanagra, Ledeza. CMS V 228 and V 682. Courtesy CMS.

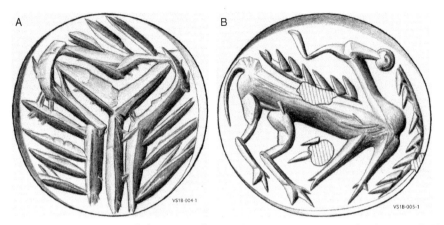

FIGURE 4.8. Two MPG seals from Megaplatanos-Sventza. CMS VS1B 4 and 5. Courtesy CMS.

(CMS VS1B 4–5; Figure 4.8a–b): although one of the latter is chipped at places and listed as "leicht berieben" (lightly worn) in Dickers 2001 (215, no. 331), the seal does not display the worn surface of the MPG seals at Thebes, Tanagra, and Chalkis. Megaplatanos-Sventza is quite probably outside the sphere of Orchomenos, and individuals here may have followed peripheral customs. MPG seals found in LH IIIA-B strata at the cult site of Kalapodi, on the other hand, appear to be well worn, suggesting they had been used during life.[25] This in turn suggests that Kalapodi may have been associated with the palace of Orchomenos in the palatial period.

Further research might refine and clarify the picture, but it should not surprise that in the provincial areas of Central Greece some people were involved with minor administration, while others, especially perhaps at places outside palatial control such as Megaplatanos, followed the peripheral custom of interring mint-condition seals.

MPG seals are found in some quantities but without other types of seals in eastern Phokis, Lokris, and Doris; they are found as single specimens in tombs in the Argolid (where they are also found on the acropoleis of Mycenae, Tiryns, and Midea), Attica, Messenia, Elis, Boeotia, and Euboea (but almost all evidence for Euboea comes from Chalkis and Lefkandi, close to Boeotia). It is tempting to read in these distribution patterns a difference in which seals are regarded in core areas versus more or less peripheral areas. Apparently in core areas (the Argolid, Messenia, but also Boeotia and central Euboea, i.e., areas under palatial control) MPG seals are actually worn during life. An individual thus gets buried with the one seal he (she?) used in life for identification purposes.

[25] Photo and brief report in the *Archaeology in Greece* database (http://www.hellenicsociety .org.uk/frame.htm), Kalapodi 2010. A worn MPG seal was found in a LH IIIC-Submycenaean context as well; in this case, the worn surface might be because of the age of the seal when it was deposited.

With increasing distance from these core areas, however, MPG seals increase in (symbolic) value and decrease in actual function, and much like the early Mycenaean elites used redundancy of status symbols (including seals) to declare their high status, individuals in, for example, western Phokis, southeastern Thessaly, and Aetolia may get buried with multiple seals that might even be made specifically for the funeral as suggested by their mint condition (Dickers 2001, 110). That MPG seals in these outlying areas were considered valuable is also suggested by a LH IIIB interment in a tholos tomb in Rachmani, who wore two MPG seals around the neck, apparently as jewelry (Dickers 2001, 112) and the burial of a child in Tomb 162 at Medeon: the little child was buried with two gold earrings as well as with an MPG seal, some beads, and spindle whorls (ibidem). In this case, the seal clearly functions as item of adornment: the child would have had no official dealings requiring administration.

The mint condition and context of many MPG seals in the peripheral areas of southeastern Thessaly and Aetolia, but also at Oxilithos, Mitrou, and Megaplatanos-Sventza, thus suggests that they functioned as status markers in death. Yet, there is no denying that the intrinsic value of MPG seals is low, since they are made of commonly found soft stone (steatite) and typically carved with schematic, linear designs. It is therefore likely that these seals conveyed status primarily because of their symbolic associations. Their symbolic associations may have been twofold, but in both cases linked to elites: elites from palatial polities used seals in transactions, and elites flaunted them as jewelry. The elites from the province may have wished to associate themselves with the high culture of the palaces and the easiest way to do so was by adopting MPG seal stones. In a period when precious materials and weapons were restricted, steatite seals thus attest to the aspirations of provincial elites and sub-elites of climbing the social ladder. The local elites reinforced their status in their communities by imitating some outer forms of palatial behavior.

At the same time that these MPG seal bearers are trying to define themselves in terms of the elites, Mycenaean administrators themselves use mostly heirloom seals to impress sealings (Younger 2010, 329). The irony is thus that MPG seals give their provincial owners the idea that they are "like" the powerful palace administrators, while the administrators themselves use mostly very different (and higher status) seals: access to the "real thing" is still very much restricted, possibly even more so than before since seals are now finite commodities. This mechanism is also visible in skeumorphic pottery and in the LH IIIA1 custom of tinning ceramic vessels: in this case, too, only the elites would have access to the real metal vessels, while humbler imitations in clay would be more widely available.

In summary, seals were in the early Mycenaean period status markers of warrior elites, then became associated with lower or non-warrior elites when they changed from primarily jewelry to have primarily administrative functions. But because of the associations of administration with the palaces, MPG seals became the status markers of sub-elites (Dickers 2001, 109–117; Krzyszkowska 2005a, 274) and elites in peripheral areas, while being mere identity markers of commoners (Younger 2010, 333) in core areas. Mycenaeans outside the palatial sphere with social aspirations tried to associate themselves with the prestige of the palaces by using seals as status markers; their cravings were satisfied by the masses of MPG seals produced just for them. It is with these late LH IIIA-LH IIIB MPG seals then that we find, for the first time, possible evidence for ideological change in the "periphery." The distribution, use, and ornamentation of MPG seals suggest that they have lost any association with a warrior culture. Not even oblique references to warrior ideals are recognizable; they are found with child as well as adult burials devoid of weapons, and they were at least in some cases actually used in administration. The associations of these MPG seals were thus rather with administration and, however vaguely formed, ideas of palatial elegance and status: the users of these seals wished to belong, even if only symbolically, to the palatial sphere.[26]

THE DOMESTICATION OF THE WARRIOR

Mycenaeans are typically viewed as warlike, and we have seen that in the early Mycenaean period martial subjects were popular on seals. This might lead one to expect that as soon as Mycenaeans start carving their own seals, they show battle scenes, weapons and armor, and other martial themes. However, a survey of MPG seals reveals that not a single one bears a reference to a martial theme: Mycenaeans do not show their belligerent side on their seals (cf. Laffineur 1990, 154). I have suggested on pp. 80–82 that a separation took place between "warrior activities" and "seal-bearing functionaries." MPG seals may simply have followed that pattern, once it was established. However, the invisibility of the warrior occurs also, as argued earlier (pp. 76–77; 83–84), in pictorial pottery, where LH IIIA and B pictorial pottery shows humans predominantly in processions with chariots and lightly armored grooms. True warlike scenes and scenes with hunters occur on pottery only after the collapse of the palaces, in LH IIIC Middle.

Other evidence, too, suggests an ideological restriction of warrior identity in favor of more "civic" expressions of status. Whereas in LH II contexts in the Argolid and elsewhere on the Peloponnese great warrior graves exist in addition to inhumations of minor warriors with seals, by LH IIIB we find

---

[26] A similar sentiment may be visible in the depictions of women, dressed in elite fashion, mourning on larnakes from Tanagra: their presence references "the participation of the palatial elite" in an ideal world (Cavanagh and Mee 1995). These larnakes have been dated to the LH IIIA2-B period, i.e., the period of popularity of MPG seals.

barely any weapons at all. The Kalapodi tombs (LH IIB-IIIA1), three tombs at Chalkis (Tombs V, VIII, and XI), and the warrior tomb in Building D at Mitrou are the last warrior tombs in the Euboean Gulf area. The tombs at Chalkis were used over long periods of time, but both Tomb V and Tomb VIII fell out of use early in LH III. Tomb XI was first used in LH II, then used until the end of LH III; it is not clear to which period the knife and dagger from this tomb date. At Mitrou, LH IIIA represents the final phase of use of built Chamber Tomb 73.

Warrior tombs were a defining characteristic of the early Mycenaean period, to the extent that the LH IIIA1 warrior tombs near Knossos have been traditionally interpreted as the graves of Mycenaean conquerors arriving on Crete (see Preston 1999 for an overview over the scholarship). Yet, warrior tombs virtually disappear from the Greek mainland in the LH IIIA2 phase and there are barely any warrior graves dating to the height of the palatial period, the LH IIIB period (Steinmann 2012).

Coinciding with the disappearance of warrior graves is a change in sword types: from the long but somewhat fragile Type A to the shorter, sturdier Types F and G, which are less susceptible to breakage and perhaps easier to handle (Steinmann 2012, 31; Figure 4.9). Type A is last attested in a LH IIIA1 context (Tholos 2 in Routsi); the first of the shorter types dates to LH IIIA2 (Steinmann 2012, 31–32). They remain prevalent throughout the palatial era. Although short versions of the Type A and B swords existed before, the new swords are characterized by wider blades, making them more suitable for cutting while still allowing thrusting. Moreover, their handle allowed two sorts of grip. A grip with the index finger curved around the shoulder and the area between thumb and index finger nestled in the curved guard was traditional. It "allowed the point to be aligned with the natural 'straight punch' trajectory of the arm for thrusts, and aligned the cutting edges with the natural cutting line of the arm for cuts" (Molloy 2008, 125). The newer swords allowed a second grip, the so-called hammer grip, in which the sword handle is held with a full fist. This allowed for "more percussive strikes" (Molloy 2008, 125; Peatfield 1999). As a result of this different grip, the new swords excelled in the confined space of close combat situations on the battlefield, whereas the earlier swords excelled at duels set in open space (Peatfield 1999, 72).

At the same time that these swords appear, the gold-embellished "ceremonial swords" disappear from the record. These developments have been interpreted as a direct consequence of palatial efforts in equipping "professional" armies (Steinmann 2012, 219–220): Linear B evidence with inventories of weapons and armor from Knossos suggest that the palace concerned itself with equipping warriors fully. For example, tablet Ra 1540 from Knossos lists 50 swords, Ra 7498 lists 18 and 99 swords, and 20 fragmentary tablets list additional unknown numbers of swords (Driessen and MacDonald 1984, 64;

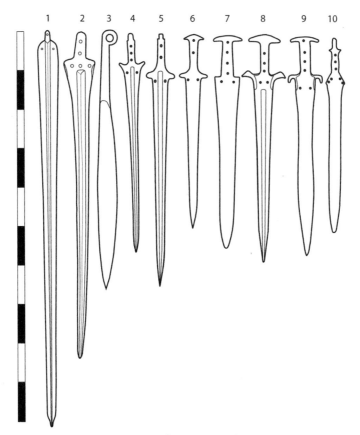

FIGURE 4.9. Major categories of Aegean swords. 1, Type A; 2, Type B; 3, single-edged; 4, Type C; 5, Type Di; 6, Type Dii; 7, Type Fii; 8, Type Gi; 9, Type Gii; 10, Type Naue ii. Courtesy of Barry Molloy.

Molloy 2010, 412–413). Other tablets in the series are concerned with other weapons: Ra 0481 lists 42 spears and Ra 0482 a number of arrows. Combined with the thousands of bronze arrowheads from chests in the Arsenal of Knossos, these records attest to a centrally organized industry overseeing the forging and distribution of crucial weaponry: whereas having a sword (and the skills to use it) in the early Mycenaean period was an individual privilege and limited to elites, now larger groups of men, not necessarily all of them elite, were equipped by the palace.

Steinmann has suggested that the newer swords were practical for men who did not have the time or opportunity to practice much, but had to be ready to fight when the palace ordered them to do so (Steinmann 2012, 221). Molloy's experimental research suggests however that each sword type does require ample practice, since incorrect use results in ineffective attacks or even damage to the weapon (Molloy 2008). Perhaps the greatest change is then not one from highly to hardly trained fighters, but from a type of individual competition among elites to mass fights. The frescoes in Hall 64 at Pylos, where Mycenaean warriors battle undefined barbarians clad in animal skins, may represent such large-scale fights. The weapons used are spears and short swords (identified by Molloy [2010, 411] as Type G and Type F) or daggers.

The individual "hero" displaying his superior skill, honed by years of daily practice, in fighting a heavily armed opponent, is no longer visible in the palatial period. Since the new swords were no longer restricted to the aristocracy, the sword may have lost some of its heroic connotations. It is notable that where long swords are depicted, as in the Room with the Frescoes at Mycenae, their function is now purely ceremonial: in the fresco at Mycenae, the long sword is held by a female figure in a context which, although not fully understood, is certainly cultic. Just like seals suggest that minor warriors were transformed into palatial functionaries, sword iconography suggests that major warriors were made obsolete, and that their traditional long sword was now purely ceremonial.

Given how symbolically charged swords were, it would certainly be in the interest of the palaces to restrict and control that symbolism: because they possessed such potent agency, they had to be controlled. Curbing the display of weaponry essentially ensured that in the system of symbolic communication the palace emerged as the only source of wealth, prestige, and military power. With the palaces overseeing the manufacturing and distribution of arms and armor, as well as monopolizing the import of tin and copper, necessary to make the bronze weapons, and actually distributing the new type of swords, no man in the Aegean could be equipped as a Mycenaean warrior from a palatial polity without active palatial support, whether he lived within the palatial polity or on its fringes. It is telling that almost all warrior graves from the LH IIIB phase are found in non-palatial areas such as the islands of the Dodecanese, Achaia, and Epirus (Steinmann 2012, 393–398): it seems likely that these areas were not influenced by the palatial rules and restrictions and continued to value traditional elite warrior display.

With the rise of the palaces, the warriors were thus "domesticated"; they were brought "into the control and hierarchy of the evolving state structure" (Ortner 1996, 250). The preferred outlet for masculine display was increasingly the hunt rather than battle: whereas in early Mycenaean iconography the two categories of warrior and hunter are often conflated (as, for example, on the lion hunt dagger where fully equipped warriors battle a lion as if it were a human foe), in the LH III period, the hunter becomes the "most popular masculine power metaphor" (Thomas 1999, 305).

As a part of this control over masculine expression, individual differences were downplayed: swords were widely distributed and no longer marked an individual as an excellent warrior. This deemphasizing of the individual after the early Mycenaean period was part of a wider social trend and is visible in the burial sphere too. Whereas the Shaft Grave individuals were fixed for eternity, laid out in extended position and bedecked in gold, and the LH IIB–IIIA1 chamber tombs at Kalapodi each still contained only one or two primary burials in extended position, the multiple burials in the LH IIIA1 Agia Triada tombs in the hills above Mitrou included males, females, and children in contracted position, suggesting that the chamber tombs functioned as family tombs. The attribution of specific grave goods to individual interments is difficult in these communal tombs, and exacerbated by the fact that secondary burial consisted of simply sweeping skeletal remains aside, sometimes into a pit, often to the side of the chamber. The individual was thus symbolically destroyed (rather than fixed for eternity), joining an amorphous community of ancestors, and skeletons and grave goods are all intermingled. This reflects a change in ideology in which emphasis shifts from the eternally fixed identity to the transient state of the individual before joining the corporate group of ancestors. Already at the moment of interment the common contracted position, which allows less room for individual display (Treherne 1995, 113; Sherratt 1994), suggests an emphasis shifting from individual to corporate identity.

The domestication of the warrior may have had positive implications for female status. Aggressive masculinity limits feminine possibilities; the warrior's prevalence as the principle of male construction is readily tied to a patriarchal social system (Langdon 2008, 248–249). In line with this, there are very few depictions of females, or clearly "feminine" goods, from the early Mycenaean period: in the Shaft Graves, seals with overt masculine iconography of battle and hunt were deposited with female burials, suggesting that female status could only be expressed in masculine terms. In other words, "female status" was a paradox: status was automatically tied to masculine prowess. But in the palatial period we find numerous frescoes with female figures of obviously high status; although some of them are portrayed in "masculine" roles, for example, driving a chariot or handling a weapon, in the palatial period we find them acting in official roles in rituals or in the mortuary sphere for the first time. This is visible, for example, on paintings of female figures handling figurines, attested at Mycenae, Tiryns, and on a larnax from Tanagra.[27] These paintings suggest that women acted as priestesses, or more broadly as officials, in various rituals.

Such portrayals are in line with Linear B evidence, which mentions priestesses associated with various cults. At Pylos, four priestesses are known in addition to seven or eight priests; at least one of these priestesses, an individual named Erita, was a wealthy landowner and legally independent enough to be engaged in a dispute over land (Billigmeier and Turner 1981, 7).

---

[27] See Immerwahr 1990, 120, figs. 33a and b for the frescoes from Mycenae and Tiryns; Kramer-Hajos 2015, 648–649; fig. 11 for the larnax from Tanagra.

It is not coincidental that women become visible in these roles only after the warrior ideology has diminished in importance.

Warrior ideology does not die out altogether. It is appropriated by the palaces and thus continues to exist in palatial frescoes. Frescoes depicting battles, warriors going into battle, or fragments of men in warrior outfit are known from Pylos, Mycenae, Thebes, and Orchomenos.[28] Yet in these cases the propaganda message does not proclaim the greatness of an individual hero, but the power and might of the palace, represented by stereotypical Mycenaean warriors operating in groups. All individual achievements are made subordinate to and in service of the palace. Any display of weaponry outside the palatial sphere, however symbolic, might have been seen as a threat to the dominance of the palace and not be accepted. In the areas outside the palatial rule, bronze weapons may have become harder if not impossible to come by, since the palaces tried to monopolize not just the trade routes but also the workshops specializing in bronze working (see Chapter 6). Even if these outlying areas could have produced bronze weaponry, their aspirations to be just like the palatial elites (or rather, like the image formed about these palatial elites), caused them to seek status in seals rather than in weapons.

CONCLUSIONS

Between LH II and LH IIIA2, the ideologies of the early Mycenaean period, with their emphasis on individual warrior prowess, make place for ideologies reflecting a more consolidated society, in which power is no longer constantly contested between individuals but has become hereditary. Iconography on seals suggests a shift from duels (contesting power) to symbols of (consolidated) power (Laffineur 1992); in graves, weapons become less prominent. In addition, certain symbols that used to be found more widely become restricted to palatial elites: chariots, for example, are no longer carved on seals even though they are painted on palace walls. This all points to an appropriation of warrior imagery by the palaces, and to a "domestication" of the early Mycenaean aristocratic warrior elites: individual warrior prowess is no longer idealized. By the LH IIIB period, warrior graves are almost exclusively found in peripheral areas, away from the palaces, whereas warrior ideologies are exclusively expressed in frescoes on palace walls.

Sometime during LH IIIA, chariot seals disappear, swords change meaning, and warrior elites as a class die out. At the same time, Mycenaean pottery and burial habits become ubiquitous throughout the mainland, an indication

---

[28] Immerwahr 1990, 192 (My. No. 11); 195 (Or. No. 1); 196–197 (Py. Nos. 4 and 10); 201 (Th. No. 2).

that "Mycenaeanization" has been completed. The spread of Mycenaean culture, as visible in the wide distribution of Mycenaean pottery and the common use of chamber tombs, suggests that the elite networks of the early Mycenaean period are now opening up: transfer of standard pottery types, but also of, for example, beads and seals, is no longer restricted to very few major centers but includes smaller, regional or local sites. However, this does not result in a free circulation of goods originating at elite centers: when the elite networks start linking to lower-level sites, resulting in a trickling down of Mycenaean goods to local centers, a restriction on certain motifs and expressions of warrior identity becomes visible. In this way the highest elites can bind lower, local elites to them by (carefully controlled) gift-giving, and at the same time maintain a clear separation between the different ranks in society.

5

PREHISTORIC POLITICS
The creation of the periphery

The coastal village of Larymna is nowadays a rather depressing place. A large nickel extraction plant spews dense clouds of brown smoke into the sky, dead fish float on the surface of the polluted Larymna Bay, and trucks drive back and forth through denuded hills in red dust. But it is likely that already in the Bronze Age the area was less attractive than most of the Euboean Gulf landscape. The Mesozoic soils here are poor for agriculture; nowadays the hills surrounding Larymna on all sides are used for grazing, because in these Mediterranean scrublands not much can grow apart from the hardy, spiny *phrygana*. And yet, for an archaeologist interested in the Mycenaean period in the Euboean Gulf area, the site is a must-see, since this is the only site on the shores of the North Euboean Gulf with evidence for Cyclopean masonry, the Mycenaean large-scale architecture used especially for fortification walls. What happened here? Why is it, of all places, at Larymna, that the Mycenaeans decided to build a fortress? And, as importantly, why is Larymna the only Mycenaean site fortified with Cyclopean masonry along the North Euboean Gulf?

This chapter analyzes the developments in the Euboean Gulf area in the LH IIIA2-B period of highest flourishing of the palaces in an attempt to answer these questions and, ultimately, understand the interactions between the palaces of Central Greece and the Euboean Gulf area. The palatial period in Central Greece was dominated by a few palatial sites, Thebes, Orchomenos, and Gla, located in large fertile plains that provided their economic base. In addition to pottery, this chapter will look at some artifacts that are associated specifically with the palaces to trace how networks of interaction in Central Greece changed. It will argue that the marginal status of the Euboean Gulf coasts during the palatial period is far from a "natural" state because of its location or a historical "inevitability," but that, instead, the coasts were actively marginalized, leading to a dearth of material indicative of a failure to thrive during the heyday of Mycenaean civilization.

FROM MARITIME TO LAND-BASED NETWORKS

The palaces of Orchomenos and Thebes are firmly land-based (Figure 5.1). Although in this traditional representation, which allows each polity a 22-km radius,[1] both have access to the sea, most of their territory consists of land, and most of the coastal areas fall outside their polities. Yet, it is only to be expected that both palaces sooner or later realized the importance of access to the Euboean Gulf and expanded their territory to include ports on the coast. When that happened, the entire coastal network, in place since centuries, seems to have fallen apart, with devastating consequences for many coastal sites.

Evidence for the process is visible at Chalkis. Rock-cut chamber tombs at Chalkis, dating to the end of LH I or LH IIA contain, among other things, Minoan or Minoanizing pottery (pp. 60–61; Figure 3.3), suggesting Chalkis had ties to the south. As early as LH IIB we find, however, more similarities with pottery from Boeotia: most notably a tall version of the straight-sided alabastron (Figure 5.2). The foliate bands in zones (left) correspond to a similar LH IIB alabastron from Thebes (Mountjoy 1999, 653, no. 28). This connection with Boeotia becomes more clearly visible in LH IIIA2, when giant alabastra turn up in Chalkis. They are at least 20 cm high with a maximum diameter of about 28 cm in contrast to the usual size with an average height of 6–9 cm (Figure 5.3; Mountjoy 1990, 257). They are elsewhere found in Boeotia, Achaea, and Elis; they have not been found in Attica, the eastern Peloponnese,

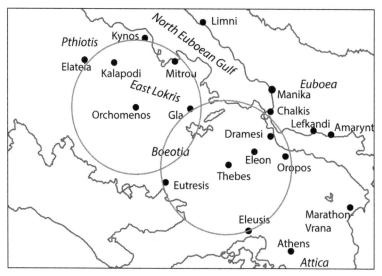

FIGURE 5.1. Hypothetical territories of Thebes and Orchomenos, with an approximate 22-km radius (cp. map in Nakassis et al. 2010, 241, which shows the two polities as not overlapping but equally land-based).

[1] Roughly a day's walk, in accordance with Renfrew's Early State Module (Renfrew 1975).

FIGURE 5.2. Chalkis-Trypa, tall-bodied, straight-sided alabastra, LH IIB. H. 0.115; 0.105 m. After Hankey 1952, pl. 18, nos. 469A and 520A.

FIGURE 5.3. Chalkis, large and giant alabastra, LH IIIA2. Left: H. 0.16, D. 0.20 m; Right: H. 0.23, D. 0.25 m. After Hankey 1952, pl. 19, nos. 486 and 541.

and Thessaly. Locally produced, they attest to the spread of a fashion in pottery making rather than to the movement of actual pots. Their distribution suggests then a major overland network of specialized pottery production cutting through the maritime network of the Euboean Gulf.[2] This is not a matter of a complete absence of Minoan influence – there is still a Minoan import in LH IIIA2 Chalkis – yet there seems to be an increasing influence from the mainland. The concurrent decreasing influence from Crete might be because of the disappearance of Akrotiri from the Aegean network: Knappett et al.'s 2011 model suggests that the removal of this hub with betweenness centrality (it owed its prominence to its place in the network) would have led over time to an increasing disconnect between Crete and the mainland. Coinciding with the increasing mainland influence is a diminishing overall amount of material from Chalkis (Hankey 1952). This culminates in the LH IIIB decline of Chalkis and other coastal sites along the Euboean Gulf.

---

[2] Although the giant alabastra that have been found are locally made, it is possible that they were inspired by imported examples that are lost. It may be more likely, however, that actual professional potters traveled and made wares at various sites.

While Chalkis appears to be in decline, Thebes rises meteorically, and the two events are probably related. Specifically important is the desire of the Theban wanax to monopolize imports for elite consumption in his polity (see also Chapter 6). This is suggested by the "hoards" of high-status, exotic prestige goods found at the Theban workshops or in storage, versus the virtually complete absence of any such goods elsewhere in LH IIIB Boeotia. A monopoly over exotic imports required control over the maritime traffic coming through the Euboean Gulf, and it seems highly likely that by LH IIIB Theban economic and perhaps political control extended to Chalkis in order to make this possible.

The political and administrative network of Thebes is traceable to some extent via the Linear B tablets from the palace. They suggest a three-tier hierarchy with Thebes at the top, Eutresis, Eleon, an unknown ku-te-we-so, and perhaps Kreusis as secondary centers, and a larger number of smaller sites (Del Freo 2009). The tablets suggest that Theban involvement extended to the west coast of Central Euboea: a shipment of wool to a female weaver in Amarynthos (a-ma-ru-to; see Aravantinos 2010, 93) suggests the presence of a textile workshop there involved in the palatial textile industry (Figure 5.4).[3]

The fortified site of Anthedon, on the North Euboean Gulf coast about 25 km from Thebes, is likely to represent the Theban harbor in LH IIIB (Hope Simpson

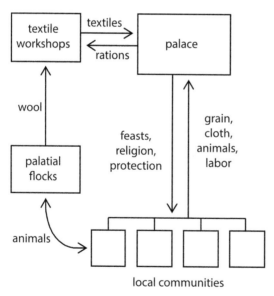

FIGURE 5.4. Simplified model of Mycenaean redistribution of staples and wool products. After Nakassis et al. 2011, 182 fig. 4 and following adaptations from Knodell 2013, 369 fig. 5.4.

---

[3] The only other identified site on Euboea to appear in the tablets is Karystos (ka-ru-to) on south Euboea, sending one pig to Thebes; as Knodell notes, this "hardly suggest a serious tributary relationship" (Knodell 2013, 144). On geographical grounds, incorporation of Karystos in the Theban polity is unlikely as well.

and Dickinson 1979, 253#G43); a hoard of bronze tools and other objects, probably dating to the end of LH IIIB, was found here but is now lost. It is a strong indication that Thebes actively expanded its economic (and probably political) control to the coasts, most likely in order to benefit from the maritime route through the Euboean Gulf. It is worthwhile comparing this scenario to developments in the Saronic Gulf, where Aeginetan pottery dominates assemblages until LH IIIA1, when Mycenaean fine ware and utilitarian vessels start dominating pottery assemblages (Tartaron 2010, 175; Tartaron et al. 2011, 630). There, the establishment of the palace at Mycenae coincided with the decline of Kolonna's export industry (ibidem) and the cultural dominance of Kolonna in the Saronic Gulf is eclipsed by Mycenaean dominance. Mycenaean interest in the site of Kalamianos specifically is also suggested by the architecture at Kalamianos, which appears to have been built in a "single, planned effort" in order to utilize it as a port (Tartaron et al. 2011, 630). In both cases the establishment of the palace negatively affects a coastal site across the water (Chalkis and Kolonna), although in different ways: Kolonna remains an independent hub but loses part of its markets, while Chalkis is subsumed in the Theban cultural sphere.

In network terms, what seems to be happening is that the increasingly important hub of Thebes co-opted existing links, growing exponentially and leading to an increasingly centralized network (Figure 5.5).[4] In Figure 5.5b, the extreme variant – a truly centralized network – is shown. Although in

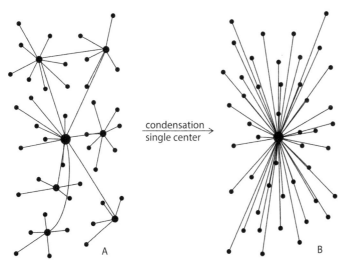

FIGURE 5.5. Transition from decentralized to centralized network between LH IIIA1 and LH IIIA2-B. Schematic representation of network types adapted from Baran 1964, Fig.1.

---

[4] This centralization is especially apparent on the mesoscale. On the macroscale, there are multiple condensation centers (Thebes, Pylos, Knossos, etc.), so that the entire network on the macroscale resembles the decentralized model in Figure 5.5a.

reality centralization was not absolute, the model is nevertheless useful to understand the ascendance and consequent collapse (for which see Chapter 8) of Thebes. The transition from a scale-free network to a centralized network happens through a process of condensation, resulting in a single center. This single central node has, in an absolutely centralized network, direct links to all other nodes in the network (that is, its eccentricity – the largest distance between the central node and any other node – is 1); all other nodes in turn are linked only to the center. Like a scale-free network, the centralized network is robust against the random removal of nodes or links, but the removal of the central node disrupts the entire network.

In reality, the network will not have been completely centralized: for example, the Theban administration would have had direct contact with a number of secondary centers, but not necessarily with every small village. Nevertheless, from a political and administrative point of view, Thebes became a superhub; in addition, as we will see in Chapter 6, it came to dominate and monopolize the distribution of prestige goods. The almost absolute palatial monopoly over exotica (which are virtually absent elsewhere in Boeotia in the LH IIIB period) strongly suggests a centralized network with Thebes as its hub.

This highly centralized network is reflected in the size of the citadels of Thebes and Gla, which are disproportionally large compared to the citadels of Mycenae, Tiryns, and Midea in the Argolid (Hope Simpson and Hagel 2006, fig. 2; Symeonoglou 1985, 33). In the Argolid, multiple elite centers (not only Mycenae, Tiryns, and Midea but also Argos, Asine, and Nauplion) crowded together around the plain of Argos in a more decentralized network structure. Although Mycenae clearly dominated, it was not allowed or able to grow unchecked the way Thebes and Gla grew as hubs in a highly centralized network.

Thebes also virtually monopolized the olive oil imports from Crete: of the 43 inscribed stirrup jars (ISJs) in Boeotia, only two were found outside of Thebes: one in Orchomenos, one in Gla (Haskell et al. 2011, 94). Such monopolies required control over the maritime traffic coming through the Euboean Gulf. The walls at Anthedon, as well as the other fortifications on the mainland side of the Euripos (Figure 5.6), seem to strengthen the theory that Thebes invested in this maritime connection, at the expense of Chalkis, on the other side of the Euripos.

The exponential growth of Thebes and the attendant increasing centralization of the network was accompanied by a reorientation of preexisting networks, from a roughly north-south coastal network to one with an east-west orientation that was essentially land-based, like the palace itself. Although I have given my reasons for being somewhat skeptical of PPA in Mycenaean Central Greece (see pp. 25–26), it is interesting that PPA by Knodell clearly shows the east-west orientation of the Theban network

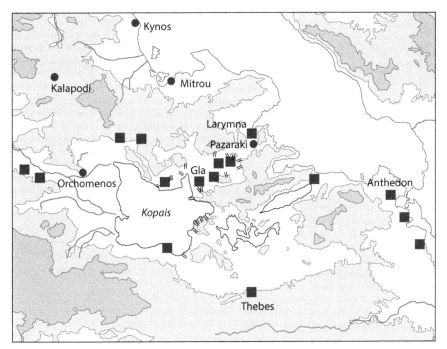

FIGURE 5.6. LH IIIB fortifications (indicated as squares) in the Euboean Gulf area (after Dakouri-Hild 2010, 620, fig. 46.3). Lake Kopais is largely drained and severely contracted (compare Figure 1.2); katavothres are indicated by parallel lines.

(Knodell 2013, 370 fig. 5.5). This new network cut through and largely replaced the old coastal network, as becomes visible by pottery from Chalkis now showing strong parallels with Thebes rather than with the Argolid or the Euboean Gulf sites. Simplified, one may imagine that Chalkis declined since it found itself increasingly on the margin of the Theban network, rather than as a central node in the coastal network: its connectivity decreased since it no longer functioned as a conduit between north and south but became the terminal station to the east for Thebes – especially since it was located on the east side of the Euboean Gulf and thus had no significance for Thebes as a port side. Chalkis lost its "betweenness centrality." When the Theban network became increasingly centralized, some former hubs diminished in importance: this was a process of scale-free network growth propelling Thebes forward and at the same time causing at least relative decline for other hubs.

DESTRUCTIONS AND ABANDONMENT

The picture of decline noted for LH IIIB Chalkis is equally visible elsewhere in the Euboean Gulf area. Already in 1966, Sackett et al. remarked that on

Euboea there was "a rather unexpected scarcity of normal IIIB among the sherds" collected by the survey in 1966 (Sackett et al. 104); in fact the surveyors were so puzzled by the dearth of LH IIIB material that they suggested in their report that certain LH IIIC Early bowls should perhaps be considered LH IIIB (Sackett et al. 1966, 105). Subsequent excavations, mostly on the mainland, seem to confirm that the pattern of diminished LH IIIB remains is region-wide.

Although the evidence is not conclusive, at Kynos, Mitrou, and Lefkandi the combined evidence suggests a gap or a period of decline, or at the very least a change in settlement at all three sites. In all three cases, the LH IIIC remains are far more impressive than the LH IIIB evidence, which I will attribute to a re-emergence of the maritime north-south network in Chapter 8.

Evely et al. speak of a "LH IIIB gap" (Evely et al. 2006, 111) in the main excavated part at Lefkandi. Although this is partially caused by extensive cutting into LH IIIB strata in the LH IIIC Early phase (ibidem 1; 9), evidence for LH IIIB occupation is at least in the center of the mound "barely represented" (Evely et al. 2006, 135).

The evidence from Kynos is scanty as well because in order to prevent the impressive LH IIIC walls from collapsing, only a very small area was dug below the LH IIIC levels, making it impossible to say anything about the extent of the LH IIIA-B occupation with certainty. An LH IIIA1 stratum is sealed by a burned layer and followed by LH IIIB2 levels with a number of clay floors alternating with burned destruction layers, possibly caused by earthquakes, which are frequent in the area. It is possible that some sort of disaster struck the settlement at Kynos at the end of the LH IIIA1 phase, but the excavated area is very small and it cannot be excluded that the evidence for burning is limited to a small part of the site. Similarly, it is difficult to conclude from the current evidence whether there was a gap in occupation at Kynos between LH IIIA1 and LH IIIB2. However, the LH IIIC walls follow a slightly different orientation than the IIIB2 walls, suggesting a break of some sort after the palatial period.

At Mitrou, many of the LH IIIA2 remains are heavily burned, and the monumental Building D as well as the settlement around it were destroyed and left in ruins; new buildings were few and flimsy. This suggests that the destruction was intentional and accompanied by a decline in population and prominence of the site. The extent of the decline during the LH IIIB phase is not entirely clear: whereas virtually no architectural remains dating to LH IIIB have been encountered, an important deposit dating to LH IIIB2 suggests continued contacts with the wider Aegean. The deposit is similar to contemporary assemblages from the Argolid but especially Thebes; it includes a Rosette deep bowl, a shape extremely unusual outside the Argolid and associated with ritualized elite drinking activities, such as libation (Podzuweit 2007). Drain tiles in this deposit imply the existence of at least one building of a certain importance.[5] The pottery from the deposit indicates furthermore that Mitrou had contacts with Boeotia, Phocis, Aegina, the Argolid, and western Crete: it was far from isolated, but continued to thrive despite earlier destructions. Yet, the LH IIIB1 period is barely represented, and the location of the hypothetical important LH IIIB2 building is yet to be found, suggesting that habitation and the elite center changed location between LH IIIA and IIIB2.

Perhaps most striking is the picture of depopulation in the Kalapodi area. Although there is evidence for cult activity in LH IIIA and IIIB,[6] evidence from excavated cemeteries in the area points to depopulation in LH IIIB. No new cemeteries were established during the LH IIIB period, and cemeteries at four locations, including Kokkalia and Golemi, do not seem to have survived the end of the LH IIIA period (Kramer-Hajos 2008, 125–126).[7] After the explosion of LH III sites, this LH IIIB decline demands explanation. Since this decline coincides with the period when nearby Orchomenos started its drainage and fortification project, it is tempting to see a correlation between the two events and relate the decline to Orchomenian expansion.

ORCHOMENOS, GLA, AND THE KOPAIS

Orchomenos was excavated early in the twentieth century by Heinrich Schliemann. Although no Linear B tablets have been found, it is generally assumed to have been the site of a palace based on the scale of public works associated with Orchomenos (about which more on pp. 116–119), the fresco fragments found, and the splendid "Treasury of Minyas," a tholos tomb competing with the Treasury of Atreus in size (14-m diameter, versus 14.5 for the Treasury of Atreus), plan, technique, and decoration. Like the Treasury of Atreus, it had a smaller chamber off the main chamber. The tholos tomb must have been highly visible in the landscape and since the form was unknown in Boeotia, it must have made a powerful impact (Mee and Cavanagh 1990, 242). At Thebes, for example, chamber tombs at Kolonaki/Agia Anna, Ismenion, and Megalo and Mikro Kastelli served the needs of commoners and highest elites alike. Two of the tombs are unusually large: 40 and 80 m² respectively, with dromoi of 18 and 25 m in length. One of these tombs was furnished with wall paintings of a funerary procession, a rocky landscape, and decorative designs, suggestive of the high status of the interred (Dakouri-Hild 2010,

[5] Vitale, AIA Meeting in Philadelphia, 2009. See also Van de Moortel 2009, 360: palatial-period pottery is abundant and of high quality.
[6] *AR* 53 [2006–2007] p. 43; 54 [2007–2008] p. 48; *Chronique des Fouilles* 2012.
[7] Although there is some LH IIIB material at Golemi and Zeli-Agios Georgios, the amounts are minimal and stand in stark contrast to the amounts of earlier material: at Zeli-Agios Georgios the only LH IIIB and LH IIIB-C sherds are from the fill of looted chamber tombs.

702). This demonstrative setting apart of funerary habits (tholos tomb at Orchomenos versus chamber tombs at Thebes) occurs elsewhere as well and seems to be a sign of political rivalry (Cavanagh 2008, 330).

In other respects, too, Orchomenos stands in stark contrast to Thebes, where exotic prestige goods abound and indicate far-flung contacts throughout the eastern Mediterranean, while no fewer than 42 Minoan stirrup jars with Linear B inscriptions and five without (far more than the 7 and 12 at Mycenae or the 20 and 0 at Tiryns) bear witness to contacts between Thebes and western Crete (and to a lesser extent central Crete: Catling et al. 1980; Day and Haskell 1995). From Orchomenos, only one Minoan ISJ is known. Orchomenos, home of the traditional MH Gray Minyan pottery and an agricultural center with less easy access to suitable harbors, seems less "international" than Thebes, turning its attention squarely to the mainland of central Greece (Kountouri et al. 2012, 468; Aravantinos 1999). Not a single extra-Aegean import has been found at Orchomenos (Burns 2010, 136).[8] Rather than ascribing the situation to the hazards of excavation, I suggest here that this represents a real difference in strategy between Thebes and Orchomenos.

Orchomenos is situated at the edge of the largest polje in Greece. The karst-polje landscape is characterized by high water inflow during the rainy season in winter and when the snow melts on the mountains in spring. Natural outflow took place through *katavothres* (Figure 5.6), natural subterranean sinkholes, channels, and fissures in the porous limestone. Their discharge capacity was limited, however, so that in winter and spring inflow was higher than outflow, resulting in a shallow but extended lake (Knauss et al. 1984). When Mycenaeans drained the lake in LH IIIA2 or early LH IIIB, they created the most fertile agricultural land in the Mycenaean world (Knauss 1987). The traces of the dams and canals, still clearly visible on the ground until ca. 1964 (see discussion in Hope Simpson and Hagel 2006, 190–197), have been thoroughly leveled by modern agricultural equipment and are no longer visible except in a single few meters'-long stretch near Pyrgos.[9]

Whereas the southern and especially the western side of the Kopaic Basin has ample flat land above water level, usable for agriculture, the northern edge is mountainous and the amount of arable land limited (Hope Simpson and Hagel 2006, 191 fig. 11). Therefore polders were created, protected from

[8] It should be noted that Gla does have some foreign imports (representing one contact in Parkinson's view: Parkinson 2010, 23 fig. 2.2). It is uncertain whether Gla acquired these foreign goods directly, or via a Mycenaean center (Thebes is the obvious candidate).

[9] Some studies of the Kopaic drainage system are, in chronological order: Kambanis 1892, 1893; Kenny 1935; Kahrstedt 1937; Lauffer 1940, 1971, 1974, and 1986, Knauss et al. 1984; Knauss 1987, 1990. Most recently the area has been investigated by the Archaeological Reconnaissance of Uninvestigated Remains of Agriculture (AROURA) project under direction of Michael Lane (Lane 2011, 2012).

inundation, on the north side of the Kopais. Dykes indicate that such polders existed between Stroviki and Kastro, around Gla, between Kastro and Agia Marina, and northeast of Agia Marina (Iakovidis 1998, 277; 2001, 155–156; Hope Simpson and Hagel fig. 11). In order to prevent the polders, as well as the naturally arable land in the western and southern parts of the basin from flooding, incoming water was channeled into two canals, one on the north (accepting the water from the Kephissos and Melas rivers) and one on the south side of the Kopais (serving the many smaller rivers there), which carried the water to *katavothres* on the eastern side of the Kopais that fed into lower lying lakes or the sea to the east of the Kopais. Both the northern and the southern canals, with an estimated depth of 2.50 m (Hope Simpson and Hagel 2006, 191), had average widths of about 45–50 m (Hope Simpson and Hagel 2006, 190, 195) and were flanked by 25–30-m wide banks of earth that were at least at some parts more than 2.70-m high (Hope Simpson and Hagel 2006, 191) and were faced with Cyclopean retaining walls of 2–3-m thickness. North of Gla, a second canal ran parallel to the first, sharing a central bank, for about 2 km between Kastro and Agia Marina (ibidem 189–190), probably to ensure protection of the important Gla polder at times when the lake itself threatened to overflow after heavy rainfall (Hope Simpson and Hagel 2006, 191–192, 198–201).

This is the most impressive engineering project known from the Mycenaean era, and after the system fell in disrepair at the end of LH IIIB, it was not attempted successfully again until the nineteenth century. The scale of the project was vast: Loader calculates that the construction of two wall faces of the fortification at Gla, the most important of the strongholds surrounding the Kopaic Basin, must have taken well over twelve years, compared to the approximate 5.5 years for the two wall faces of the citadel at Tiryns (Loader 1998, 65).[10] She estimates that it must have taken at least 825 years for one man to construct the dams of the Kopais (Loader 1998, Appendix 4 p. 181), so 100 men would have taken a little more than eight years. Loader concludes from these data that experienced stone masons would travel from one project to the next (ibidem, 65). The style of the Cyclopean walls in the Kopais is different from those in the Argolid, however: the Kopaic style is more polygonal and uses fewer interstice stones (Fossey 1990a, 23; 1990b, 72–89; Hope Simpson and Hagel 2006, 82). It is thus likely that experienced masons would have traveled from one site in the Kopais to the next, but it is less likely that such masons came from the Argolid. What is more, in addition to these experienced masons, most of the heavy manual labor – the quarrying, carrying, lifting – was probably carried out by

[10] The calculations on the time it would cost to transport enough stones to build one face of the circuit wall from quarry to work site (about 16.5 years at Gla, almost 5 years at Tiryns: Loader 1998, 69–70) are highly speculative, based on various unprovable assumptions, as admitted by Loader herself (ibidem 70–72).

hundreds of men from the area. Were these local peasants who were recruited to work in exchange for stable rations? It is interesting that an almost 10-km wide belt north of the string of fortifications, an area with dense mortuary evidence in the LH II-IIIA periods, seems virtually deserted in the LH IIIB period (Kramer-Hajos 2008, 125–128).[11] One may wonder if these were the areas from which labor was recruited, first to build the forts, then to work the newly created fertile polders around Gla (see pp. 122–123).

The scale of the project suggests that Thebes and Orchomenos, despite indications of rivalry between the two ruling families, may have joined forces in the draining of the Kopais; at the very least, the drainage works could only have been completed in a time of peace (Hope Simpson and Hagel 2006, 209). Indirect evidence of Theban involvement in the project can perhaps be seen in the lapis lazuli fragments in frescoes at Gla (Brysbaert 2008, 133); given the rarity of lapis lazuli, Brecoulaki tentatively suggested a connection with the Kassite seals found at Thebes (2010). It seems undeniable, however, that it was Orchomenos that benefited most from the creation of the Kopaic polders.

In order to maintain and protect these drainage works, a large number of fortifications was built on limestone outcrops along the northern, eastern, and southern sides of the basin (Figure 5.6). Along the southern border only Kastri/Haliartos has Cyclopean-style circuit walls.[12] Since Haliartos is neither close to a polder nor to a *katavothra*, the fortification here suggests a Theban attempt to defend its northern border at its westernmost point, rather than the drainage works. Several authors have expressed their surprise at the lack of fortifications on the border between Thebes and Orchomenos.[13] This lack may support the idea that the drainage was a joint effort; it should also be borne in mind, however, that Lake Kopais was never fully drained: in summer, much of it remained a wetland, while in winter and spring, a large part of it was a shallow lake (Knauss 1990, 371). Together with lakes Hylike and Paralimni, it did serve, therefore, as a highly visible border between the two polities.

[11] The large (45 tombs have been excavated) prepalatial cemetery at Kolaka-Agios Ioannis is, if not discontinued in LH IIIB, severely retracted in the palatial period: Kramer-Hajos 2008, 125. In the Kalapodi area, the apparent abandonment of sites (with the important exception of the site of Kalapodi itself, already a center for cult activity in LH IIIA-B) stretches north as far as Agnanti.

[12] Hope Simpson and Dickinson 1979, 237–242. It should be noted that the other southern settlements are all on steep hills or spurs or otherwise strategic locations. Fossey moreover described the walls at Daulosis-Kastraki, east of Haliartos, as "of Cyclopean style" (Fossey 1988, 312–313); Hope Simpson and Hagel express their doubts about this and favor a Classical or Hellenistic date, although they agree that a Mycenaean fort would be expected at this site (Hope Simpson and Hagel 2006, 80).

[13] Recently Dakouri-Hild 2010, 620. One would expect Onchestos to have been fortified, since it is located at the pass between the hills that led from Thebes into the Kopaic Basin.

More fortifications are found along the northern side of the Kopaic Basin, where Poligira, Pyrgos, Stroviki, Kastron/Topolia, Gla, Agia Marina, Chantsa, and Agios Ioannis are all characterized by Cyclopean walling on a hill.[14] Given the density of polders in the northeastern part of the Kopais, it is perhaps unsurprising that most fortifications are centered on this area: they protect the most important area, as well as the most vulnerable part of the Kopaic drainage works, the *katavothres* (Fossey 1990b, 87; also Hope Simpson and Hagel 2006). Fossey has argued convincingly for all these strongholds that, since they are all in visual range with each other and, ultimately, via relay stations, with Orchomenos, they served to protect the Kopaic Basin and its drainage works from attacks from the north (Fossey 1990b, 84–88).

Of all these strongholds, Gla is the best known. It is a fortified administrative center and military stronghold built on a low limestone island rising up from the floor of the Kopaic basin near its northeast corner. Its circuit wall has an average thickness of 6 m and is with a length of 3 km the longest of all known Mycenaean citadels, encompassing at least 200,000 m²; in comparison, the fortification wall of Mycenae enclosed at its greatest extent less than 40,000 m².[15]

Gla's purpose may have been to oversee the protection of the drainage works, whose focus, after all, lies not far to the northeast of the site, and administer the storage of produce generated on the polders; a dual purpose is among other things suggested by its "melathron," the main domestic building that consists of two equal and roughly symmetrical corridor-and-room systems connected to each other and forming an L shape (Iakovidis 2001, 150).[16] Storage took place in the Central Enclosure (or South Enclosure), a series of rooms accessible via ramps, whose storage capacity is estimated at minimally 2000 tons (Iakovides 1998, 195, 274). Grain samples recovered from Building H in this enclosure are largely einkorn (*Triticum Monococcum L.*), a hardy glume wheat type that stores well, with a few representing emmer wheat (*Triticum Dicoccum Schübl*: Jones 1995; Iakovidis 1998, 172–176, 263–265). It is likely that most of the grain was harvested from the polders

[14] Poligira is described by Fossey (1988) but not by Hope Simpson and Dickinson 1979, 237 as having Cyclopean walls, and Kastron/Topolia is not noted as having Cyclopean walls in Hope Simpson and Dickinson 1979, 238–239, but is included in a list of walled settlements by Hope Simpson and Hagel 2006, 187.

[15] The thickness of the walls is given in Loader 1998, App. 2 p. 173. At Mycenae the thickness ranges between 5.50 and 7.50 m (Mylonas 1999, 13). The area encompassed by the walls at Gla is estimated by Loader 1998, App. 2 p. 173 at 200,000 m²; Hope Simpson and Hagel 2006, 205, estimate 235,000 m². For the estimated area enclosed by the wall at Mycenae, see Mylonas 1999, 13 (30,000 m²) and Loader 1998, App. 2 p. 169 (38,500 m²).

[16] Castleden refers to it as a "keep" with towers on its south and west ends (Castleden 2005, 61), and assumes as a major function for Gla to hold all people and livestock of the area in times of attack or emergency (ibidem, 63 fig. 2.19; repeated in Schofield 2007, 96).

along the northern and northeastern edge of the Kopais. There is limited evidence of storage of olive oil in the form of parts of relatively few storage stirrup jars (Iakovidis 1998, 151–153, 256–257). Until recently, the melathron and the southern storage complex were the only buildings known from the citadel, but recent geophysical survey work under direction of Christophilis Maggidis has brought to light traces of far more buildings, somewhat modifying the traditional picture of Gla as a largely empty citadel (Maggidis 2014).

Sherds from the agricultural storage complex date the occupation of Gla to between the very beginning and the end of the LH IIIB periods, i.e., almost a century.[17] Since Gla clearly depended on the drainage of the Kopaic (and vice versa), and drainage works are centripetally arranged around Gla, the construction and destruction of the drainage works must be dated to the same periods (Hope Simpson and Hagel 2006, 207; independent evidence from the canals themselves is not yet available). The construction of dams and canals "has all the marks of a single coordinated design, implemented within a single period of time" (Hope Simpson and Hagel 2006, 188) that most likely took place at the very end of LH IIIA2 or early LH IIIB1.

It is in the light of these fortifications that Larymna can be understood. Its Cyclopean wall (Figure 5.7a), of which a stretch of about 80 m is preserved, stands at approximately 2.5-m high and is 4.5-m thick (Oldfather 1916, 37) and would have bounded a low acropolis. It is built in a rough polygonal style exactly comparable with the walls at Gla (Figure 5.7b; Loader 1998, 27) and Agios Ioannis (Fossey 1990a, 23; 1990b, 72–89). Although the exact date for the Larymna fortification is disputed (see Kramer-Hajos 2008, 55–56), LH IIIB sherds found inside the walls (Hope Simpson and Dickinson 1979, 243–244) provide a *terminus post quem* for the construction, and the wall must have been built at some time in LH IIIB. It seems undeniable that it is the last extension of the series of strongholds extending from Orchomenos via Gla to the coast, securing Orchomenian access to the Euboean Gulf and extending its defenses. Orchomenos would certainly have tried to gain access to the important North Euboean Gulf, and Larymna would have been a logical choice. The nearby site of Pazaraki controlled the access route between the sea and a well-watered plain; a Mycenaean settlement or outpost here would be in visual contact with the fortification at Agios Ioannis. As such Pazaraki would have been in an ideal position to relay warnings of intrusions from the bay at Larymna to this fortification system. Although Larymna is located east from the point where the water drains into the Megali Katavothra, it is clear that it forms in fact part of the same network.[18] This

---

[17] Iakovidis 1998, 278: "The earlier sherds are late LH IIIA2 or incipient LH IIIB1. The destruction layers contain nothing later than advanced LH IIIB2 examples."

[18] Already Oldfather (1916, 40–41) connected Larymna with Orchomenos; though part of his argument for this is based on his assumption that the remains of a road at Pazaraki, consisting of wheel ruts, is "Minyan" (it is in fact more likely Classical: Jansen 2002, 20. See

FIGURE 5.7A–B. Cyclopean masonry at Larymna (a) and Gla (b).

explanation for the existence of Larymna (and Pazaraki) explains Larymna's odd location, as noted on p. 107: it is one of only very few sites that is not located in or adjacent to fertile soil (Skroponeri is another example). Larymna was not an organically developing settlement, but, as it were, "custom-built" by Orchomenos as part of an elaborate defensive system. The parallel with Korphos-Kalamianos (see p. 111) is obvious.

also Kramer-Hajos 2008, 57 for an overview of the evidence for dating this road), the part where he connects the two based on topography and fortification is valid, and he was certainly right in his conclusion.

The southern part of the Kopaic Basin forms a striking contrast to its northern side: although many sinkholes are located on the southeastern side of the Kopaic Basin, they are all left undefended. The relative lack of fortifications on the southern side of the Kopais suggests two things: first, that there was no need for a strong border between Thebes and Orchomenos (the visible, if somewhat symbolic border of Lake Kopais sufficed), and second, that there was no need to defend the southern dams and *katavothres*. Both of these suggest that Thebes was not perceived as a military threat, possibly because it had invested in the drainage works itself.[19]

The question remains why Orchomenos felt it necessary to invest in defending the northern border of the Kopaic Basin; the fortifications suggest, however, that the relationship between Orchomenos and its northern neighbors was far from ideal. It should be noted that, even with the most conservative estimate of building time, the works cannot have been thrown up as a defense against any immediate threat: instead, they must be viewed as "part of an offensive programme where authorities visually displayed their sovereignty over the surrounding territories" (Loader 1998, 72–73).

The string of fortifications may have served a practical purpose, but from a phenomenological viewpoint, it was also highly symbolic and charged with meaning, separating the Kopaic polders from the area to the north, a permanent expression of the power and might of the palace of Orchomenos. These fortifications represent an attempt to intimidate forces that are anticipated as a long-term threat and reflect unease, at least, of the close presence of a perceived "other" to the north, suggesting that the area of East Lokris, north of the Kopais, was not fully incorporated into the polity of Orchomenos. These fortifications may then have served as a border between the palatial core area under control of Orchomenos and the more provincial parts to the north.[20] It is possible that the LH IIIA2 destruction at Mitrou as well as the decline in the Kalapodi area should be attributed to Orchomenos.

The effect (the agency) of these walls on the people in the area should not be underestimated and may have led to two reactions from local people that were not associated with the palace: on the one hand, one may imagine a desire and attempts to be incorporated in the palatial sphere with its mighty walls and promise of order and protection, and, on the other hand, an increased feeling of alienation and exclusion from the palatial sphere. Especially the first reaction could have resulted in the change in settlement

[19] A third possibility is that Thebes was ultimately responsible for all Kopaic drainage works. Given the little benefit it received from this, however, this seems unlikely. Moreover, Linear B evidence seems to support a territorial division between Thebes and Orchomenos (Del Freo 2009).

[20] Whereas a single citadel, such as Mycenae, served as the center of a territory, a string of smaller fortifications is more likely to be perceived as a border. In line with this, whereas Mycenae is surrounded by roads, cemeteries, and smaller settlements, the forts along the Kopaic Basin, with the exception of Gla, seem to lack such satellite settlements.

pattern just north of the forts, as observed on p. 118. Farmers from these areas who had perhaps already worked for the palatial power on building these very forts may have relocated to work the newly established polders, perhaps lured by prospects of secure rations and safety, thus adapting to expanding palatial power by identifying with it. On the other hand, there may have been people who remained outside of the palatial economy and viewed the expressions of palatial power negatively. Especially if Orchomenos was, as speculated, a cause of destructions, it is easy to imagine the rancor felt by people coming from such areas and viewing these outward expressions of palatial invincibility.[21] Either way, the apparent effect of a "wasteland" or a "no man's land" north of the forts would have strengthened the idea of a visual separation between the domain of Orchomenos and the area to the north. It is a visible testimony to an increasing alienation between palace and province, which may well have escalated during the period of destruction of the palaces around 1200 BCE and the following decades.

Mitrou may have come under control of Orchomenos at the end of LH IIIA2, when widespread burned deposits suggests destruction. The LH IIIB2 evidence suggests ties with a palace, but also a drastically changed architectural landscape, within which the center of habitation shifted. Similar developments are visible at Iklaina, where LH IIIA destruction of the megaron was followed by LH IIIB building of a new megaron with a different orientation. Iklaina, too, lost its independence, attested by an LH IIIA Linear B tablet, to become a secondary center in the Pylian realm by LH IIIB. The extreme centralization characterizing the Pylian polity is visible in Boeotia as well, especially in the power of Thebes.

The drainage works supplied Orchomenos with enough fertile farmland to allow it to build up a surplus stored at Gla, ensuring that the inhabitants of the benefiting communities had enough food year round. This surplus suggests that Orchomenos, as other palaces, specialized in large-scale monocultures emphasizing the easily storable einkorn, of which at least 2 metric tons may have been stored at Gla. This sort of agricultural specialization is extremely vulnerable: if for some reason (weather, infection) one type of produce fails to produce a harvest, a mixed system always has other products to fall back on. When these other products are not cultivated, shortage and famine are imminent. Kroll has established that grain (wheat and barley) quality decreased drastically in the Argolid in LH IIIB, and that many noxious weeds intermingled with the grain (Kroll 1984; Deger-Jalkotzy 2008, 389): a situation typical for large monocultures as seem to have been practiced in the polders. The palaces "may have undermined the viability of

---

[21] It seems unlikely that the possible movement of people toward the palatial territory went hand in hand with a counter movement north, away from the palatial area. Most people must have been subsistence farmers, bound to their land, which they would not leave without clear promise of a better existence.

traditional risk-buffering agricultural strategies" (Tartaron 2008, 134) such as reliance on mixed systems.[22] Orchomenos was even more vulnerable since its fertile land was won from the water. In the event of dykes breaking through or *katavothres* being blocked, its land and therefore its crops would be inundated in a matter of hours.

With the Kopaic drainage works, Orchomenos represents a palace and power structure that is very different from the other known Mycenaean palaces. The other palaces were, at the end of the day, unnecessary for the local population; each *wanax* may have been well aware of this and this may be one of the reasons for the almost neurotic restriction of symbols of power. Their wealth finance system, prevalent at Pylos (e.g., Galaty and Parkinson 2007) but also, judging from the many exotic prestige items and workshops specializing in elite materials and items, at Thebes, was critical to maintain power: "elite status items manufactured under palatial supervision acted as markers of affiliation that legitimized and advertised the authority of the palatial elite" (Schon 2007, 143). The control over these items, emblematic for the palace itself, allowed the elites to legitimize and propagate social inequality (Schon 2007, 143).

At Orchomenos, there was no or much less need for wealth finance in maintaining social hierarchies. Once the polders had been formed, settlements had been founded on former wetlands, and farmers were working the polders, the central power at Orchomenos, via its delegation at Gla, was suddenly indispensable. The central authorities made themselves essential to farmers by creating the polders, which needed maintenance but virtually ensured large harvests and thus alleviated "a major source of risk and unpredictability" (Foxhall 1995, 240). In general, as Foxhall has noted, this was difficult in the Aegean, where "farming was (and is) at the mercy of erratic and unpredictable rainfall (among other things) no matter what central authority may or may not have been in control" (ibidem). Since the central power at Orchomenos was thus indispensable to the local inhabitants, it may have had less need to proclaim its authority in ways that were standard in other palaces that lacked this "natural" advantage. There is thus a possibility that the patchiness of Orchomenian remains is not merely because of the hazards of excavation or the less-than-perfect records kept by early excavators but that a real difference with other palaces underlies this situation. Despite its access to the North Euboean Gulf via the port of Larymna, Orchomenos does not appear to have assimilated a seafaring spirit or have benefited significantly from expanding its network into the long-

---

[22] After the collapse of the palaces, grain quality improved again in the LH IIIC Argolid, and in Messenia the tree population increased (Kroll 1984; Wright 1972). At LH IIIC Kalapodi the large variety in the samples of grains found was noted (Lemos 2002, 221; Felsch 1996, 102–103).

distance maritime routes. Instead, it focused all its energies on the engineering miracle of the Kopaic drainage, becoming a major agricultural center.

CONCLUSIONS

In any schematic representation of Mycenaean territories, the mainland is
divided up into chunks allowing for the presence of one palace. All of Euboea,
as well as the Euboean Gulf coasts in some models, happen to fall outside any
of these palatial territories (e.g., Galaty and Parkinson 2007, fig. 1.1; Nakassis
et al. 2010, 241): these areas are shown as peripheral to the palatial civilization
of Mycenaean Greece. It is not impossible, of course, that palatial centers
existed in these areas but have not been found yet; but the evidence available
suggests that the coastal areas, including Euboea, were provincial. Yet, these
same areas had not been peripheral in the early Mycenaean period, when
competing elites vied for power similarly to the elites in core areas. I have
suggested in this chapter that the area was actively marginalized by the
actions of the palaces. This marginalization can be explained by applying
the theoretical framework of network theory: when the palaces created networks extending to the Euboean Gulf coasts, these palatial networks inter-
rupted the preexisting coastal networks, causing them to disintegrate and
causing the hubs in them to become marginal nodes.

The formation of land-based networks linking the palaces with coastal
sites is visible in the pottery from Chalkis and in the fortifications between
Orchomenos and Larymna. Chalkis' increasing ties with Thebes went hand
in hand with a general decrease in material from Chalkis: the opening up of
networks witnessed in the previous period, when Thebes and Orchomenos
may have actively invested in local elites in attempts to win their loyalty, was
checked in the high palatial period, when the palatial elites attempted to
monopolize access to long-distance links. Once a status quo had been
reached, Orchomenian investment in the area to its north ceased as
Orchomenos turned its attention to the Kopais. This resulted in
a marginalization of the area to the north, which was placed behind
a highly visible border: the periphery here was, far from being a "natural"
and inevitable consequence of its location or resources, created by human
agency. Only Kalapodi, as a sanctuary, received palatial investment; the
cemeteries in the area, however, were all but abandoned.

The reorientation of networks was accompanied by a change in their
structure: whereas in the prepalatial periods multiple centers flourished,
suggesting a network of decentralized (scale-free) properties, in the palatial
period the number of centers declined drastically and the center of Thebes
dominated trade and exchange relations. This suggests that the network
became far more centralized. The cause of the change in networks has been
sought in the agency of palatial rulers, who cut through existing coastal

networks and marginalized coastal centers in order to control the long-distance weak ties. I have viewed palatial elites as knowledgeable actors, purposefully manipulating networks (and, as the next chapter will argue, material goods) to their advantage. Far from "natural causes" – its location, lack of resources, or size of area – being the reason for the peripheral status of the Euboean Gulf region, the area was artificially restricted to the extent that not only did it not thrive more than before but actually saw a cultural decline.

In contrast to the situation at Kalapodi, Lefkandi, and Mitrou and Kynos, developments in the Gulf of Volos show a flourishing LH IIIB phase, when a number of Mycenaean settlements coexisted in a heterarchical system (Pantou 2010). At Dimini, two megaron-type buildings and a central court, workshops, storage rooms, and domestic quarters have yielded evidence for jewelry and tool production in the form of stone molds, as well as actual jewelry, weapons, and "a stone object inscribed with Linear B script" (Adrimi-Sismani 2006, 468). Linear B tablets have been identified at Kastro. These finds suggest that it was indeed the agency of the palaces of Thebes and Orchomenos that led to a marginalization of the Euboean Gulf coast in LH IIIB: their influence did not extend to Volos.

When the palaces emerged, sites around them could be affected in multiple ways. The most straightforward is perhaps the situation when sites were already part of the sphere (the network) of the palatial center before it started expanding: such sites, like Eleon, saw relatively little change. Sites that were, however, first incorporated in the palatial network changed significantly. Larymna and Anthedon benefited from palatial investment, visible in the erection of fortification walls. In the case of Mitrou the presence of drain tiles and palatial-type pottery, after destruction of the LH IIIA buildings, suggests the site lost its independence and came under palatial control. Yet another possibility is exemplified by sites like Chalkis, and by the abandonment of cemeteries at Limni, Kolaka, and around Kalapodi, suggesting a marginalization of sites that fell on the borders of the palatial territory without being of importance for the palace. In the case of Chalkis, it may simply have been on the "wrong" side of the Gulf; Kolaka and the Kalapodi areas were both on the "wrong" side of the Kopaic fortification line without having the advantage of a coastal location.

Since the beginning of the Late Bronze Age, Mycenaean society had been in transition. In LH IIIB there is a certain regional stability: the mainland of Greece was divided into territories each ruled by the local palace. However, internally this system was rather fragile, because of some inherent weaknesses in the Mycenaean states. Although the Mycenaean polities had a centralized and internally specialized administration and are therefore rightly characterized as "states," they had in fact a lot in common with chiefdoms: they were small, emphasized the rank of the chief, and were highly dependent on the flow of prestige goods (Parkinson and Galaty

2007, 123). In fact the territories of Mycenaean states are generally assumed to be no larger than about 50 km in diameter, and this falls well within Spencer's maximum size for a chiefdom (Spencer 1990). This has to do with the highly competitive origins of the Mycenaean states (emerging elites at many places); perhaps with the fragmented nature of the Greek landscape, promoting small polities focused on a geographically clearly defined unit; and with the seeming inability of Mycenaean kings to delegate (except, perhaps, at Mycenae, if the administration at Tiryns is interpreted as that of the port of Mycenae, and at Orchomenos, with its delegation at Gla). All administration is centered on the palaces, and, with the exception of the polity of Pylos with its Further Province, most sites in the polity can be visited within a day by an official from the palaces, resulting in a marked gap between primary and secondary centers: characteristics of a highly centralized political and administrative network. Finally, unlike Orchomenos, the other palaces and their officials depended on the constant influx of prestige goods to advertise their status and reward lower-level officials. It is this dependence on prestige goods that will be the focus of the next chapter.

6

PALATIAL CONCERNS
Ships and exotica

The reorientation of networks and change in network topology, from a decentralized to a highly centralized type, has been ascribed to Theban expansion into the Euboean Gulf area, allowing Thebes to plug into the preexisting maritime routes through the Euboean Gulf. This chapter will examine more closely Theban motivations for doing so, ascribing them to control over the weak ties responsible for the import of more or less exotic prestige goods. The exploitation of weak ties allowed the Theban ruling elites to consume imported exotica, which in turn enabled them to legitimize their status at home. This chapter thus focuses more on the agency of the ruling palatial elites, who, as knowledgeable actors, purposefully manipulated material goods to their advantage. Within the established *habitus* of the Mycenaean culture, the consumption of exotic prestige goods enhanced status, and it is therefore not surprising that the palatial elites attempted to increase their consumption of such goods: this was ultimately the main motivation behind the changes in social-political networks. In exploring the motivations for changing the social-political network, this chapter will ask two questions: Why is there such a dearth of ship iconography in official art dating to the palatial period? And what does an analysis of import consumption by the palatial elites suggest about palatial relations to coastal areas?

MISSING SHIP AND SEAFARING ICONOGRAPHY

In 1980 Maria Shaw identified two small LH IIIB fresco fragments from Pylos, published originally by Lang in 1969, as depicting part of a mast and rigging of a ship (Figure 6.1; Shaw 1980, 177–178). The reconstruction is convincing, and one may wonder why it took until 1980 to identify the depiction. One major reason is that the fragments were unique. After the Akrotiri miniature fresco, ships largely ceased to populate the frescoes of the Aegean world, and the Mycenaean palace walls mostly lack, with only very few important

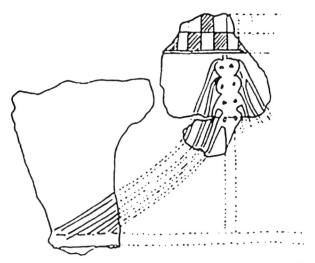

FIGURE 6.1. Mast and rigging of a traditional sailing ship on fresco fragments from Pylos. After Shaw 1980, 178, fig. 12.

exceptions, references to ships and seafaring. Apart from the fragment mentioned above, the evidence consists of a possible hull on an LH IIIB fragment from Pylos found to the northwest of the palace (Morgan 1988, 132; Wedde 2000, no. 699), a group of seven fragments from Room 31 at Pylos that are associated with the fragments identified by Shaw and depict a mast of a second ship, part of a hull, and parts of rigging (Brecoulaki 2006; Brecoulaki et al. 2015, 282, figs. 14–15), a group of four ships, three of them partially overlapping, from Hall 64 at Pylos (Brecoulaki 2004, 2005, 2006, 2007; Petrakis 2011, 194; Brecoulaki et al. 2015), and a probable *ikria* (ship's cabins) frieze at Mycenae (Shaw 1980). Almost all fresco evidence for ships to date thus comes from Messenia.

Before assessing the significance of this, we must take a closer look at the sort of ships depicted in the Late Bronze Age Aegean. The Akrotiri fresco is populated by traditional, Minoan-type sailing ships, even though most are, anachronistically and obviously painfully, paddled, suggesting a ceremonial voyage (see Figure 2.6: the paddlers have to lean over the gunwhale awkwardly, a painful and ineffective position that indicates clearly that these ships are not meant to be paddled). The traditional sailing ship, used throughout the Aegean, is characterized by a crescent-shaped hull (Figure 2.6) with ample cargo space and a boom-footed rig, recognizable in depictions by the multiple pairs of deadeyes (pairs of loops at the masthead) and halyards, ropes used to support, raise, and lower the boom and yard and thus to maneuver the sail at the top of the mast (Figures 2.6 and 6.1). This boom-footed rig was awkward to manipulate; the sail was spread by raising the yard to the masthead, and Wachsmann postulates that the clumsy rig, lateral cables, and inboard-projecting keel together imply that seafarers used the sail only when the wind was astern (Wachsmann 1998, 251). The fragment identified by Shaw (Figure 6.1) suggests, with its multiple deadeyes, this type of ship.

The sailing ships could be rowed, and indeed must have been rowed occasionally, for example when maneuvering into or out of a harbor, or possibly during hostile encounters; their strength was however their sailing capability, coupled with the fact that they could be operated by a small crew, leaving ample space in the hull for cargo (Wedde 2005, 30). When used as warships, they could have been outfitted with a larger crew of rowers (ibidem). The evidence for military use of these ships in the Aegean is however limited to the North Frieze in the West House at Akrotiri, which depicts a shipwreck, possibly as a result of a coastal battle (Doumas 1992, 27 fig. 26). An LH IIIB krater from Enkomi on Cyprus (Wachsmann 1998, 141 fig. 2.28) depicts two ships carrying warriors, but in a static and seemingly peaceful environment. Although not exactly crescent-shaped, bow and stem are only distinguished from each other by stem devices that are similar to those on the Thera ships and the single preserved masthead has three pairs of deadeyes: these are examples of traditional ships. With their dotted robes, the sword-carrying figures are similar to those on the krater from Ugarit (Figure 4.2) and not so much martial as ceremonial.

By LH IIIB the Mycenaeans had invented a new type of ship: the Mycenaean oared galley (Wedde 1999, 165; 2005, 31–32; Wedde's Type V). Although most depictions of the new ship type date to LH IIIC, Wedde suggests reasonably that the few depictions of LH IIIB and IIIA-B date are evidence that the type was known well enough by that time to be depicted, which in turn suggests that the creation of the new design may have taken place in LH IIIA (Wedde 2005). Since the new design represents a completely different concept with a different hull, and it is therefore unlikely that Minoan ships were gradually adapted to evolve into Mycenaean galleys (ibidem), I assume that the hypothetical LH IIIA examples were typologically the same as the LH IIIB and IIIC examples, and use the abundant LH IIIC iconography here as evidence for palatial-era galleys.

The new Mycenaean galley design was characterized by a smaller, lighter hull that seated more rowers,[1] allowing for greater speed at the cost of sacrificed cargo space: whereas the older Minoan ships had their hull designed around their sailing function (Gillmer 1985; Basch 1986, 425), the new oared galley had the hull designed around the propulsive unit of rowers. On depictions, the open rowers' galleries are often emphasized, suggesting that to the Mycenaean artists the single most striking feature consisted of

---

[1] Wedde estimates the overall length of the Mycenaean galley as about 25–30 m, as opposed to about 35 m for the Minoan sailing ship (Wedde, personal communication March 2015).

these galleries (Wachsmann 1998, 130–131, 140). Rowers' stanchions or oars number between 9 and 26 pairs on depictions, with most depictions showing around 20–25 pairs (see Wachsmann 1998, 131–144). Raised platforms in the bow or aft and subsequently the addition of a deck covering most of the hull protected the rowers while creating a fighting platform. The shape of the hull is different: the bow is no longer curving, but raises more or less vertically in a reinforced stempost, often combined with a pronounced keel extending into a short spur. This facilitated beaching at speed without compromising structural integrity (Wedde 1999, 466; Crielaard 2000, 59); more generally, it would have allowed withstanding greater impact. There are two scenarios in which that would have been advantageous, that is, in case of a maritime battle, in which ships were at close quarters, and when exploring unknown rocky coasts: barely submerged rocks under the water would easily tear open the crescent hull of traditional ships (as seems to have happened to the Cape Gelidonya ship around 1200 BCE: Bass 1967), but the square, reinforced bow with protruding keel of the new galley would be less susceptible to sustain damage severe enough to result in sinking. Thus these ships may have been more suitable, due to their increased maneuverability as well as their sturdiness, for exploring unknown coasts (Wedde 2005), seeking out new territories (and creating new weak ties) in order to acquire small prestige items.

The new ships are further recognizable by an improved steering mechanism (Wedde 2005, 31) and a brailed rig. The steering oar of these galleys represented a marked improvement over the steering gear of the Minoan ships: the oar blade is triangular (Figure 6.2), and the helmsman maneuvers the oar via a tiller (a projection fixed to the head of the steering oar to give the helmsman leverage or allow him to steer when the rudder head is out of reach: Wachsmann 1998, 381), visible on Figures 7.2 and 7.3. These improvements allowed the Mycenaean galley to turn more quickly and meant that a team of rowers with the helmsman could quickly maneuver a ship in battle-ready position. The helmsman thus held an important job, and his importance is reflected in the iconographical emphasis he receives: he is seated above the rowers in a protected area with a good view of the sea and the sail (Wedde 2005, 31), and may be shown as large and prominent as the warriors on deck (see Figures 7.2 and 7.3).

FIGURE 6.2. Mycenaean galley on an LH IIIC Middle stirrup jar from Skyros. After Wedde 2000, no. 655.

The newer brailed rig is identifiable in depictions by the absence of a boom and the limited number of deadeyes (typically only one pair; Wedde 2000, 85 and see Dakoronia 2006, 27 fig. 6). This system allowed one to furl the sail upward much like a Venetian blind; it allowed for quick adjustments to the sail, and was therefore suitable for naval combat and raiding activities, where speed and maneuverability are of the essence. Under full sail a ship could surprise another ship or a coastal settlement, and after quickly furling the sail (in the process creating space on deck for battle; cf. Casson 1958 for a historical parallel), rowers could maneuver the ship into place. As a result of these changes, the new Mycenaean galley was a less successful sailing ship, but it could move at high speed under oars handled by warriors, which made it excellent for executing quick coastal raids, although it may have been used for trade as well. The limited cargo space suggests that trade focused exclusively on small quantities of prestige goods (and not, for example, on bulk trade of metals).

Its light open hull appears suddenly in the pictorial record in LH IIIA-B. A boat model from Tanagra, dated to LH IIIA-B, is perhaps the earliest representation of this new galley type, recognizable by its offset bow ending in a bird-head device (Demakopoulou and Konsola 1981, 87); two more early examples are depicted on an LH IIIA2-IIIB sherd from Ashkelon (Mountjoy 2011) and a LM IIIB larnax from Gazi. A gold diadem from Pylos with embossed decoration, too, represents this type, recognizable by its flat hull with a tall vertical bird-headed stempost (Blegen and Rawson 1973, 16 fig. 108a-d; Wachsmann 1998, 136 fig. 7.18; Wedde 2000, no. 6006).[2] Assuming that the depictions of these galleys postdate their actual invention somewhat, the galleys would have "been part of the great increase in activity in LH IIIA, when the major citadels found their extended form" (Wedde 1999, 468).

Yet, all ships depicted on palatial frescoes are of the traditional Minoan type. In the small fragment in Figure 6.1, the number of deadeyes indicates that this ship was of the traditional design; the fragments associated with this depict a boom-footed rig (see Brecoulaki et al. 2015, 282 fig. 15), indicating that the second ship was of the same type. The ships depicted in Hall 64 at Pylos are interesting. The fragmentary fresco, dubbed the "Naval Scene," decorated the northwestern section of the northwestern wall of Hall 64, stretching over 3.20 m in length (Brecoulaki 2009), which makes it only slightly shorter than the 3.90 m-long Flotilla Fresco from the West House at Akrotiri (Doumas 1992, 68 fig. 35).[3] In other respects, too, the fresco seems comparable to the Akrotiri Flotilla Fresco; for example, the four ships, of Minoan hull shape,

[2] Bouzek 1994, 230, notes the European inspiration for this diadem, and Wachsmann 1998, 137, connects the bird-head device on the stem with the bird-boat ornaments in Urnfield art.

[3] Younger (2011, 169) has suggested that the West House fresco from Akrotiri may have been based on a map of the sea and its coasts, noting the existence of such maps on papyrus and the similar heights of papyrus documents (0.40 m) to the frieze (0.42 m). The Pylos frieze

move to the right and are surrounded by dolphins (although at Pylos the dolphins, unrealistically, move in opposite direction to the ships rather than with them, suggesting the speed with which the ships move). The ships are represented with two steering oars, typical for sailing ships (compare, for example, the boat under sail on the Thera fresco: Doumas 1992, 69, fig. 35; 76, fig. 37); Mycenaean galleys are, on the other hand, invariably depicted with just one steering oar. The decks, too, are with their awnings reminiscent of Theran, rather than Mycenaean ships, and the ships lack rowers' stanchions. Despite this, the ships are rowed instead of sailed (Brecoulaki et al. 2015, 274-277, figs. 8–9),[4] leading Tartaron to suggest they may represent an intermediary stage between Minoan sailing ships and Mycenaean oared galley (Tartaron 2013, 60). However, although artistic elements do show a mix of Minoan and Helladic features, the publication by Brecoulaki et al. 2015 shows the ships themselves as purely Minoan; as mentioned before, these ships must have been rowed on occasion so there is no reason to assume that they represent anything else than the traditional sailing boats. The reason for this mode of propulsion here is unclear, but the small number of oars (between five and seven pairs per ship) suggests a non-military occasion.[5] Therefore, if the fresco served as a naval equivalent to the battle frescoes in Hall 64 (as suggested by Brecoulaki et al. 2015), which have been taken as instrumental in projecting Pylian identity and supremacy (Davis and Bennett 1999; Bennett 2007) and led Kilian and Hiller to consider that Hall 64 was the domain of the *lawagetas*, the Pylian general (Kilian 1987, 38),[6] it did so without obvious militaristic overtones.

Tartaron suggests the rowers may be backing the ship into anchorage (Tartaron 2013, 60), although the presence of dolphins and complete absence of landscape features may rather suggest an event taking place on the open sea. Of course, artistic representations may well favor convention and esthetic concerns over realism. Another possibility is that the ships

was described as 0.49-m high in the field notebook entry dated June 29, 1953 (HS7-Ext. 6: Brecoulaki 2006), but it seems no landscapes are depicted in addition to the ships.

[4] The same is true for a recently (2009) discovered LH IIB-IIIA1 fresco fragment with a ship from Iklaina (Cosmopoulos 2009, 14, fig. 33a; 2015, 251-254). The fragment shows the crescent-shaped bow of a ship with two rowers, leaning forward (and thus at the beginning of their stroke, as on the Pylos frescoes). Although immensely important and interesting, this fresco is not considered here for the following two reasons: Iklaina, although an important district center in the "Hither Province" and find spot of the earliest known Linear B inscription, was not, on current evidence, a palace; and the fresco predates this chapter's concern with established palatial ideology. It is however striking that this particular iconography is on present evidence limited to Messenia.

[5] The crescent-shaped Egyptian ships shown engaged in a coastal battle on the Medinet Habu relief (see Figure 7.5) have between 9 and 11 pairs of oars: on the lower end, but still within the range for Mycenaean galleys.

[6] For the iconographic program in the megaron, which appears to be overwhelmingly ceremonial in character, see, e.g., Bennett 2007, 12–15, 17–18.

participated in "an event or ceremony of religious character" (Brecoulaki et al. 2015, 288) and indeed some decidedly old-fashioned or traditional design elements in the ships suggest a ritual or ceremonial occasion. Like Neopalatial glyptic representations of "ritual craft" (Wedde 2000, 339–340 nos. 901–912), the rightmost ship lacks a mast (Brecoulaki 2005; in Brecoulaki et al. 2015, all four ships are restored without mast). Two of the ships carry a cabin in the stern, and awnings cover the decks. The leftmost ship bears a circular decoration on the bowsprit, possibly an emblem of the sort that is also found on the ships from Akrotiri and Agia Irini. The hull of the ship on the right displays a regular zigzag decoration (Brecoulaki 2005, 2006), also present on, e.g., two longboats on an Early Cycladic "frying pan" from Chalandriani (Coleman 1985, 199 no. 27; Wedde 2000, nos. 403–404), two small sherds from Iolkos that have often been taken to portray ships (although Wedde 2000, 239, notes that their topology would be unique for their MH-LH I date), and (as restored) on a ship from Agia Irini (Morgan 2005, 33 fig. 1.18). As Broodbank (1989, 328) notes, the exact meaning of the zigzag is difficult to determine; it may have been structural or a ritual marker (Brecoulaki 2005). It seems to be important, however, that the few examples of (possible) ships with such zigzags are all examples of great antiquity compared to the Pylos ship, suggesting that the Pylos ship is emphatically archaic (see also Petrakis 2011, 194).

Thus fresco evidence from Pylos shows exclusively the older, traditional Minoan sailing ship. This is surprising, since Linear B evidence from Pylos shows that the palace invested heavily in the new Mycenaean galley. The employment of the galley by the palace at Pylos is suggested by tablets PY An 1, An 610, and An 724. Although remarkably few texts pertain to Mycenaean war-fleets (Palaima 1991, 285), the few texts that are known suggest the importance of the organization of the fleet for the Pylian *wanax*: inscribed by the master scribe, these three tablets record the compulsory draft of no fewer than 600 rowers for the fleet in return for the use of land (Palaima 1991, 286); the sheer numbers of rowers suggest they served on oared galleys. Assuming there would be no more than 50 rowers per ship, these rowers would represent the crews for at least 12 galleys.

Another indication that the fleet was of paramount importance for the palace at Pylos is found on tablet PY Na 568, on which shipbuilders are given the largest exemption from contributing flax (50 units) of any group on 101 tablets (Palaima 1991, 287; other groups are bronze smiths, hunters, and a group connected to the military leader). Since this is the most generous release from payment in the entire series, Wachsmann states that this indicates a "pressing need" for ships by the palace (Wachsmann 1998, 227). It is certainly interesting that shipbuilders receive a greater exemption than craftsmen responsible for manufacturing, for example, bronze weapons, suggesting that galleys may have had an important military function.

The term *na-u-do-mo*, shipbuilders, occurs on two other tablets (Ventris and Chadwick 1973, 123, 298–299, 562; Palaima 1991, 287–288). It heads PY Vn 865, which contains a list of 12 male names; on KN U 736 it appears in connection with 181 "oar straps" and 93 units of an item whose name is lost on the fragmentary tablet. The fact that PY Vn 865 lists personal names suggests the importance of these men, whether they were shipwrights themselves (if the header is to be understood as a nominative plural) or were given to the shipwright as assistants (if the header is a dative singular: Petrakis 2011, 208). In addition, PY Vn 46 and 869 contain lists of construction materials that might refer to timbers used for construction of an average ship of 10–15 m in length (Wachsmann 1998, 227). The existence of an ideogram for ship in Linear B suggests that the palatial scribes recorded maritime matters on a regular basis (Palaima 1991, 287). The Linear B evidence thus implies that the palaces oversaw at least some of the shipbuilding and that maritime matters were of great, probably military, interest to the palaces.

The rowers named in the PY An series, apart from getting large tax exemptions and being recorded by their personal name rather than as a collective, all come from important coastal centers and are associated "with several individuals of prominent status in the Pylian social and political hierarchy" (Palaima 1991, 285). For example, five rowers on PY An 724 are associated with a prominent leader called e-ke-ra$_2$-wo, possibly to be equated with the *wanax* himself (Palaima 1995, 134–135; 2006, 62–63; Nakassis 2012, 14–17). Even if e-ke-ra$_2$-wo was not the *wanax*, it is clear that he was of high status and associated with the *lawagetas*, the military leader and second in command (Petrakis 2008). One more rower on PY An 724 is associated with the *lawagetas* directly. Since the *lawagetas* is assumed to be the leader of the armed forces, it is likely that these rowers were warrior-rowers and the galleys were indeed used, at least on occasion or when the situation demanded, for military engagements.[7]

Rowers were granted land in return for their service (Palaima 1991, 285) and one text implies that they are married to weaving women at the palace; Palaima suggests that the palace may have supported the rowers' families during their term of duty (Palaima 1991, 286). As a result of this palatial engagement with the rowers and their families, their children are the only ones in the Linear B tablets whose parents are both known by name (Shelmerdine 2008b, 147). The evidence indicates clearly that the galleys

[7] Perhaps we may imagine the use of these galleys as similar to what Broodbank has proposed as a role for the Early Cycladic longboats: vessels meant primarily to intimidate and establish military supremacy, which may have played a role in raiding or forceful collection of small prestigious items (Broodbank 1989; 2000, 247–258). Possibly similar "warrior-rowers" (with oars and spears) are depicted on an MH pithos sherd from Kolonna (Siedentopf 1991, no. 162).

and their rowers were of interest to the palatial elites: they invested in their building and in their crews and kept a palatial fleet at hand.[8]

The galley was, according to Wedde (1999, 468), instrumental in the creation of palatial civilization, and indispensable for the growth of the palaces. As part of the LH IIIA economic and political growth, the galley extended "the range of maritime forays in search of raw materials and trade contacts" (Tartaron 2013, 68). In network terms, galleys forged new links, many of them long-distance ties that were instrumental in procuring the prestige goods on which the palatial elites depended for their legitimization. Therefore it is surprising that the fresco evidence from Pylos does not picture the new galley but instead the older, traditional, Minoan design of the sailing ship in a non-military setting. Even the image of the ship doodled on the verso of PY An 724 shows, like the Linear B ideogram itself, a crescent hull, like the Minoan ships, without mast (Wachsmann 1998, 125). Although it seems oddly incongruous to draw this ship type on a tablet dealing with warships, this may simply be because of the Minoan (Linear A) origin of the Mycenaean Linear B script. A Minoan heritage is certainly the reason for the curving hull on an LH IIIB sealing made by a metal ring dated tentatively to LH IIIA1 (CMS I Suppl. 193).[9] The evidence suggests that palatial ship depictions were ultimately conservative, failing to take important design innovations into account; the only exception from the palace of Pylos that I know of consists of the gold diadem with embossed decoration depicting a galley mentioned on p. 132. Whatever the exact reason, references at Pylos show overwhelmingly the older Minoan type, whereas the texts themselves, mentioning rowers, seem to refer exclusively to Mycenaean galleys. Tartaron (2013, 69) already raised the question why galley depictions peaked in the postpalatial period rather than during "the heyday of Mycenaean overseas contacts and international trade."[10]

Even more striking, however, is the virtually complete absence of ship iconography at other palaces. Although fresco fragments from Thebes are numerous, and themes include marine scenes with dolphins, hunting scenes, and a miniature scene of a bearded and helmeted warrior in a window, not a single ship has been found to date.[11] This seems the more surprising since Thebes had far-flung international connections and would thus be expected

---

[8] Harbor facilities involving some hydraulic engineering have been discovered at Romanou, near the Tragana tholos tomb. Dated to LH IIIA1-B, these facilities are chronologically concurrent with the flourishing of the palace of Pylos and it is likely that they were built on instigation of the palace. See Zangger et al. 1997, 613–623.

[9] See Wedde 2000, 242, for possibly another sealing from Pylos with a curved hull.

[10] He suggests tentatively that this may have to do with the inward-focused MH societies from which the palaces emerged (Tartaron 2013, 292, note 15).

[11] A possible ship appears on a stone mold from Thebes. It, however, "produces a vessel which has no parallels in the evidence," reason for Wedde to doubt that the image is meant to represent a ship (Wedde 2000, 240).

to have been especially invested in ships and seafaring. Fresco fragments from Orchomenos, too, include hunting scenes but lack ships. A series of fragments that may depict the siege and attack of a citadel shows, apart from architectural features with greaved legs on top of them and parts of chariots, possible swimmers (Immerwahr 1990, 217, note 13 identifies them as Cretans), suggesting a coastal town. These fragments are the closest we have to the narrative ship frescoes from the earlier part of the Late Bronze Age; they seem close in theme (a siege) to a frieze from the megaron at Mycenae (Kontorli-Papadopoulou 1999, 332) as well as one from the House of the Oil Merchant (Immerwahr 1990, 125). Any ships, if they were ever part of the scene, are, however, not preserved. The *ikria* frieze from Mycenae is emblematic rather than narrative, repeating just one part of a ship imbued with symbolism (see p. 140) or perhaps simply in a pleasing decorative rhythm; moreover the *ikria* refer to traditional Minoan-type ships.

Ships are frequently modeled in clay; Wedde provides a catalogue of no fewer than ten boat models from the palatial periods on the mainland and an additional four models of possibly LH III date (Wedde 2000, 310–312). Among the sites where these boat models were found are palatial centers: Mycenae, Tiryns, and Thebes are all represented by several examples. Aegina, Methana, Nichoria, and Tanagra have yielded LH IIIA-B ship models as well. However, these ceramic models are not associated with high culture and cannot be taken to convey specifically palatial concerns. The same is true for pictorial pottery dating to the LH IIIA-B periods, on which ships are rare. Thus three sherds of two kraters showing rowers from Tiryns, dated to late LH IIIB2 or LH IIIC Early and found outside the citadel (Güntner 2006, 179), cannot be taken to reflect palatial concerns; and neither can two sherds, both dated no more precisely than "LH," one from Mycenae and one from Eleusis (Wedde 2000, nos. 639 and 648).[12] A possible ship or boat in the underworld (?) painted on a larnax from Tanagra Tomb 47 (Wedde 2000, no. 697) is equally useless for reconstructing palatial ideologies. The depiction on a pottery sherd from Mycenae (Vermeule and Karageorghis IX 88) is unlikely to represent a ship: Wedde 2000, 239). For an important sherd from Ashkelon, see Chapter 7.

Absence of evidence cannot, of course, be equated with evidence of absence, and the possibility that fresco fragments of ships will still turn up at other palatial centers cannot be discounted. Yet, the fact remains that whereas battle scenes, hunting scenes, and processions are commonly found on the walls of the palaces at Mycenae, Tiryns, Pylos, Thebes, and Orchomenos, ships seem exceptional and are on present evidence limited to Pylos. Since Linear B evidence for ships is likewise limited to Pylos, one

---

[12] Evidence from LM IIIB contexts is equally poor: a Mycenaean ship is drawn upside down inside a LM larnax (Gray 1974, G47, fig. 11; Wachsmann 1998, 131, fig. 7.7), and another ship is painted on the outside of a LM IIIB larnax from Gazi (Wachsmann 1998, 136, fig. 7.19).

explanation for this might be that only at Pylos, ship manufacturing and outfitting were under palatial control. I find this unlikely, however, given the crucial role ships played in sustaining palatial legitimization (more about this in the next section) and the obsessive control exercised by the palaces in other economic, military, and religious matters. Therefore I operate here under the assumption that Mycenae, Tiryns, and Thebes would have controlled their ships much like Pylos did.[13] Frescoes illustrate palatial concerns and consolidate palatial propaganda: the themes frequently found can be assumed to have held significant meaning for the palatial elites commissioning them. Is it possible, then, that with the exception of Pylos, ships did not have the specific significant meaning required to be portrayed on palace walls?

In summary, although the palaces were invested in the building, manning, and operating of ships, they seem surprisingly reluctant to depict these ships on their walls. One reason for the absence of contemporary ships is indubitably the fact that palatial frescoes were conservative, hence the long-lived popularity of stock themes like female processions and battle and hunting scenes. This conservatism, possibly reinforced by the use of templates with examples, may have led fresco painters to eschew the contemporary design in favor of the traditional Minoan ship. However, conservatism does not explain the more general dearth of palatial ship iconography. Ships were relatively prominent in prepalatial frescoes in the Cyclades and on Minoan seals, so it is possible that, as Tartaron suggests (Tartaron 2013, 292, note 15), the traditional mainland inward focus plays a role: the grave stelae from Grave Circle A, which are among the first Mycenaean-crafted representations, show chariots and horses, suggesting that from the beginning of the Mycenaean culture these were valued symbols. I would like to suggest yet another possibility here, seeking the answer in aristocratic values.

At first sight, the communal venture of military rower crews under control of the palace seems to fit palatial values well: the prepalatial glorification of the individual warrior gave way during the palatial period to an ideology in which individuals were subsumed under the palace. Yet it seems that, despite the importance of ships for the palaces, ships did not convey the image the palace wished to convey. A comparison with chariots, which did end up represented prolifically in palaces, may be useful.

Chariots are common on palatial frescoes: they are prominent at Mycenae (Crouwel 1981, 170–171 W1–30), where they decorate the megaron and houses inside as well as outside the citadel, at Tiryns (Crouwel 1981, 171–172 W38–69), Pylos (Crouwel 1981, 171 W 35–37), and Orchomenos (Crouwel 1981, 171 W31–34). Schon has summed up the other evidence for

---

[13] Since the corpus of Linear B tablets from Pylos (1087 tablets) dwarfs that at Mycenae (73 tablets), Tiryns (27 tablets), and even Thebes (337 tablets), and only a small fraction (eight tablets, or 0.7%) of Pylian tablets deals with ships, it is conceivable that such tablets once existed at the other palaces.

the importance of chariots for the palatial elites (Schon 2007). Although it is debated and indeed difficult to maintain that chariots were manufactured at the palace of Pylos itself, in the so-called North Eastern Building (Bendall 2003), their manufacture was nevertheless tightly controlled and administered at Pylos (Lupack 2008, 469–470). Attached production, common in the production of wealth items, allowed the palace to control not just production but also distribution and to some extent consumption (Costin 1991). Wide roads emanating from the palaces suggest, too, that chariots were focused on the palaces. Schon notes that there are no depictions of chariots fighting against other chariots (Schon 2007, 140); instead they are always shown battling poorly equipped foot soldiers. They are thus ideologically similar to the swordfighters of the early Mycenaean period: attributes of superior and invincible heroes. Whether chariots were actually used to conquer people in the region, as Schon suggests (Schon 2007, 140), or merely conveyed a symbolic image of superior civilization against fictitious but uncivilized and non-heroic enemies, their depictions fit the desired identity of the (palatial) elites.

Chariots were not only an effective symbol of elite status; they were also a great asset in increasing the power of the palaces. Chariots were difficult to produce, costly to maintain, highly restricted, and a powerful symbol of technological sophistication, and therefore meet several of the criteria that allow an object to be understood as elite (Schon 2007, 143). Schon suggests reasonably that only elites could afford to keep and train horses, and training charioteers would require chariot racing, which in turn by its exclusivity would emphasize the elite connotations of the chariot; non-elites would be excluded. It is possible that palatial chariots would traverse the road networks around Mycenae and that the short stretches of wide, paved roads around the prepalatial Building D at Mitrou were likewise used to parade chariots (Maran and Van de Moortel 2014, 537). Chariots were thus made and used only or primarily in the immediate vicinity of the palaces and played a crucial role in the construction of elite (palatial) identity as well as in supporting palatial power.

Ships could not do this to the same extent. Even if their manufacture was controlled by the palace, the coastal location of manufacture removed them symbolically as well as physically from the palace. A large crew was needed to operate the galley, and we know from Pylos that these crew members were recruited from important coastal centers, thereby enfranchising large groups of men from outside the palace. Therefore, ships did not provide the sense of palatial exclusivity needed to communicate palatial elite ideology. Chariots were charged with symbolism as well as highly mobile; whether they were largely restricted to the immediate vicinity of the palace or found throughout the polity, as Schon suggests (Schon 2007), they were more visible to most Mycenaeans than ships. Although ships were costly to manufacture and required specialized knowledge, they could not be visible throughout the polity (or even abundantly and consistently abroad, like the stirrup jars with perfumed oil), and therefore did not function in this "network of symbolic communication" (Schon 2007, 144) to any great extent.

It appears to be significant that at Mycenae the only known possible (and indirect) palatial references to ships are a series of painted *ikria*, ship's cabins (Shaw 1980), on the traditional sailing ships. It is generally assumed, on the basis of evidence from Akrotiri, where *ikria* are visible on board of ships (they also appear as emblematic motifs, as at Mycenae), that they indicate the seat of the captain (Doumas 1992, 49). Thus it is this emblem which finds its way onto the walls at Mycenae, rather than the entire ship: this is the only part of the ship which has elite connotations. On the South Frieze in the West House at Akrotiri, the captain's spear is protruding from the *ikria* in six out of seven cases and his helmet is mounted on one of the poles in at least four cases (Figure 2.6). Yet, in the *ikria* friezes at Akrotiri and Mycenae these pieces of warrior equipment are not shown, precluding a strong association with warriors. Davaras has connected the *ikria* with ritual implements such as the altars or shrines shown aboard several Neopalatial boats on rings (Davaras 2003, 7–9). Shaw's suggestion that these *ikria* at Mycenae function as symbols of maritime power is certainly correct (Shaw 1980), yet these *ikria* were painted in a bedroom or at least a private room, like the *ikria* at Akrotiri, suggesting that they were not used in a system of communication with a larger audience; as the *ikria* themselves have a sense of privacy to them, they are found in private contexts.

Ships are thus not suitable vessels for elite ideology, and I consider that this may be one of the reasons that they are so rarely depicted on palace walls. In Hall 64 at Pylos, where perhaps a larger Pylian identity was created and reinforced (Davis and Bennet 1999), ships may have been more suitable. Yet the ships depicted are of the traditional type, avoiding references to a military function of ships. In addition to conservatism, there may be another reason why the Mycenaean galley is never present on frescoes. As Wedde speculates (2005, 32–33), the groups of highly trained armed men, forged into a tight community by their service on board, would, even if nominally under direct control of the palace, in reality, given their physical distance from the palace, owe loyalty only to their captain and helmsman and thus pose a potential threat for the palatial officials. Should they ever turn against the palace, they constituted a force to be reckoned with.[14]

---

[14] Is that perhaps a reason that their wives are dependent personnel: craftswomen (weavers) linked to the palace?

Since no wrecks of Mycenaean galleys are known, the evidence for the use of ships is indirect, consisting of depictions and of the goods they must have brought in: the many small prestige items of exotic origin. It is to these that we will now turn, since they provide additional insight into the question of the relationship between palaces and ships.

PALATIAL MONOPOLIES ON ELITE GOODS

The "Treasure Room" in the New Kadmeion at Thebes is aptly named: it contained a staggering 47 imports, among which onyx jewelry, fragments of ivories, and, most impressive, a cache of 34 deep-blue lapis lazuli Near Eastern cylinder seals (another three imported seals were made of faience with gold foil, and two were stone other than lapis lazuli: Kopanias 2012). These seals had their origins in Syria-Palestine, Mesopotamia, and Cyprus and depict striking figural scenes with animals, humans, and deities. Several, originally created by Hittite or Old Babylonian craftsmen, were already antiques when they were recarved on Cyprus. For the palatial officials of the New Kadmeion, however, their age, level of artistry, and perhaps even their exotic origin (symbolic of contact with an eastern power) seem to have been of little value. Their find context suggests that, instead, they were treated as raw material, stored temporarily in the Treasure Room in order to be reworked by palace artisans into Mycenaean artifacts (Burns 2010, 39; Kopanias 2012, 398) – jewelry, perhaps, such as has been found in Thebes (Aravantinos 2010, 81). That the Mycenaeans had a penchant for blue jewelry is suggested by the many blue glass beads.

At least five workshops on the Kadmeion, the palace of Thebes, specialized in crafting goods from mother of pearl, gold, ivory, glass, and various exotic or more common stones, among which are lapis lazuli, agate, quartz, and steatite (Dakouri-Hild 2012). The Loukou and Tzortzi workshops (LH IIIB1 and LH IIIA2-B1, respectively) specialized in ivory and gold working; the Koropouli workshop (LH IIIB1) produced stone (quartz, agate), bone, and metal jewelry; the Kordatzi workshop (LH IIIB1) worked lapis lazuli, mother of pearl, and gold. The Cultural Center site (late LH IIIB2), finally, provides evidence for production of ivory artifacts and boar's tusk harvesting – now an industrialized enterprise under palatial control, far removed from its origins of individual hunters killing the boars required for a helmet. Glass was worked as well, though it is unclear where: the evidence consists of a mold for making glass jewelry, glass artifacts in several workshops, and chemical analysis of glass artifacts found elsewhere (Nikita and Henderson 2006). Another four sites are storage contexts: the House of Kadmos (LH IIIA2-B1) stored agate, steatite, quartz, bone, and gold; the Kordatzi "hoard" (LH IIIA2-B1) contained ivory; the "Arsenal" (late LH IIIB2), ivory; and the

Treasure Room (late LH IIIB2), as noted before, lapis-lazuli and gold orientalia.

Theban evidence for imports is largely limited to the palace: outside the Kadmeion, only a single rich chamber tomb on the Gerokomeion Hill was furnished with an Egyptian glass vase and a Canaanite jar (Cline 1994, nos. 324 and 737). Outside of Thebes, extra-Aegean imports are equally rare: a Mitanni faience cylinder seal at Tanagra (CMS VS1B 360), one in Pharos-Dexameni, close to Chalkis (CMS VS1B 359), and two at Chalkis (CMS V 230 and 231), and a fragment of an ostrich-egg rhyton at Gla (Cline 1994, no. 946) constitute the extent of evidence for circulation of imported goods outside of Thebes. Kopanias notes that, in general, we find only Mitanni, Syrian, Cypro-Aegean, and Aegean cylinder seals, while Kassite cylinders are entirely and Mesopotamian seals are mostly limited to the palace at Thebes (Kopanias 2012, 399). This suggests that only relatively easy to obtain seals were distributed to non-palatial elites.

Parkinson rightfully notes that the sheer number of imported goods does not necessarily give an accurate measure of extra-Aegean trade. He reduces these numbers to the minimum number of contacts necessary to account for the foreign goods and calculates a minimum number of only seven contacts for Thebes (Parkinson 2010, 19). Yet, this is still far more than the evidence for the four palatial-period imports in the Euboean Gulf area (at Tanagra, Chalkis, and Pharos), which equate to at most three contacts – if, that is, they were acquired independently rather than distributed from Thebes. Their small numbers and distribution, at sites close to Thebes, make independent acquisition suspect. Thebes virtually monopolized all international exchange in the region and seems to have maintained even tighter control over craft and industrial activity (Dakouri-Hild 2012, 475). This stands in stark contrast to the prepalatial period, when Mitrou, Perati, Chalkis, and Thorikos all have imports (Parkinson 2010, 23).

In the Argolid, the situation is different: in addition to Mycenae several centers and elite families at Tiryns, Argos, Midea, Asine, and Nauplion engaged in the consumption of exotica. But even in the Argolid, there is evidence for palatial control. Whereas in the LH IIIA phase imports are common outside Mycenae (at Prosymna, Asine, Dendra; see Burns 2010, 181–182), in the LH IIIB period imports are heavily concentrated at Mycenae. Voutsaki has argued that even when valuable goods are consumed outside of Mycenae, it is likely that elites at, e.g., Tiryns and Midea acquired these goods via Mycenae: in other words, the elites at Mycenae controlled distribution of prestige goods and used such goods to create and maintain alliances, which Voutsaki sees as a key element in the process of centralization itself (Voutsaki 2001, 204–207; 2010a, 103). Mycenae, Tiryns, and Thebes account together for more than 90 percent of the orientalia found in LH IIIB contexts (Cline 2007, 191). In addition, examination of the workshops at Mycenae, Tiryns, and Midea suggests that in addition to bronze, lead, glass, faience, wood, and bone and antler, the most precious materials, gold and ivory, were worked exclusively at Mycenae, while at Tiryns other metals (bronze, lead) and bone were worked and at Midea glass and semi-precious stone (Voutsaki 2010a, 101).[15]

Burns gives a compelling history of "import consumption" in the Argolid, illustrated by the import of ivory. In the early Mycenaean period, ivory as an exotic raw material was desirable and prestigious in its own right: an unaltered piece of elephant tusk was deposited in Shaft Grave IV (Burns 2010, 95). In the early palatial period, the "most powerful imports [. . .] were those that made specific reference to foreign lands and exotic cultures" (Burns 2010, 193), as visible on a carved elephant tusk from an LH IIIA context in Mycenae Chamber Tomb 55. The tusk is decorated with an exotic landscape including a volute tree with blossoming lotus tendrils and a male figure wearing an Egyptian pectoral and bracelet, suggesting its Levantine origin (Burns 2010, 173): its exotic origin is emphasized. But the LH IIIB Chamber Tomb 27 in the Panagia cemetery contained nearly a hundred ivory inlays, decorated with themes coming from the Mycenaean tradition, such as warriors wearing boar's tusk helmets (Burns 2010, 187). These items were almost certainly locally crafted at Mycenae, where several workshops give evidence for ivory working (Voutsaki 2001, 196). The proximity of this cemetery to the citadel – it is located just behind the Treasury of Atreus – thus suggests "domestication" of foreign objects closely associated with the palace. Such intended domestication is also suggested for the lapis lazuli cylinder seals at Thebes, found in a storeroom and possibly meant to be converted into typically Mycenaean blue beads.

Dakouri-Hild has recently (2012) traced production and mortuary consumption of ornaments in Late Bronze Age Boeotia, and her findings are similar. Until LH IIIA1, elite graves in Boeotia display a preference for finished goods acquired via long-distance exchange. In LH IIIA2-early IIIB1, "exotic" goods are still associated with elites, but by this time such goods were reworked by the palaces. In the later LH IIIB1 period, sumptuary practices in the mortuary sphere between elites and non-elites diverged in interesting ways: in elite graves, there is less emphasis on distant origins, and artifacts of local materials are now included as well. This may be related to LH IIIB1 earthquake destructions at the palace (for which see Dakouri-Hild 2010, 698), which may have weakened the palace. It also accords with the idea of palatial domestication. In contrast, in non-monumental Theban tombs and elsewhere in Boeotia, there are more exotic furnishings: "ivory, gold, and certain *original* imports are found only in [non-monumental] tombs" (Dakouri-Hild 2012, 476; my emphasis). She notes that "[d]espite possible

---

[15] Evidence for ivory working at Tiryns is uncertain (Krzyszkowska 2005b).

palatial restrictions and sumptuary monopolies, a relatively wide range of such artifacts are consumed in the non-elite ambit" (Dakouri-Hild 2012, 479) and suggests that this may mean that such artifacts now trickled down to lower elites. Alternatively, this may suggest that palatial restrictions on the consumption of (reworked) exotica were strongest in the immediate vicinity of the palace, whereas more outlying areas continued to be able to consume exotica and – importantly – valued original imports. In the LH IIIB2 to early IIIC periods (Dakouri-Hild 2012, 477), non-ceramic goods disappearing from high-status graves and lower-status tombs including a limited range of other grave goods, suggesting a general decline following the destructions at the palace in LH IIIB1 and late LH IIIB2 (Dakouri-Hild 2010, 698).

It seems that similar mechanisms were at work at Thebes and in the Argolid. Both involved monopolizing imports, and then erasing their exotic connotations by reworking in palatial workshops, effectively domesticating the foreign items. This restriction of access to exotic prestige goods, and subsequent domestication of these goods, suggests that exotic goods were important for the palatial elites to ensure their continued power: palatial elite ideologies depended to a great extent on restricted access to exotic prestige goods. Similar political control of distribution of rare and exotic items (such as precious metals and semiprecious stones) has been noted at LH IIIA-B Nichoria in Messenia (Aprile 2013, 434).

Burns (2010) has thus already emphasized how the palatial restrictions on access to prestige goods and the palatial reworking of exotica constitute evidence for the crucial importance of such goods for the palaces. He has also drawn attention to import consumption by local elites in reaction to these palatial restrictions. I would like to go further here and suggest that not only do local elites react to the palaces – for example, by continuing to furnish graves with "exotica" when palatial elites turn to domestic goods – but the actions of the palaces may in turn constitute evidence for a palatial reaction to what is happening in outlying, coastal areas.

Ships were instrumental in procuring exotic goods and evidence from Pylos shows that the palaces invested heavily in keeping a fleet. However, shipping was never completely under control of the palaces. Apart from the obvious possibility of foreign traders arriving to coastal settlements on the Aegean shores, there were probably always independent traders from within the Mycenaean world as well (Van Wijngaarden 1999, 30; contra Sauvage 2012, 161). In either scenario, coastal centers had a distinct advantage and functioned as gateway communities: they would be the first place of contact with foreign ships, and would be the point of departure and arrival for independent and palatial traders alike. It is likely that the Mycenaean expansion to incorporate the coastal center of Kalamianos into its economic and political influence sphere (Tartaron 2010; Tartaron et al. 2011) was motivated at least in part by the desire to monopolize entry points for maritime trade goods; similar developments are visible at Anthedon, Mitrou, and, most clearly, Larymna. However, total control over maritime trade would have been impossible, although it is conceivable that one of the galley's tasks was to control piracy. In the early palatial period (LH IIIA), the presence of exotica in non-palatial centers may thus have various causes: the goods may have arrived as gifts from the palatial center or may have bypassed the palace altogether and have been independently acquired. I suggest that the embellishment of exotica in palatial workshops, which not only ensured palatial monopoly over the sphere of exotic goods but also symbolically subordinated the exotic to palatial domination, may have been one response to the potential threat posed by independent traders: it ensured that it was no longer enough to possess exotica, since your exotica only acquired value after having been reworked at a palatial workshop. The marginalization of ship imagery may be seen in the same light. Both strategies deemphasized the importance of the world outside the palatial sphere, and manipulation of exotica and ship imagery was thus employed by the palaces for ideological purposes. This reconstruction of events accords the provinces agency and the influence to change palatial behaviors. Although staying firmly within the established *habitus* of Mycenaean culture, in which control over elite exotica was of paramount importance, the palatial treatment of such exotica changed, possibly in response to perceived rivalry from the coastal communities.

With the probable exception of amber (Harding et al. 1974), the acquisition of exotic goods took place largely or even exclusively over sea, giving coastal settlements an advantage in the early Mycenaean period. Even the palaces could not prevent adventurous individuals from going out and maintaining or establishing contacts abroad and acquiring prestige goods. However, the palaces were able to change the perception of what was prestigious. Partially this may have been a natural process: when more of a certain commodity reached the mainland, its intrinsic value decreased and only by embellishing the material could it regain its prestige. However, one consequence of this was that, since the palaces controlled the workshops, any exotic goods circulating outside the palatial sphere lost value.

I suggest that, perhaps in addition to this natural process, the palatial officials acted as knowledgeable and rational actors. By marginalizing the ideological importance of ships, lowering the value of raw and finished exotic goods, and monopolizing the creation of prestige goods, the palaces effectively marginalized the coastal societies: the rules dictated by the palace meant that the coastal elites were dependent on the palaces for their prestige. As Burns has suggested, competing elites in the Argolid could subtly resist the power of the palace by consumption of exotic goods and formation of alternative identities (Burns 2010); I suggest that in Boeotia palatial (Theban) manipulation of the value of exotic goods formed a response against elite aspirations of coastal centers, as did the production of "exotica" such as glass objects. The Theban glass industry may suggest attempts by the palace to become independent from trade or exchange: whereas at, e.g., Pylos glass with an origin in Egypt and Mesopotamia was found (Polikreti et al. 2011, Walton et al. 2009), at Thebes glass was not just worked but even produced locally (Nikita and Henderson 2006). Only the secondary elites enfranchised by the palaces could obtain, via the palaces, exotic prestige objects. This effectively sidelined coastal communities who had, due to their location, by definition a natural advantage in establishing foreign contacts.

In this respect it is interesting that most evidence for ships comes from Pylos, where only very few imports were found (Burns 2010, 132): Cline's catalog lists just five imports (versus 85 for Mycenae, 35 for Tiryns, and 41 for Thebes: Cline 1994, 277). Although 11 glass beads from Pylos have been traced by chemical analysis to Egypt and Mesopotamia, the dearth of other imports from these regions has led to the suggestion that these glass beads were acquired via other Mycenaean centers (Polikreti et al. 2011). Despite its fleet, Pylos thus seems less active in foreign trade and exchange than Mycenae, Tiryns, and Thebes, which coincides with a greater prevalence of ship iconography, possibly in ritual contexts: when ships are less mundane and practically useful, their symbolic value increases. Galaty and others (2014) have recently shown that Pylos was less well connected to the other Mycenaean palaces (including Knossos) than those were to each other, and that in addition Pylos was preoccupied with bringing the Further Province, with its fertile valley, under control. Together these two factors account neatly for the "inward looking" character of Pylos; Orchomenos was in a similar position.

If Thebes, the "superpower" in Central Greece, had near total control over production and distribution of prestige goods in LH IIIB, it is likely that the process of marginalization of other sites had started much earlier. An indication of this may be visible at Mitrou. There is currently no evidence for craft activity from LH IIIA onwards at Mitrou, and if this absence of evidence is not coincidental, the ramifications of this may be that the emerging palaces of Thebes (and Orchomenos?) had started to mono-polize the production of prestige goods and exotica. Especially the cessation of the purple dye industry after the prepalatial period (Vykukal 2011, 12) could be important, since it could constitute an example of tight palatial control over the production of "royal purple" (the term is found in an LH IIIB Linear B tablet at Knossos [KN X 976]: Ventris and Chadwick 1956, 321, 405), which seems to have been concentrated at Mycenaean Knossos (all four Linear B references to purple cloth are from the Knossos archives: Palaima 1991, 290).

The late prepalatial/early palatial cessation of industrial activity at Mitrou is followed by the LH IIIA2 destruction of its elite center. Parallel developments took place in Messenia and Laconia: in Messenia, Iklaina, a peer-polity of Pylos and a proto-palace, was destroyed at the end of LH IIIA1 (Cosmopoulos 2009, 2010, 2011, 2012), and in Laconia, coastal Agios Stephanos thrived in LH I, declined in LH II, was destroyed early in LH IIIA2, and has hardly any LH IIIB due to activity from the inland palace of Agios Vasileios (Taylour and Janko 2008).

CONCLUSIONS

Ships were, unlike chariots, rarely depicted on palatial frescoes. More strikingly, only the traditional, Minoan sailing ship is ever depicted in palatial settings, despite the fact that probably in LH IIIA, certainly in LH IIIB, the palaces made use of the new invention of the Mycenaean galley. This may reflect simply a certain conservatism on the part of the fresco painters (who may well have worked from pattern books based on traditional designs) or the palatial officials commissioning their work; however, there may have been ideological reasons as well, and I have argued that ships, and especially the new galleys with their crews of rowers, were unsuitable vehicles for palatial propaganda. Following Wedde, I have further argued for the existence of a tension between the subculture of the coastal centers, focusing on the galleys, and the land-based palaces, a tension exacerbated by the inability – or at the very least the difficulty – of the palaces to keep the galleys completely under their control.

Although galleys were necessary and useful – bringing exotic goods to the palaces and expanding their network – they were also potentially threatening. The landlocked palatial centers of central Greece may have feared as much as they needed sea captains, who possessed nautical skills and navigational knowledge that allowed them access to the sea and thus to all things exotic. This differential access to maritime knowledge is likely to have given rise to competition and tension between coastal groups and palatial centers.

This tension is further suggested by the way the Mycenaean palaces attempted to regulate and restrict imports. Attempts by the palaces to control the import of foreign goods are visible, first, in the palatial expansion to the coast and incorporation of certain coastal centers (Mitrou, Larymna, Anthedon) in their polities, allowing access to maritime routes; second in the marginalization of other coastal centers; and third in the creation and maintenance of palatial fleets of galleys. However, unable to prevent non-palatial centers from acquiring foreign goods completely, the palaces responded by changing the meaning and the value of these foreign goods by ascribing them value only after their reworking in palatial workshops.

Thus non-palatial centers were, even if they were able to get the raw material or finished exotica, unable to emulate objects created by and in the palaces.[16]

The relative scarcity of prestige goods in non-palatial LH IIIB contexts suggests that the palaces severely restricted the circulation of prestige goods, ensuring their rarity and thus their desirability. This ensured the complete dependence of non-palatial, local elites on the palace: in order to compete on a regional level, they required the sort of goods the palaces controlled.

Ships were thus both necessary for the palaces and a potential threat. The deployment of galleys in the LH IIIC period, after the collapse of the palaces, indicates they not only survived the downfall of the palatial system but thrived in the chaotic years thereafter, contributing significantly to a quick economic and socio-political recovery of the Euboean coasts. The role of the galley in the post-palatial era will be the subject of Chapter 7.

[16] Broodbank notes a not dissimilar response to competition in Early Bronze Age Daskaleio-Kavos: access to raw materials could not be controlled, but the manufacture of marble into prestigious objects was taken to a new level, "enabling the creation of objects that others were unable to emulate" (Broodbank 2000, 169).

7

REACTIONS TO COLLAPSE
The rise of a sailor-warrior culture

Perhaps the most famous piece of pottery from Lefkandi is the LH IIIC "griffin pyxis" (Figure 7.1). Decorated in a light-on-dark technique, the pyxis is dramatically different from all preceding and most contemporary pottery. It owes its name to the subject on the main side of the pyxis:[1] a lively scene of two griffins that are standing on either side of a nest, feeding the two hungry chicks whose heads emerge from the nest. Slight differences between the two griffins suggest a parental pair: the left griffin is more ornate, with an outline of stipples covering its entire body and its body entirely striped, and it has been suggested that this represents the father, with the somewhat plainer griffin on the right, representing the mother (Vermeule and Karageorghis 1982, 144). Minor differences in pose could be attributed to this as well: the front leg of the "father" rests on the ground, whereas the "mother" holds it above ground level, touching the "father's" front paw in what looks like a gesture of greeting. Despite this slight difference in pose, their position is roughly heraldic, with both parents focusing on their chicks between them. It is this heraldic position, in combination with the strongly charged meaning of griffins, which offers a suggestion how to interpret this scene.

REACTIONS AGAINST PALATIAL DOMINATION

On frescoes, griffins frequently convey a supernatural, awesome power indicating the divine status of the person whom they accompany. Thus the griffin accompanying the "Goddess" in Xeste 3 at Akrotiri and that carried by

---

[1] I take this to be the main side since its scene occupies the space between the two handles completely and without crossing over into the next field (see Crouwel 2006, pl. 67 for a drawing). The other two groups consist of (1) three goats and (2) a sphinx with two deer; Crouwel has suggested that like the griffins, the deer and the goats form family groups (Crouwel 2006, 244).

FIGURE 7.1. LH IIIC Light on Dark "Griffin pyxis" from Lefkandi. Reproduced with the permission of the British School at Athens.

the helmeted female figure on the plaque from Mycenae have been taken to argue for the divine status of the female figures with which they are associated (e.g., Davis 1986, 402; Rehak 1984, 541; 1998, 228). The griffins' importance is further suggested by their frequent portrayal in heraldic positions as in the Throne Room at Knossos, where they guard and protect the person seated on the throne. Ivory plaques and pyxides, exotic luxury objects limited to elites, also depict griffins: griffins attack a deer on an LH II pyxis from the Athenian Agora (Poursat 1977, 25, pl. 1), a griffin battles a lion on the lid from an LH II-IIIA1 pyxis from Tiryns (Krzyszkowska 2005b, 183–184, 199, pl. 1.5), and a griffin strides on a large ivory plaque from Mycenae (Papazoglou-Manioudaki 2012). Although seals occasionally portray griffins with their young, suggesting that they were thought of as actual animals, the rarity of their depictions combined with the precious material or rare, eastern shape of the seals on which they occur suggest that they were nevertheless emblems of authority or possibly even divine status. On a metal ring, CMS I 304, two large griffins in heraldic position are each topped by a small (baby?) griffin in the same position. The heraldic element not only overshadows any "parental" element ("parents" and "babies" do not interact) but the duplication of the heraldic position (echoed by the "babies") strengthens this element of power in the way that the doubling of motifs in "primitive" societies doubles the power and attribute of the image (see Broodbank 1989, 328). On the Lefkandi pyxis, however, the conventionally awesome creatures, guardians of palatial power when shown in heraldic positions, are domesticated. Rather than guarding the *wanax* or the palace itself, they guard their helpless chicks: their fierceness is gone together with the palaces of the LH IIIB period.[2] Palatial iconography is thus turned upside down and powerful symbols are rendered not only harmless but even comical.

This is admittedly a very specific interpretation for a single piece of pottery, and it depends on the assumption that the painter of the scene would have been familiar with palatial conventions. However, two other fragmentary vessels may strengthen it. On a krater fragment, a large parental sphinx stands over a small baby sphinx. Both sphinxes wear the headdress (though without plume) of earlier Late Bronze Age representations, but the composition, indicative of a family group (Crouwel 2006, 244–245, no. G2), tames and domesticates these previously awesome creatures. Sphinxes were associated with (palatial) elites: they occur on three gold signet rings, two at Mycenae (CMS I 87 and 129), one at Ialysos (Laffineur 1990, 153), as well as on an ivory pyxis from Thebes (Aravantinos 2010, 88). The intended meaning of another two krater fragments is less clear due to the uncertainty surrounding the identity of the animals.[3] They might be dogs attacking their prey in antithetical positions, as the composition suggests; but the dogs are oddly lion-like; the prey, sporting claws like a lion, like "nothing that ever pastured in Euboia" (Vermeule and Karageorghis 1982, 140), so that the alternative suggestion that we are seeing once again a family group, this time of a "parent lion on each side taking its cub out for a frisky stroll" (*ibidem*), cannot be discounted. Since in the throne room at palatial Pylos lions guarded the throne, and on the Lion Gate at Mycenae they heraldically guarded the pillar representing the House of Mycenae, if the alternative interpretation of the krater fragments would be correct, this would constitute the third example of an animal emblematic of palatial power shown in a domestic context, stripped of its power. The LH IIIC artists at Lefkandi thus may well have intentionally domesticated the three creatures most associated with palatial and divine higher power – the griffin, the lion, and the sphinx. In a period when the palaces are no longer in existence, this pyxis may then represent a reaction to palatial iconography by downplaying, even mocking, powerful palatial symbols.[4] This suggests a disassociation and dissatisfaction of at least this artist or his patron with the Mycenaean palace system.

Less explicit but equally important reactions suggesting disassociation with the palatial era are visible in the architectural layout of Kynos and Mitrou. At Kynos, occupation continues from LH IIIB, but the LH IIIC occupation follows a different plan, suggesting a break with the palatial-

---

[2] Rutter, Aegean Prehistoric Archaeology (http://www.dartmouth.edu/~prehistory/aegean/) Lesson 29.

[3] Popham and Sackett 1968, 19, and Popham and Milburn 1971, 340, thought they were lions; Vermeule and Karageorghis 1982, 140 no. XI.79, and Crouwel 2006, 242, lean toward an interpretation of the creatures as dogs.

[4] Cf. Younger 2011, 172: "It would be tempting to view [themes that exist in only a few depictions] as artistic renegades that escaped the censorship of social propriety, perhaps attesting even to a resistance against it."

period occupation.[5] At Mitrou, the evidence is more telling. After the "palatial gap," the postpalatial settlement at Mitrou followed the basic plan of the early Mycenaean settlement with the construction of a major building (Building B) on top of the old, prepalatial elite building D. Although Building B's walls were less impressive than those of Building D, it was very similar in size and layout, and was undoubtedly a building of high importance in LH IIIC Mitrou (Van de Moortel 2009, 361). This suggests a conscious reverting to older and more glorious times, by assimilating the old elite symbol and incorporating it into a new elite structure: the LH IIIC elites attempted to legitimize their rule by co-opting prepalatial power structures, much like the LH IIIC elites at the palace site of Tiryns did by reviving architectural symbols of kingly power (in Megaron B), thereby "claiming descent from the strong kings of palatial times" (Maran 2006, 143). The difference between Tiryns and Mitrou is telling. At the former palatial site, elites refer to the glory of the palace, whereas at Mitrou elites go back to prepalatial glory days. This is understandable if Mitrou had been, as suggested, under palatial control, losing its independence. Together with the iconographic record at Lefkandi, this suggests that at least some individuals in the Euboean Gulf region actively resented the previous, palatial-era situation. This sentiment is visible at Mitrou, Lefkandi, and perhaps at Kynos: on both sides of the Euboean Gulf and on both sides of the Euripos. In the postpalatial period, as in the prepalatial, Mitrou is a well-organized settlement with a dense, urban character, similar to contemporary settlements at Kynos and Lefkandi (Van de Moortel 2009, 361). Mitrou does not manage to return to its full prepalatial glory, however: in the postpalatial period it is overshadowed by Kynos, which has supplied the most spectacular LH IIIC finds.

KRATERS FOR WARRIORS

A clumsy drawing on two joining pottery fragments from Kynos constitutes, despite its limited artistic value, arguably the most important postpalatial Bronze Age document from the Euboean Gulf area (Figure 7.2). The artist has attempted a scene not attested anywhere else in the Bronze Age Aegean: a battle taking place on board a ship. The ship is being rowed, and while the helmsman maneuvers his steering oar, two warriors with two different shields duel with spears or javelins on deck. A third warrior stands at the vertical stempost at the ship's bow and seems to be ready to fire an arrow at an unseen enemy. Dated to LH IIIC Middle, or roughly the mid-twelfth century BCE, the depiction belongs to the postpalatial era and seems to offer a glimpse into the life and circumstances of the period after the collapse of the Mycenaean palaces.

---

[5] Dakoronia 2002a, 42–43; 2003, 38; 2006, 23. At Lefkandi, too, the LH IIIC settlement rarely reused the LH IIIB walls (Popham et al. 2006, 8; Sherratt 2006, 304–305).

FIGURE 7.2. Two joining pictorial krater sherds from LH IIIC Middle Kynos, depicting a shipboard battle. After Dakoronia 2006, 28 fig. 8 and Dakoronia 2002, 99 fig. 3.

The Euboean Gulf region fared surprisingly well in this period. Whereas the LH IIIB period was characterized by decline and contraction, a visit to the Euboean Gulf coasts in the LH IIIC period would reveal a surprising number of flourishing settlements – a situation very different from most of Boeotia, Attica, the Argolid, and Messenia, where one would notice decline and depopulation. Major sites in the LH IIIC phase are Lefkandi, Kynos, Mitrou, and Kalapodi, as well as Perati on the coast of Attica. The cemetery of Perati was newly established in the postpalatial period, and the other sites seem to have expanded after the collapse of the palaces: their poorly represented LH IIIB phases are followed by important LH IIIC Middle remains. Thus the LH IIIC period is in this area not, as it is at other areas in Greece (the Argolid and other parts of the northeast Peloponnese, Messenia, Kea, and eastern Phokis), a period of abandonment of settlements, of population decline, and of contraction, but quite the opposite.

The postpalatial settlement at Kynos was thriving: pithoi with seeds and round clay storage bins must have been used for storage of the produce grown on the fertile plain of Atalanti (*ArchDelt* 40 pl. 59); a mudbrick pottery kiln with many pieces of misfired but high-quality LH IIIC sherds, spindle whorls, and psi- and animal figurine fragments around it constitutes evidence for a local pottery industry; ceramic and stone spindle whorls and one bronze and several bone needles suggest the presence of a textile industry (although not necessarily on a larger scale than that of the household level) with weaving and sewing activities; and the remains of an oven and mineral slag, most likely in connection with copper smelting, suggest metal working.[6]

---

[6] Copper ore could have been imported from Thessaly, southern Attica, or the southeastern tip of Euboea (McGeehan Liritzis 1996, fig. 3.2.1). LH IIIC finds at Kynos include a bronze axe, three bronze arrow heads, and a bronze chisel.

At Mitrou there is an elite building again, and at Lefkandi, another high mound site with evidence for bronze working (Evely 2006, 265–290), possible textile production (Evely 2006, 296–300), and agricultural storage (Popham, Evely, and Sackett 2006), a fortification wall that had been used through the LH IIIB period was now converted into a house wall: the expanding settlement apparently felt secure enough to do away with fortification. Extensive cutting into LH IIIB strata in the LH IIIC Early phase is attributed by Popham and Sackett to an influx of population, possibly from destroyed centers elsewhere (Popham and Sackett 1968, 34).

These coastal sites along the Euboean Gulf are highly visible and easily accessible (Crielaard 2006, 278), unlike coastal "refuge settlements" on Crete, which were tucked away in sheltered locations behind fortification walls, probably to protect themselves against sea raids (Rutter 1992, 68–69). Lefkandi and Kynos are, as prominent mound sites, conspicuous to anyone sailing through the Euboean Gulf, so the abandonment of the fortification wall at Lefkandi suggests a degree of confidence that may seem surprising in these unsettled times. These were not, as Crielaard has also emphasized (2006), refuge settlements: they are dominant centers that had apparently little fear of attack. The reason for this may be sought in their apparent maritime dominance, suggested by their pictorial pottery.

Pictorial pottery is a new art form in this area, appearing first in LH IIIC (Dakoronia 2006, 24; Crouwel 2006, 240). Almost exclusively limited to kraters, it provides the clearest evidence for a warrior culture along the Euboean Gulf. Figure 7.2 shows only one of many krater drawings that advertise this warrior culture; pictorial kraters with similar themes have been found in settlement contexts at Lefkandi, Kynos, and Volos, as well as at the sanctuary of Kalapodi.[7] Something all this pottery has in common is an adherence to thematic unity: unlike earlier pictorial pottery, which displays what Petrakis (2011, 197) calls "thematic unawareness," the LH IIIC Middle kraters are more similar to fresco painting in their focus on a single subject and setting (maritime or terrestrial). These krater depictions are essentially narrative, rather than emblematic.

Kraters were elite display vessels that were used, much like in Archaic and Classical Greek symposia, for high-status ceremonial wine consumption: ritualized drinking is depicted on a krater fragment from Lefkandi (Crouwel 2006, 240). This suggests that the depictions on kraters advertised an elite self-image, the desired identity of the Mycenaean elites in the LH IIIC phase. That may explain the scarcity of female representations in pictorial vase painting in the Late Bronze Age: the male elites who used the vessels

---

[7] See, e.g., Crielaard 2006, 279 fig. 14.2 and 283 fig. 14.4 for relevant figures.

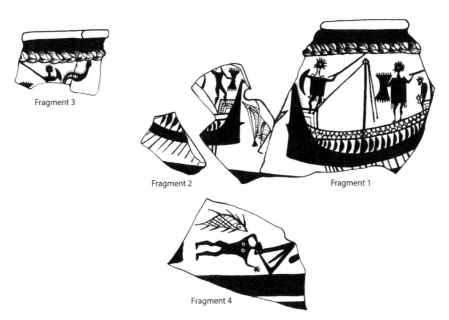

FIGURE 7.3. Pictorial krater fragments from LH IIIC Middle Kynos, depicting warriors on ships. After Dakoronia 2006, 25 fig. 1.

with pictorial decoration during their symposia, wished to promote their own heroic activities, not focus on the world of women.[8]

The evidence from Kynos is most instructive. Fragments from at least five locally produced figurative kraters are decorated with depictions of ships carrying fully armed warriors brandishing javelins or swords and shields, sometimes engaged in battle on board of a single ship (Figure 7.2); elsewhere preparing to engage the enemy on another ship (Figure 7.3).[9] Although the themes on these sherds are the same, they appear to have been produced by at least three different painters (Dakoronia 2006 and Figures 7.2–7.4). Thus the decoration does not represent the quirks of an individual artist, but constitutes a popular theme in postpalatial Kynos. Other krater fragments depict (parts of) ships, rowers, helmsmen, and so on but without preserved warriors. These narrative scenes of maritime battle occur only on kraters (Dakoronia 2007a, 119): pictorial decoration and narrative are linked with high-status consumption of wine in a symposium setting. For LH IIIC inhabitants of Kynos, ship-board battles were an important iconographical theme, which in turn suggests that these elite LH IIIC Mycenaeans valued their own (perceived) role as warriors: they wished to promote a self-image of fearless sailor-warriors who took to their ships to fight on foreign coasts or, if necessary, on board of their ships (Kramer-Hajos 2012a).

[8] See Steel 2006 for some exceptions to the general rule of rarity of women in pictorial vase painting.
[9] Dakoronia 2006. See also Dakoronia 1987, 1996b, 1999; Dakoronia 2002, plates 3–5; Wachsmann 1998, 130–137; Crouwel 1999; Wedde 1999. Dakoronia 2007a, 125 fig. 1.4, shows ships with helmeted(?) figures, but no certain weaponry.

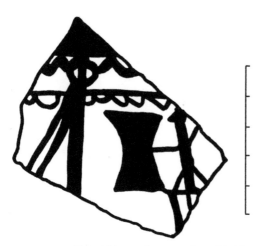

FIGURE 7.4. Pictorial krater fragment from LH IIIC Middle Kynos, depicting a warrior on a galley. After Dakoronia 1999, 127 fig. 1.

In itself, this does not necessarily mean that the elites would also actually perform such acts: as Whitley has emphasized for a different context, a warrior burial does not equate to the burial of a warrior. Instead, a warrior burial makes "ideological claims about status, hierarchy, authority and gender" (Whitley 2002, 227). Yet, even if we acknowledge that each individual buried as a warrior did not necessarily live a warrior lifestyle (and Whitley's examples of historically known persons are convincing enough), the very existence of swords, weapons invented specifically for human combat, suggests that the general practice of warfare, combat, or dueling did exist and was associated with status, especially when such swords appear newly in the material record (i.e. when they are not yet ceremonial "fossils"). Similarly, we might suppose that the pictorial themes on the kraters refer to epics, myths, or legends, rather than referencing an everyday historical reality, but the very presence of certain specific and new types of equipment suggests that, even if the specific narratives on the kraters were meant to represent legends, an everyday real practice informed the pictures. In the case of these depictions, the ships, weaponry, and armor are all new enough equipment to suggest that maritime battles were actually fought during the LH IIIC period.[10]

[10] Petrakis (2004) remarks that in an era where regionalism reigns, the similarities between ship depictions are remarkable. The two features of his focus, the bird (or monster) prow ornament and the "horizontal ladder pattern," are, however, features that can be easily explained by the actual form of galleys in this period. Crielaard 2006, 282, also assumes that the Kynos depictions are informed by real life. Papadopoulos supposes that these depictions probably reflect actual contemporary events, given the generally unstable and chaotic times, but refrains from explicitly connecting them with an elite lifestyle (Papadopoulos 2009, 75). Pottery from the tombs at Perati does not bear such depictions: it seems they are reserved for display among the living. Few Perati tombs actually contain weapons – a sign of economic restraint at times when weapons were rather "recycled" than deposited among the dead?

THE MYCENAEAN GALLEY REVISITED

The ships depicted on the Kynos kraters represent the Mycenaean oared galleys, a design recently invented by the Mycenaeans (Wedde 1999, 465; Crielaard 2000, 59; 2006, 280, and see Chapter 6) and excellent for "speedy seaborne attacks on coastal settlements" and "naval engagements at sea" (Crielaard 2000, 59). Although a few depictions of the Mycenaean galley are dated to LH IIIA-B, most date to LH IIIC. A sherd from Ashkelon now seems to form an important exception to this general rule: produced in the Argolid (Mycenae-Berbati) during LH IIIB (Mountjoy 2011, 483–484) and apparently exported to Ashkelon, the sherd depicts a warrior on a ship's prow similar to many LH IIIC galleys. LH IIIC Middle examples are depicted on krater fragments from Kynos, Kalapodi, and Athens, and on a stirrup jar from Skyros (Figure 6.2) and one from Asine; an LH IIIC Late Mycenaean pyxis from tholos Tomb 11 at Messenian Tragana completes the mainland sample. The type also occurs once at Phaistos and Gazi on Crete, and several times at Phylakopi and Seraglio on Kos. The ships are not necessarily shown in a military setting (Crouwel 1999, 459) and they could be used for a number of purposes (Wedde 2005, 34), although they are especially suited for military endeavors and are shown together with warriors not only at Kynos but also on a krater found at Bademgediği Tepe (Mountjoy 2005).

All LH IIIC depictions have the brailed rig, suggesting that the older ship type did not survive the invention of the galley. Since the older type was a better sailing ship with more cargo space (the galley sacrificed cargo space for a sleeker design housing more rowers), this suggests in turn the changed circumstances between the palatial and the postpalatial periods: focus shifted from large-scale trade to war and raiding. It seems that the new design of Mycenaean galley became popular around the time of the collapse of the palaces, when long-distance trade in bulk raw materials between palatial centers gave way to more frequent combat and raiding and piratical activities.

The Kynos ships are oared, and although the ship in Figure 7.3 has a mast and rigging, in this battle it is rowed (as were the much later triremes of classical Athens). The lunate shapes below the deck are the torsos of the rowers, conceived in a way similar to the helmsman at the stern of the ship (Wachsmann 1998, 132), although only in one case they are shown rowing as they would in reality: facing the stern of the ship. The oars of the ship in Figure 7.2 reach the deck, suggesting the ship was rowed from the upper deck, an important development that may indicate a first step toward a two-banked ship (Wachsmann 1998, 137, 155).

The depictions show that these Late Bronze Age ships had no ram, and their positioning in Figure 7.3 – with the left ship placed higher and slightly smaller than the right ship – probably indicates that they are not about to collide head-on, as ships with a battle ram would, but move next to each other so that the warriors on board of both ships can board the other ship and on-board battle can commence (Dakoronia 1999, 123; cf. Wedde 1999, 470). Figure 7.2 shows the battle in full swing; the warriors are fighting on the deck of the ship as they would on land. The absence of a mast is here no doubt to accommodate the rather complex scene of warriors engaged in hand-to-hand combat.

The tall vertical stemposts on the ships, indispensable for maintaining structural integrity during impact or when beaching at speed, are characteristic for the Mycenaean galley. On the ship depiction from Skyros (Figure 6.2), the top of the stempost represents an animal head; Wachsmann draws attention to the common occurrence of bird heads on stemposts of ships in the Late Bronze Age through the Roman period (Wachsmann 1998, 177–197) and has connected them with European Urnfield cultures (ibidem 178). Many of the figure heads are less bird- than dragon-like, however (Petrakis 2011), and may have had apotropaic meanings as well as have been intended to inspire fear in the victims of the raids for which the galleys were used (cf. Basch 1986). The vertical stempost with bird head is visible on the Sea Peoples' ships on the Medinet Habu naval battle relief (Figure 7.5),[11] recording the victories won by Ramesses III over the Philistines and other Sea Peoples in 1179 BCE (Drews 1993, 158). Another similarity between Sea Peoples' ships and the Kynos ships consists of the brailed rig, visible by the way the sail is drawn up on the mast.

FIGURE 7.5. Sea battle between Egyptians and Sea Peoples, Medinet Habu. Courtesy of the Oriental Institute of the University of Chicago.

---

[11] Wachsmann observes that the Sea Peoples' ships on the Medinet Habu relief "are virtually identical in nearly all surviving details to [the right ship on Fragment 1]" (Wachsmann 1998, 172).

The observed similarities between the Kynos depictions and the Medinet Habu relief could simply mean that the people at Kynos – as elsewhere – had adopted the latest techniques (such as the brailed sail, which may have originated in the Levant: Emanuel 2014) and equipment common for the period. Against a close similarity between the Mycenaean galleys and the Medinet Habu ships argues the double bird-headed stempost depicted on the latter. The Sea Peoples' ships, moreover, are depicted with crow's nests, and these are lacking on all Mycenaean depictions. Since the first galley depictions are Mycenaean, it is assumed that the design was invented by the Mycenaeans. However, it was taken over and improved upon by, probably, people in the Levant (Wachsmann 1998, 51, 56; Emanuel 2014, 30). Although the correspondences between the Mycenaean galleys and the Sea Peoples' ships are not exact, the activities in which they are engaged are remarkably similar, making it not unlikely that Mycenaeans were among those elusive Sea Peoples themselves (so, e.g., Wood 1987). Thus discussions of the (ethnic) identity of the Aegean and Sea Peoples' ships (e.g., Wachsmann 1998, 176–177) seem to miss the point: rather than trying to differentiate the two on the basis of distinguishing characteristics of ships or crewmembers, it may be more fruitful to view the Mycenaean galleys as part of the same phenomenon as the Sea Peoples' ships on the Egyptian reliefs.[12] The new type of ship was used by parties willing to battle and raid throughout the eastern Mediterranean, and to the Egyptians it may have mattered little where exactly the northerners with these galleys had their origins.

Whether or not Mycenaeans from the Euboean Gulf area were among the Sea Peoples attacking Egypt's shores is in fact unimportant. Their own documents – their pictorial kraters – tell us that they took pride in their sailor-warrior lifestyle, and their flourishing, unfortified settlements suggest that they conceived of attack as the best form of defense: rather than waiting to be raided, they took to their ships to wreak havoc on other communities themselves. This explains the continuity as well as the location of sites like Kynos, Mitrou, and Lefkandi right on the coast: these settlements did not fear attacks from the sea, since their ships efficiently controlled the Euboean Gulf, and they used these coastal settlements as bases from which to raid and pillage.[13] They engaged in the sort of activities credited to the Sea Peoples – raiding, maritime battles, and piratical activities – and were among the aggressors in the postpalatial period, causing some of the turmoil and benefiting from the breakdown of organized

---

[12] Likewise, Merrillees has argued that the Egyptian records refer not so much to "Sea Peoples" as to pirates (Merrillees 1992, 90–91). See also Luraghi 2006. The Warrior Vase from Mycenae may lead to similar questions. The warriors carry small shields and wear "hedgehog helmets" on one side and helmets with horns, not unlike those worn by the Shardana bodyguards of Ramses II at Kadesh, on the other.

[13] As suggested for Cycladic and Cretan sites: Nowicki 2000, 264–265; 2001, 29–31, 37.

society, rather than suffering as the passive recipients of it. They were proud of their raiding pursuits: they chose such scenes to present a self-image, and such activities were part of the elite lifestyle, rather than occurring on the fringes of society.[14]

Although the depictions from Kynos are unique in their unequivocal depiction of a combination of ships and warriors, similar fragments have turned up at Lefkandi and elsewhere along the maritime route of the Euboean Gulf. Two Lefkandi LH IIIC Middle pictorial krater sherds depict ships with human figures interpreted as warriors. One sherd shows two human figures, somewhat crudely drawn in silhouette with outlined heads, holding their oars with both hands (*AR* 51 [2004–2005] 51, fig. 90). Although lacking helmets, shields, or identifiable corselets, they have been interpreted as warriors based on the parallels in theme with the Kynos and Kalapodi sherds. Vertical lines in front of them may represent the individual stanchions of the rowers' galleries, as on the Tragana ship; given the lack of contemporary parallels, it is less likely that they represent spears as on the much earlier Kolonna pithos fragment. Another krater fragment shows the image of a warrior, with round shield, in silhouette with outlined head and neck but without ship (*AR* 50 [2003–2004] 39). A small krater fragment from Kalapodi shows part of the curving stern of a Mycenaean galley (Jacob-Felsch 1996, 133 pl. 36: 233). Graffiti of at least eight ships on an anta of a tomb from Dramesi (Wachsmann 1998, 143–145) may date to LH IIIC as well. The tomb itself dates to early LH I, but the open rowers' galleries – with at least 22 windows, suggesting the possibility that a penteconter was the subject of depiction – suggest an LH IIIC date for the graffiti.[15]

The additional finds of three terracotta ship models (one a toy) from a slightly later time period (LH IIIC Late) are evidence for the continued importance of ships and sailing at Kynos. The presence of the ship model on wheels, interpreted by the excavator as a child's toy, is especially interesting, since it suggests that ships were both common and important for the people at Kynos. Although it may be premature to think of a fleet of Homeric-type

---

[14] A different relationship with the sea is suggested on another krater from Kynos showing a unique charming scene of five fishermen standing in shallow coastal water and hauling in long nets while smaller and larger fish are leaping out of the water (Dakoronia 2002, 100). In the small part which is preserved, there is no hint of danger, and it would be interesting to know what was depicted on the rest of this krater. Fishing in shallow waters at the shore as opposed to offshore deep-water fishing seems an oddly humble theme for elite symposia.

[15] Early LH I date for the tomb: Blegen 1949, 41; Papadimitriou 2001, 166. Penteconter: Wachsmann 1998, 144. LH IIIC date for the graffiti: Buchholz and Karageorghis 1973, 94, no. 1168, followed by Crielaard 2006, 279 fig. 14.2(a). (Earlier: Crielaard 2000, 56, no. 47: the ships date "presumably" to LH IIIB). Wachsmann 1998, 144 figs. 7.30–31 does not commit himself to a date, but discusses the depictions amid LH IIIB-C evidence. Since the majority of Mycenaean galley depictions postdate the collapse of the palaces, an LH IIIC date for the graffiti may be most likely.

penteconters stationed at Kynos,[16] it is more than likely that Kynos was an important port, given its excellent location on the shore.

Although depictions of oared galleys occur elsewhere, the prevalence and distribution of these depictions strongly suggests that oared galleys played an especially important role among the communities of the Euboean Gulf coasts, evidence that they were closely connected in a small world.[17] In a reversal of the domestication of the warrior elites during the palatial era, now the palatial symbols of power (griffin, sphinx, and lion) are domesticated, while warriors rule once again supreme.

WEAPONS AND ARMOR

Not only ships but weapons and armor, too, differ from that of earlier Mycenaean periods. The two warriors with javelins in Figure 7.2 are accompanied by a probable archer: the top of his bow is just visible on the far right of the preserved sherd fragment (Wachsmann 1998, 137). Although arrowheads are frequent finds in tombs throughout the Late Bronze Age and archers were popular during the prepalatial period (on for example the Siege Rhyton [Figure 2.7], the lion-hunt dagger, and a gold seal ring [CMS I 15]), depictions of archers are exceedingly rare on pottery as well as on frescoes: a fragment from Pylos contains the only clearly identifiable archer (a female) on a fresco fragment, although three additional fragments, one from Mycenae and two from Tiryns, may depict archers (Brecoulaki et al. 2008, 372, note 15). The *only* two archers depicted on Mycenaean mainland pottery date to LH IIIC Kynos and Volos (Vermeule and Karageorghis 1982, XI. 58) and are painted on kraters,[18] suggesting that they were now (and in this area) seen as warriors worthy of depiction.[19]

The spears used (Figures 7.2 and 7.3) are a far cry from the early Late Bronze Age maritime lance. Whereas the latter was about twice the length of

[16] Dakoronia estimates that one of the terracotta ship models from Kynos representing a war galley may have had at least 25 oars on each side, thus fitting the definition of the pentecounter (Dakoronia 1996b, 160). In the Catalogue of Ships, Kynos heads the entry for the Lokrians, who provide 40 ships for the expedition against Troy (*Iliad* 2.527–535). See Kramer-Hajos 2012b.

[17] Their style likewise suggests a regional koine focused on the Euboean Gulf and its immediate hinterland. The depictions are drawn in a solid silhouette style with only the eyes spared out (the only exception is one warrior on Figure 7.3 whose neck (or neck guard?) is drawn in outline), which displays similarities with pottery from Kalapodi, Lefkandi, Volos, and Amarynthos (Jacob-Felsch 1996, 87; Crielaard 2006, 282).

[18] Only two other vases, both from Cyprus, show archers: one dates to LH IIIA2, the other to LH IIIB2 (Karageorghis and Vermeule IV.16 and V.28).

[19] On seals and stone vessels they are more common; since both are Minoan art forms, it seems possible that the bow-and-arrow was a typically Minoan weapon. In the *Iliad*, Lokrians are portrayed as archers, possibly a literary reflection of a tradition going back to LH IIIC times (Kramer-Hajos 2012b).

a man if not more, the spears used now are at most as long as a man's height and probably somewhat shorter. One might speculate that they were used as javelins and hurled; however, they are only shown as used in hand-to-hand combat. The weapons are drawn sketchily enough not to rule out an interpretation as swords; however, the way the figure on the left holds his weapon suggests that it is a spear.

The LH IIIC warriors wear "hedgehog helmets" (Figure 7.3) and carry small shields, clearly no longer representing the earlier Mycenaean tower shields or figure-of-eight shields; small round shields are a common feature of LH IIIB-C pictorial vase painting, possibly gaining popularity due to contact with the Near East (Vermeule and Karageorghis 1982, 109). Since they are small, they indicate "a shift in fighting tactics toward mobility, away from set standing duels" (ibidem). Some of the shields on the Kynos fragments are concave like a proto-Dipylon shield.[20] Thus not only ships but shields, too, point forward to the eighth-century geometric depictions on Dipylon vases. In other instances, the Kynos shields are lunate or round. It is likely that the lunate shields represent a sophisticated way of showing a round shield in a side view: the less accomplished artist of Figure 7.2 has refrained from attempting to depict a round shield in a side view, instead using the easier frontal view. The two shield types do not appear to correlate to two different groups or armies, let alone ethnicities: although in Figure 7.2 two warriors with the two different shield types fight on opposite sides, in Figure 7.3 two warriors with two different types of shields appear to join forces against two other ships sailing in the opposite direction and carrying at least two warriors, one with concave and one with round shield.[21]

Additional depictions of warriors, hunters, and charioteers (Crouwel 1999) imply that the values of the LH IIIC elites were similar to those of the prepalatial elites in the area: masculine heroic ideals reigned.[22] These

[20] A similar concave shield seems to be portrayed on the aforementioned krater from Volos (Vermeule and Karageorghis 1982, XI. 57). In their 1982 publication, Vermeule and Karageorghis were understandably puzzled about the exact meaning of the "dark object [...] shaped like the blade of a double axe" but the subsequent evidence from Kynos corroborates their hunch that it was a shield (Vermeule and Karageorghis 1982, 135). They note that "not dissimilar" shields "appear among the allies of the Hittites on the Luxor reliefs of the Battle of Kadesh" (ibidem).

[21] On the Medinet Habu relief, the Sea Peoples all have round shields, while the Egyptians carry shields that are more rectangular. Vermeule and Karageorghis remark that small round shields are attributes of the Shardana and the Peleset, both constituents of the Sea Peoples, but are depicted on the Pylos frescoes as well. They are typically accompanied by javelins, as they are depicted here (Vermeule and Karageorghis 1982, 109). The Kynos depictions are more in line with the Shaft Grave dagger showing hunters with two different types of shields.

[22] For such depictions from Kynos, see Dakoronia 2006; for Lefkandi, see Popham and Sackett 1968, 19, and Sackett et al. 1966, 103, fig. 28 no. 65; for Kalapodi, see *AR* 55 [2008 2009] 44 fig. 72; for Volos see Vermeule and Karageorghis XI. 57–58; for Amarynthos, see Sackett et al. 1966, 103 fig. 28 no. 66.

depictions are, however, common staples of palatial imagery as well: fresco fragments from Tiryns and from a miniature fresco from Orchomenos depict boar hunts, and frescoes from other Mycenaean palaces show warriors, charioteers, and hunters (Crouwel 1999). They might thus be taken as attempts of postpalatial elites to identify themselves with the glory of palatial times.[23] The emphasis on ships, on the other hand, is characteristic for the pre- and postpalatial periods only. Thus, toward the end of the Mycenaean era, we encounter elites boasting to be fearless sailors and warriors: the local chiefs, the *basileis*, return to their natural power bases.[24]

The LH IIIC phase appears thus in some respects to share the same characteristics and values as the early Mycenaean phase: the values of a warrior class, oriented toward the sea, who used their prowess in seafaring, trading, or looting and pillaging to establish their prominence. The importance of sailing in this period puts Lefkandi back on the map: it occupies an extremely important position, where the South Euboean Gulf transitions into the Euripos (Sherratt 2006, 303). Many ships sailing north through the Euboean Gulf must have stopped at Lefkandi, beaching at one of the two bays flanking the mound in order to wait for favorable tides or winds or perhaps, as today, simply to wait their turn to pass through to the North Euboean Gulf. Thus it is not surprising that Lefkandi should be a prominent player in this period.

Deger-Jalkotzy has suggested that peripheral areas, like Phokis and Euboea, suffered less from the collapse of the palace system, because already in the palatial period they had enjoyed a certain degree of autonomy or had never been much affected by the sociopolitical organization of the palaces (Deger-Jalkotzy 1994, 14, 19; 1995, 375; see also Foxhall 1995; Crielaard 2006, 282). In similar vein, Lemos notes that the coastal location of the enterprising communities forming the new regional koine improved their chances for survival in an era when the protection of the palaces had been lost (Lemos 1999, 21). The evidence suggests, however, that we can go further than this: in some regions of the periphery, the collapse of the palace system was not merely inconsequential, but a positive influence, and coastal sites were at an advantage not merely because they needed to forge ties in these chaotic and unsettled times but because their location allowed them to capitalize on the collapse of organized trade and fill the power vacuum left by the palaces.

RETURN OF THE WARRIOR TOMBS

In line with this renewed emphasis on warrior prowess and personal (military) achievement is a return of warrior tombs. After the palatial intermezzo

[23] See also Deger-Jalkotzy 1995, 376; Crielaard 2006, 281; Maran 2006, 142.
[24] Since the qa-si-re-u or *basileus* was always a local chief, he was, it seems, the only official known from Linear B tablets to survive the collapse of the palaces (Palaima 1995).

in which status display was limited to rather tame "civic" emblems of
authority such as seals, local chiefs now returned at least ideologically to
prepalatial strategies of the sword. Although no warrior tombs have been
found along the Euboean Gulf coasts, the cemetery of Perati in Attica, just
south of the entrance into the South Euboean Gulf, includes three LH IIIC
warrior tombs, and weapons found outside tomb contexts on Euboea (LH/
LM swords were found at Avlonari and Palioura, northeast of Chalkis:
Deger-Jalkotzy 2006, 167) suggest that the phenomenon of warrior tombs
extended to Euboea as well. A spearhead from a built tomb at Rachita
(Vardates) dating to LH IIIC Early suggests that the warrior society extended
also into the Spercheios Valley (Lewartowski 2000, 11).

At Perati, the LH IIIC Late Tomb 38 contained an F2-type sword
(Figure 4.9), five stirrup jars, an arm-ring of bronze, and an iron knife
(Deger-Jalkotzy 2006, 156); the LH IIIC Middle or Late Tomb 12 contained
a type G sword and a Syro-Palestinian bronze knife with a handle in the shape
of a duck-head (Cline 1994, 226, no. 838) as well as seven silver rings, a mirror,
steatite cones, and many vases; and the LH IIIC Middle Tomb 123 yielded
a large krater, several drinking vessels, a razor, a pair of tweezers,
a whetstone, and a spearhead. Given the small size of the spearhead and
the small dimensions of the chamber, the shaft must have been short, so that
the weapon may have been a javelin or a spear, rather than a large lance; this
of course accords well with the contemporary pictorial evidence from the
area.

LH IIIC warrior tombs are common especially in Achaea (Deger-Jalkotzy
2006). This is another "peripheral" region that was more densely populated
in LH IIIC than in LH IIIB: another example of a marginal region that gained
importance after the collapse of the palatial system. Although here we do not
find the pictorial imagery of sailor-warriors as is so prevalent along the
Euboean Gulf coasts, we do witness a return to a warrior society.[25]
Moreover, from chamber tombs in these peripheral regions of the northwestern Peloponnese come an unusual number of pictorial-style pottery
pieces dated to LH IIIC Late (Crouwel 2009, 44). Among the most interesting
are krater fragments from Voudeni, northeast of Patras, in Achaea, which
depict warriors and chariots (ibidem; Mountjoy 1999, 365, 405).[26] These
similarities in ethos, even if expressed in different ways, between the two
regions attest to the shared values of these two peripheral communities in the

[25] As an aside, Odysseus, a representative of a galley captain, is located in the Ionian isles not
far off the coasts of Achaea.
[26] Possibly the krater with prothesis scene from Agia Triada in Elis dates to LH IIIC Late,
rather than Middle, too (Crouwel 2009, 44), based on the silhouette drawing of the various
motifs (ibidem note 5). The silhouette style is, as we have seen, a common characteristic of
LH IIIC Middle around the Euboean Gulf, but on the Peloponnese most pictorial pottery
displays a more open, ornamented style. The Elis krater functioned as a grave marker.

postpalatial period. The swords from the LH IIIC warrior graves are generally Naue II swords: the preferred cut-and-thrust sword of the period, superior to the traditional Aegean swords. The pictorial tradition continued into the Submycenaean: the only two Submycenaean pictorial vessels known to date are two duck-askoi from graves at Kanghadi in Achaea and Lefkandi, respectively (Crouwel 2009, 44 figs. 15 and 16); the Lefkandi example is the more convincing of the two.

On the other hand, there is a marked lack of warrior tombs from Messenia, which Deger-Jalkotzy ascribes to the depopulation of the region after the fall of the Pylos palace (2006, 167). She suggests that the same may be true for Boeotia and the Volos region. In addition, a difference between former palatial and non-palatial areas in terms of values and ideologies, with the "civic" values more strongly internalized in palatial areas, might be another reason.

CONCLUSIONS

After the collapse of the palaces, the Euboean Gulf coastal settlements returned to celebrating warrior values. Kraters, as elite display vessels, used in a symposium setting at all-male elite drinking parties, were used to advertise a self-image of sailor-warriors. With that, the break with the palatial period and its values, but also the return to prepalatial values, is clear. The themes that are depicted center on elite male occupations of hunting, chariot driving, and, most spectacularly, seafaring and maritime battles. These suggest that the elites in the area fell back on similar tactics as in the early part of the Late Bronze Age. This return to warrior values is notable in other peripheral regions, such as Achaea, as well.

8

MODELING COLLAPSE AND REVIVAL

In Chapter 6 I have argued that the Theban *wanax* monopolized imports in order to cement and legitimize his reign. In order to do so, he extended his reach (economically at least, if not politically) to coastal sites on the Euboean Gulf, and by LH IIIB the palace of Thebes effectively exerted economic and possibly political control over most of East Boeotia, including the area of the Euripos. This effectively changed the preexisting network structure to become increasingly centralized. Thus individual motivations affected the entire network structure. It is ironic that these motivations, rooted in individuals' desire to safeguard their power, resulted in an inherently vulnerable network and, ultimately, a complete loss of their power.

The weakness of any centralized network is its vulnerability to coordinated attack: if the hub is taken out, the entire network falls apart. This can be easily imagined in the model of the centralized network in Figure 8.1: without the central hub, all other nodes are left unconnected, in a vacuum. Such a "coordinated attack" apparently happened around 1200 BCE, when all Mycenaean palaces (with the possible exception of Athens) collapsed; one result of this collapse in Central Greece was a drastic decline in the number of settlements in the fertile plains (Figure 8.2).

Many sites along the coasts, however, not merely survived, but apparently increased in size and significance, whether due to an influx of population from elsewhere, as has been argued, for example, for Perati, or to immediate economic success. Pottery from Lefkandi suggests that the Theban network remained in place for a short period of time after the collapse of the palaces: early LH IIIC pottery from Lefkandi is similar to that from Orchomenos, Eutresis, and Anthedon (Sherratt 2006a, 219), all associated with the Theban palace in LH IIIB. These sites thus stayed connected, albeit briefly, after the central hub of Thebes was taken out, suggesting that at least the LH IIIB pottery production network was never completely centralized (even if the political network was), since it was not immediately affected by the fall of the palace.

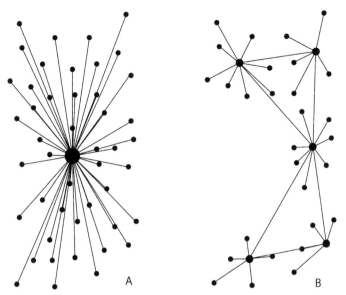

FIGURE 8.1. Transformation of sociopolitical network structures during the LH IIIB-C transition in the Euboean Gulf. Depiction of network types adapted from Baran 1964, 2, fig. 1.

The extent to which pottery production was controlled by the palaces seems to have differed by region. For Messenia, Galaty has suggested that the Pylian state may have controlled the production of certain fine wares (especially kylikes) while the production of "utilitarian" wares remained local and uncontrolled (Galaty 2007, 2010). Mycenae, on the other hand, seems to have controlled both the Petsas House workshop at Mycenae itself (Shelton 2010) and the Mastos workshop in the Berbati Valley (Åkerström 1968). Parkinson and others have argued that these regional differences may reflect the circumstances under which these palatial polities emerged: in Messenia, the palace of Pylos ruled supreme, while in the Argolid, a large number of competitors (Lerna, Asine, Tiryns, Argos, Prosymna, and Midea) may have been an incentive for Mycenae to intrude more into local economies, resulting in the attachment of specialized pottery workshops to the palace (Parkinson et al. 2013). It remains to be investigated to what extent pottery production was controlled by Thebes, but the similarities in LH IIIC Early pottery from Orchomenos, Eutresis, Anthedon, and Lefkandi suggest that it may not have been to any great extent. Since Thebes was a palace without local competition, just like Pylos, it should not surprise to find that economic production followed similar strategies in the two polities.

The temporary survival of the pottery network in LH IIIC Early was emphatically short-lived: Anthedon, Eutresis, and Orchomenos have not so far yielded pottery of the Lefkandi 2 phase (Sherratt 2006a, 218–220). Since these three sites represent, respectively, a site under palatial control benefiting from palatial investment, a second-order center in the Theban polity, and

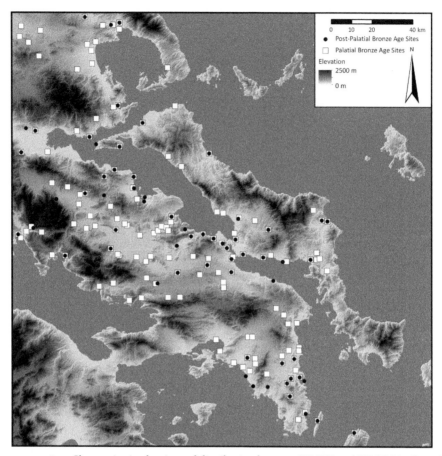

FIGURE 8.2. Changes in site density and distribution between LH IIIB and LH IIIC in Central Greece. Courtesy of Alex Knodell.

a palace, this constitutes a strong indication that, even though the pottery network was not directly affected by the collapse of the palace, the large-scale disruption in the political and administrative network resulted nevertheless, after a while, in decline severe enough to erase these sites more or less from the map.

In LH IIIC Middle, ca. 1150 BCE, Lefkandi had become part of a different network, a regional koine that focused on the coasts and stretched from Volos to Perati. This regional koine is most spectacularly visible in the pictorial pottery style found at Kynos, Kalapodi, Lefkandi, Amarynthos, Perati, and Volos (Crielaard 2006). The depictions on the pictorial pottery attest to the pervasive warlike ethos of the owners and users, as well as to the importance of galleys, and suggest the means by which elites at these sites rose to prominence (Chapter 7).

Apart from the similarities in themes between pictorial pottery from Kynos, Lefkandi, and Kalapodi, the style of these depictions displays remarkable similarities, too. A silhouette style and checkered designs occur on kraters at Kalapodi and Lefkandi (Jacob-Felsch 1996, 87; Felsch et al. 1987, 30 fig. 51). The warriors on kraters from Kynos, the hunters from Kalapodi, and the warrior from Lefkandi all wear fringed skirts. Given the similarities between the Kynos material and that from both Kalapodi and Lefkandi, this regional style seems to have focused on the Euboean Gulf and its immediate and easily reachable hinterland.[1]

Volos, too, was part of the same pictorial tradition; similarities include the concave shield type and the spared-out "breasts" on one of the figures. The archer from Volos is similarly silhouetted (Vermeule and Karageorghis 1982, no. XI.58), but the style is not limited to central Greece: Mycenae and Tiryns also yield examples (Vermeule and Karageorghis 1982, nos. XI.1, XI.4, XI.15.2, and XI.26). Indeed, it has been noted that at Volos the LH IIIC pottery is "almost identical" with that from Lefkandi (Sherratt 2006a, 219), evidence for an LH IIIC "coastal koine" focusing on the Euboean Gulf. Moreover, three LH IIIC Middle sherds from the Mitrou surface survey, belonging to one krater, display marked similarities with a PG krater from Volos, which has many LH IIIC characteristics (Kramer-Hajos and O'Neill 2008, 213–214): both have panels consisting of carelessly executed multiple wavy lines and both use dots to frame motifs. A close connection between the two sites is thus expected; in fact, the North Euboean Gulf provides an easy route between the two.

Although Mitrou, on current evidence, did not participate in the pictorial pottery tradition, in other respects its pottery is remarkably similar to that of Kynos and especially Kalapodi. Patterned kraters at Mitrou and Kalapodi "could easily have been produced at the same locale, even in the same workshop," according to Rutter (2007, 295). Lis also notes the strong similarities between pottery from Mitrou, Kynos, Kalapodi, and Lefkandi (Lis 2009, 209–212). Close connections between Kalapodi, Mitrou, and Kynos are suggested by the impressed pithoi (Lis and Rückl 2011). Pithos fragments from Mitrou with impressed decorative bands have parallels with pithoi from Kalapodi, and it is likely, as Lis and Rückl have argued based on inspection of the fabric used for these impressed pithoi, that Kalapodi and Kynos both exported locally made pithoi to Mitrou (Lis and Rückl 2011). Decorating pithoi in this way is time consuming, and points to more than simply utilitarian storage: these pithoi, some of them of monumental size (one at Kynos stands about 1.60-m tall with a rim diameter of slightly more than 50 cm: Lis and Rückl 2011, 161), allowed mass storage of agricultural produce, but were also objects of display, emphasizing the symbolic value of storage. They date to LH IIIC-PG and were extremely common at Kalapodi and at Mitrou. Another type of pithos, the "button-based pithos," was common in

---

[1] Desborough suggested already in 1964 that an LH IIIC Middle Euboean koine existed (Desborough 1964, 20, 228).

LH IIIC levels at Lefkandi (Sherratt 2006a, 219) and is also found at Kynos (*ArchDelt* 45 pl. 84).[2]

The large impressed pithoi are associated with increasing social-economic complexity, suggesting that sites like Kynos, Kalapodi, and Mitrou were in the postpalatial period arenas for display of social differentiation, even if at Mitrou there is so far no evidence for sailor-warrior elites. Since pictorial pottery is so far not attested at Mitrou, the pottery networks did not overlap completely: even within an artifactual category, one class of pottery (impressed pithoi) functioned in a different network than another (pictorial pottery), while both networks are included in a larger koine. This is an example where network differentiation on different scales is visible.

Another indication of the existence of a regional koine focused on the Euboean Gulf is the frequent occurrence of White Ware, first identified at Lefkandi (Popham and Sackett 1968, Popham and Milburn 1971) but also common at Kynos in LH IIIC Middle (Dakoronia 2007, 120). The light-on-dark style of the griffin pyxis from Lefkandi, rare in the palatial periods but more popular after the fall of the palaces, is also known from Kynos: Dakoronia notes a black-glazed skyphos with white dilute spirals (Dakoronia 2007a, 120 fig. 2.9). Other examples were found in graves at Chalkis (Papavasileios 1910, 27 fig. 27).

The role of Kalapodi in this coastal network deserves further attention. Kalapodi, the only non-coastal site in the koine, is located in the center of a highly contested space (McInerney 2011, 101). It seems to have been under influence of Orchomenos during the palatial period (p. 98 and Chapter 5) but was, after the palaces collapsed, assimilated by the coastal elites. Evidence for cult activity during the LH IIIC period consists of ash altars below an altar in the cella of the small archaic temple (Felsch 1981, 83 fig. 2; Jacob-Felsch 1996, 104), as well as offerings and dedications. Sea shells, collected from the shores of the Euboean Gulf, are among the votives left behind by the participants. The pictorial krater fragments from Kalapodi form part of a large assemblage of vessels suitable for drinking and feasting: kylikes, skyphoi, deep bowls and cups, ladles, amphorae, pithoi, and cooking- and kitchen wares, all associated with ritual meals in the sanctuary. This is thus where the LH IIIC coastal elites gathered for communal meals and sacrifices. That Kalapodi functioned as a locus of elite display is suggested by the sheer number of animal bones from the LH IIIC-Submycenaean levels, more than from any other period (Stanzel 1991). This suggests that (ceremonial and ritual) feasting at the sanctuary was at its peak during the postpalatial period, a situation that would be expected when power relations are in flux and elites aim to legitimize their position. The strong presence of coastal elites at Kalapodi

---

[2] It may be noted too that at both Kynos and Lefkandi storage facilities contained pithoi as well as unbaked clay bins (Evely 2006, *passim*).

served to incorporate the sanctuary in their koine, indicating their investment in (if not necessarily control over) the sanctuary. The vessels used in their feasting and drinking ceremonies proclaim their values: the ethos of a warrior society. In line with this, the number of deer bones, though far fewer than those of domestic animals (Stanzel 1991), is significant for the postpalatial period: the feasts were not merely feasts celebrating the harvest (Lemos 2002, 221) but furthered elite ideologies. They may also have been instrumental in forging a sense of a common identity, visible by the similarities in the material record at Kalapodi, Kynos, Lefkandi, and other sites making up the koine. That the Kalapodi settlement may have played an active role in forging communal ties is suggested by its export of impressed pithoi to Mitrou.

The sites of importance in the postpalatial era are generally the same as those that were prominent in the prepalatial period: the Lefkandi/Dramesi cluster, Mitrou, Kynos, and Kalapodi. This suggests that after the collapse of the palaces the age-old, decentralized networks fell back into place and a more heterarchical organization with multiple centers resumed: coastal sites formed a koine, once again oriented toward each other rather than toward the interior hinterland. The nodes that constituted this LH IIIC decentralized network were fewer in number than previously, although along the coasts many nodes remained the same.

GALLEYS AND THE FORMATION OF NEW LONG-DISTANCE NETWORKS

The very fact that the cultural koine is most immediately recognizable by looking at the pictorial pottery suggests that it was the elites and their activities that forged this koine in the first place. The similarities among the pictorial pottery from the LH IIIC Middle period allow us to trace the connections between sites forming part of the same network – the Euboean koine – and the long links this network has with far away regions in the southeastern Mediterranean. All these depictions are characterized by a similar focus on elite lifestyles defined by living the life of a warrior and seafaring. The pottery was, however, locally made (Jones 1996; Mountjoy 1999, 639; Mommsen and Maran 2000–2001). The emphasis on galleys suggests that they formed an important part of the desired identity of the elites that formed the new network; indeed we can go further and say that the galleys contributed significantly to the formation of the new coastal network.

Suitable for quick raids, and in the Kynos iconography associated with sea battles, these galleys help explain the prominence of the Euboean Gulf sites after the collapse of the palaces: they were the means by which the coastal communities co-opted the preexisting ties with the southeastern Mediterranean. Thus, capitalizing on the power vacuum left by the political collapse of Thebes, the Euboean Gulf coastal sites took over the preexisting trade routes: is it coincidence that LH IIIC pictorial pottery with ship depictions occurs along the Euboean Gulf as well as on Melos, Kos, and the coasts of Asia Minor? These ship depictions, so different from what we see in LH IIIA-B, suggest a strong reaction against palatial values: rather than an unmitigated disaster, for the coastal communities along the Euboean Gulf the collapse of the palaces may have been a burden lifted.

Ties with the southeastern Mediterranean are also suggested by the occurrence of a light-on-dark technique. This pottery style, found at Lefkandi, Chalkis, and Kynos, is most common in the Dodecanese and is likely to have reached Euboea and Kynos from there (Dakoronia 2007, 120–121). Thus the LH IIIC pottery from Kynos attests both to a strong regionalism and to far-ranging (trade) networks, e.g., to the Dodecanese; Kynos is part of a small world centered on the Euboean Gulf, but also benefits from long links with the southeastern Aegean. The pictorial themes are also shared with krater fragments from Kos.

An indication of the reestablishment of the exchange network with Crete after the breakdown of the Theban network is suggested by the presence of at least one Minoan transport stirrup jar in the postpalatial levels at Kynos, one of the few mainland sites that have yielded Minoan transport stirrup jars in postpalatial contexts (Stockhammer 2007, 280). In LH IIIA2-B Boeotia, Minoan transport stirrup jars were strongly concentrated in Thebes, with additional single examples at Gla and Orchomenos (Haskell et al. 2011, 94); they also occur with some frequency at the palatial centers of Mycenae and Tiryns (Catling et al. 1980, 100). A similar picture arises for Cypriot imports: in LH IIIB 23 Cypriot imports are equally divided between Tiryns and Thebes, while in LH IIIC they occur only at Perati (nine) and Anthedon (two; Cline 2007, 195), both coastal sites on the Euboean Gulf.

It is likely that the coastal elites used their galleys to take over the southeastern trade routes, and in fact these galleys are depicted not only in the Euboean Gulf area but form a chain from Phylakopi on Melos to Kos in the Dodecanese and the coast of Asia Minor (Miletos; Bademgediği Tepe). A number of kalathos sherds from Phylakopi depict a galley with an animal-headed stempost at the bow, a forked sternpost, mast, oars, and steering oars (Wedde 2000, nos. 656–663); three large joining skyphos fragments depict a clumsily drawn oared ship with prominent stempost (Wedde 2000, no. 664). From Seraglio on Kos comes the well-known krater sherd with rowers, possibly wearing feathered helmets, bent backwards as they strain on their oars (Wedde 2000, no. 654); they seem to feature in the same tradition as a number of soldiers on four krater fragments from the same site (Vermeule and Karageorghis 1982 nos. XII.29–32). From Asia Minor come a couple of extremely simply drawn oared ships depicted on a krater fragment from Miletos, which may be somewhat earlier (LH IIIB-C: Vermeule and

Karageorghis 1982, no. XIII.6; Wedde 2000 nos. 694–696), and a transitional LH IIIB-C Early or LH IIIC Early large krater fragment from Bademgediği Tepe (Mountjoy 2011). This last depiction shows rowers below deck in much the same position as the rowers from Kos, with much larger warriors, wearing hedgehog helmets, standing on deck. Although the two depictions from Asia Minor may predate the fall of the Mycenaean palaces, the certain LH IIIC evidence traces a long net of connections stretching from the Euboean Gulf to the Dodecanese, with the largest concentration of such depictions clustered around the shores of the Euboean Gulf. Although generally the evidence for a break-up of trade with the southeastern Mediterranean is overwhelming, this network of galley depictions suggests that not all contact ceased, as also indicated by the commonalities in pottery: the galleys, operated by coastal elites and their retinue, kept lines of communication open even if scale and character of acquisition, trade, and exchange differed.

The galleys could do this not merely by their virtue of being capable of crossing large distances over sea but also by the fact that the galley community presented a group of organized and trained military individuals ready to spring into action. Although the palaces would have employed the newly invented galleys as a means of importing high-status low-volume goods in a relatively safe way, their very existence required the creation of armed, and therefore potentially dangerous, male groups with a high team spirit (Wedde 2005) who were, as sailors, not under immediate control of the palace. Once the central palatial authority collapsed, local captains or chieftains (the *basileis*, whose authority was always rooted in the local community rather than granted by the authority of the palace) with enough initiative and authority could call on their rower-warrior teams to dominate their stretch of coast: the galley communities were perhaps the only parts of the previous palatial infrastructure still fully intact and able to operate without palatial oversight. It is thus not surprising that it is especially in the coastal areas of the Euboean Gulf that we find an immediate recovery after the palatial collapse, nor that that recovery is marked by an emphasis on sailor-warrior iconography. The continuation of contacts with the southeast Mediterranean is visible in the shared themes as well as styles or techniques between the Euboean Gulf communities and the Dodecanese, and continues on a grander scale in the Early Iron Age, when an Early Protogeometric grave from the Skoubris cemetery contains Egyptian and Near Eastern grave goods.

During and after the collapse, these galleys enabled individual power centers to keep supply lines protected and open, but when one center became predator on another, this would have accelerated the downfall from within (Wedde 2005, 36); after the flourishing of the LH IIIC Middle, the LH IIIC Late period seems rather dreary. Nevertheless, the continuity of galley depictions – LH IIIC Middle galleys evolve organically into Geometric galleys –

suggests that the galley and the social infrastructure around it contributed to a partial "system survival" (Wedde 2006). It is striking that among the last pictorial evidence from the Bronze Age are ships with warriors equipped with proto-Dipylon shields, a theme that pops up again in the Middle Geometric period, when the first real (Geometric) Dipylon shields are shown in combination with Geometric galleys (on a Middle Geometric II skyphos from Eleusis: Archaeological Museum of Eleusis, inv. no. 741, and on an Attic Middle Geometric II krater: New York, Metropolitan Museum of Art, inv. no. 34.11.2). This suggests that galley and shield formed part of a sailor-warrior package that survived the Late Bronze Age-Early Iron Age transition intact, which in turn suggests that this package contributed to the partial continuity between the two eras.

POSTPALATIAL TRADE

Galleys were fast, but due to their limited cargo space they were not great trading vessels. This is reflected in the sort of imports found in postpalatial contexts. Imports found in the LH IIIC settlement of Lefkandi include an iron knife, probably from Cyprus, a bronze knife with Alpine and Italian associations, and a bronze pin of northwest-Balkan or Italian origin; raw materials include emery from Naxos, volcanic stones from the Saronic Gulf, obsidian from Melos, as well as the exotic ivory and the precious gold, alloyed bronze, and lead. The items are all low volume, and of various types and origins. Pottery and figurines suggest that Lefkandi had connections with Cyprus, Crete, the Dodecanese, and Phylakopi, as well as with closer sites such as Perati. In addition to the bronze Alpine/Italian knife, a bowl and a cup are of Italian handmade burnished ware. These three LH IIIC Early Italian imports are assigned by Parkinson to three different contacts and thus attest to relatively frequent but low-key contact with Italy (Parkinson 2010). The range of goods from the Aegean and Cyprus suggest that the people at Lefkandi played an active role in acquiring these goods (much like the Shaft Grave princes), rather than waiting for ships from Cyprus, the Aegean, or Italy to visit their shores. Perhaps these imports should rather be understood in terms of personal possessions of sailors, acquired on various trips, than as "trade items."

All these imports represent items casually lost in ordinary domestic buildings throughout the site and not retrieved. This makes it likely that ownership of such items was dispersed and common: though living in modest dwellings, the inhabitants of Lefkandi constituted a relatively egalitarian but prosperous society. The society of LH IIIC Lefkandi appears thus to have been at once fairly decentralized and unexpectedly rich (Sherratt 2006b, 309). The same decentralized character is visible at Perati, where 42 imports are spread over 22 tombs, with 14 tombs having just one import each

TABLE 8.1. *Imports in the Perati tombs (after Cline 1994)*

Tomb	Cyprus	Egypt	Syro-Palestine	Cypriot or Syro-Palestine
1		1 faience cartouche	1 hematite seal	
9	1 gold earring			
11	1 gold earring			
12			1 bronze knife	
13		5 faience scarabs		
24	1 hematite seal/ bulla			1 steatite seal
28				1 iron knife
30		3 faience amulets; 4 faience figurines	1 hematite weight	
34		1 glass vase		
38				1 iron knife
49			1 gold amulet	
75		2 faience scarabs		
90		1 faience scarab		
100			1 hematite weight	
104	1 bronze tripod stand	1 faience cartouche		
108	1 iron pin			
142	1 hematite seal			
145		1 faience scarab		
147		1 faience scarab	4 gold amulets	
152	1 gold earring		1 quartz weight	
157	1 gold earring			
Σ19	1 gold earring			

(Table 8.1). This decentralized character seems to have been true for the region as a whole: the very fact that kraters with martial imagery have turned up at various sites along the Euboean Gulf suggests multiple centers of power. Thus we witness a return to less centralized networks in the postpalatial period. The LH IIIC social pattern visible in the Euboean Gulf on a regional scale, that of peer polities in a heterarchical (rather than hierarchical) organization, is thus propagated on the microscale within communities.

In the palatial period Mycenae, followed by Tiryns and Thebes, accounted for the vast majority of imports; in the postpalatial era this honor befalls Perati, on the east coast of Attica, with Lefkandi and Tiryns following at a distance (Cline 1994; Parkinson 2010). Perati thus overtook Mycenae as hub for foreign contact, evidence for the importance of formerly provincial coastal sites in general and of sites on the maritime route of the Euboean Gulf in particular. Whereas in the palatial period the Euboean coasts may have lacked extra-Aegean imports altogether, after the collapse of the palaces two of the three sites with the vast majority of imports are located in or near the Euboean Gulf. The data compiled by Parkinson (2010) are telling: for LH I-II, Mycenae dominates foreign exchange, but two of a total of ten sites with extra-Aegean contacts are located on or near the shores of the Euboean Gulf (Thorikos and Perati).[3] In LH IIIA-B, 19 sites, dominated by Mycenae, Tiryns, and Thebes, have extra-Aegean contacts; none are along the Euboean Gulf. For LH IIIC the picture is similar to that of LH I-II: of ten sites, two are on the Euboean Gulf coasts (Perati and Lefkandi). The difference between LH I-II and LH IIIC is that the center for imports shifts from the Argolid (and, to a lesser extent, the rest of the Peloponnese) to the Euboean Gulf area (and, to a lesser extent, the coastal Argolid).

The numbers of imports overall stay more or less the same between the palatial and postpalatial eras: Thebes counts 47 imports from the palatial period, whereas Perati has 39 (Cline 1994) or 47 (Burns 2010, 39) imports in its LH IIIC chamber tombs. Although overall numbers are similar, the location where imports are found changes and it is unlikely to be a coincidence that Perati, Lefkandi, and Tiryns are all coastal sites. It seems likely that centers with direct access to galleys could benefit from extra-Aegean exchange after the collapse of the palaces.

The character of these imports is strikingly different as well. The large cemetery at Perati (219 tombs have been excavated) was established in LH IIIC and endured into the Early Iron Age. In addition to goods from the Cyclades, extra-Aegean imports include gold earrings, hematite seals, and a tripod stand from Cyprus; a glass vase and faience figurines and amulets, cartouches, and scarabs from Egypt; and gold amulets, a hematite seal, a bronze knife, and a quartz and two hematite weights from Syria-Palestine (Table 8.1). All are finished goods – trinkets for the most part; the large-scale import of raw materials to the palaces, evidence for organized trade and exchange between the Mycenaean palaces and Cyprus and the Levant, has completely ceased. Two factors contributed to this shift in imports: first of all the galleys themselves, which were not conducive to large-scale transport of bulk items, and second the collapse of hubs and centers throughout the Eastern Mediterranean. The large-scale (trade) network in the eastern Mediterranean fell apart since these routes constituted the long-distance ties in a decentralized network.[4] When the hubs failed, the ties connecting the hubs (the long-distance ties in a decentralized network) failed as well, resulting in the network falling apart into a group of scattered "islands." However, new long-distance ties were formed almost immediately, between different nodes in the network.

The number of imported goods is thus roughly the same as that at LH IIIB Thebes. However, whereas Thebes' imports can be accounted for by a limited

---

[3] Note that Mitrou now joins this small group with its Balkanian horse bridle piece (pp. 46–47).

[4] On the regional scale, networks were centralized. Each regional centralized network formed a cluster in a supra-regional network; these clusters were connected by long-distance links between the hubs.

number of contacts (just seven, according to Parkinson's calculations), the number of contacts for Perati may have been as many as 26 (Parkinson 2010, 19), suggesting relatively frequent but low-level contact rather than the rare contacts with high stakes characterizing palatial Thebes. In palatial Thebes, sporadic contacts accounted for large numbers of goods, whereas in post-palatial Perati, fewer but diverse (in terms of material, origin, and type of artifact) goods are brought in per occasion: exchange is smaller in scale, but more frequent.[5] This difference between palatial and postpalatial exchange is visible also when comparing Parkinson's contacts with Cline's number of items in the palatial and the postpalatial periods at Mycenae and Perati, respectively: at LH IIIA-B Mycenae, 28 contacts are responsible for 61 imports, whereas at LH IIIC Perati, 26 contacts are associated with 39 imports. In other words, at palatial Mycenae, two contacts were responsible for at least four foreign imports, whereas at Perati, on average two contacts resulted in three imports. Although palatial Mycenae imported more goods, its foreign contacts were not more frequent than those at postpalatial Perati. Although sample size is small and calculations are rough, the trend that nevertheless emerges is a shift toward a lower-stakes and less organized trade and exchange (or possibly acquisition without reciprocity!) in the postpala-tial period.

Equally important is that the wider distribution, in relation to the number of imported items at postpalatial Perati, suggests a more egalitarian society: there is no evidence for "hoarding" imports, which are instead distributed over 19 (of 219) different tombs. This constitutes 8.7 percent of the excavated tombs, suggesting that only a minority of the population (less than 10 percent) had access to imported goods. This suggests that the structure within the settlement resembled that of the regional decentralized network. Within the tombs with imports, the imports are unequally divided: Tomb 30 stands out with eight imports from two different areas, Tombs 13 and 147 each have five, while all other tombs have one or two. With the exception of the knife in the warrior tomb, all other imports are small prestige and luxury items or trinkets. It should be noted that there is no direct correspondence between imported items and warrior tombs at Perati: with the exception of the Syro-Palestinian bronze knife (the only imported weapon) in Warrior Tomb 12, all other imported items in Cline's catalogue (38 items) are found in non-warrior tombs.

[5] I have no doubt that these conclusions are basically correct. It should be pointed out, though, that Parkinson's methodology represents just one way of looking at the data and is not without problems (e.g., are Syro-Palestinian items in an LH III context at Thebes acquired on a separate occasion from those in an LH IIIA2-B context or not?). Nevertheless, Parkinson's approach represents significant progress toward our under-standing of exchange (Parkinson 2010, 17–18).

Once central hubs had been taken out, long-distance trade networks fell
apart. For Mycenaean Greece, this meant that the import of exotic raw
materials (metals, ivory) and luxury items to the palaces stopped. As soon
as the palatial system has collapsed we find in Perati a thriving international
hub, trading with the Levant, Cyprus, and Egypt (Crielaard 2006, 281, note
36). The coastal site of Perati thus takes over the preexisting maritime routes,
but instead of rebuilding the vast, interconnected exchange network that
spanned the eastern Mediterranean in the fourteenth and thirteenth centuries, its sailors focus on collecting small, portable trinkets: a seal here, a few
scarabs there. This is probably largely a result of the aforementioned widespread collapse of exchange networks, but it also has to do with the character
of the Mycenaean galleys the LH IIIC Mycenaean used: these galleys were
unfit for carrying large cargo loads, favoring small objects. These ships would
also have allowed for the acquisition of such objects in quick raids, something
that seems not inconsistent with the warrior ethos visible on the kraters from
the Euboean Gulf area.

That Perati not only was a hub in a long-distance trade network but also
gained prominence locally is suggested by the lead and silver objects, which
were made from Laureion ore. Finds from Mine no. 3 at Thorikos attest to
occupation as well as metallurgical activity in the postpalatial period.
The unstratified ceramic material belongs to two distinct groups, one dated
to transitional LH IIIB2-LH IIIC Early, the other to LH IIIC Middle. The first
group displays parallels with Attica and the eastern Peloponnese (Corinthia,
the Argolid, Laconia); the second duplicates shapes and decorations known
from Athens and Perati. Thus, similar to what happened in Boeotia and
Central Greece, the mines at Thorikos were in the beginning of the postpalatial period still part of a network with long links to palatial areas; in LH
IIIC Middle the ties with the Corinthia and the Argolid and beyond have
been severed and replaced by local and regional ties. The similarities between
pottery from mine no. 3 at Thorikos and pottery from Perati suggest that the
inhabitants of Perati exploited the mines at Thorikos, 25 km away, in the
postpalatial period (Laffineur 2010, 719). The prominence of Perati thus
seems linked to the exploitation of the silver mines as well as to international
trade and contacts.

CONCLUSIONS

When around 1200 BCE the Mycenaean palaces were destroyed, the social
organization of the Mycenaean state fell with the palaces. Although Thebes
and Orchomenos (as well as a number of other Mycenaean palatial sites)
continued to be inhabited, the palace system was wiped out by the early
twelfth century. This total collapse of state structures was a direct consequence of the extreme centralization of the palatial networks, both in political

and in social-economic terms: the destruction of the centers of administration was the equivalent of taking out the hubs in the network, and the elimination of the highest social structures (officials who, if not destroyed directly, did not survive the interruption in trade networks on which they depended for the legitimization of their rule) meant that the social hierarchy fell apart, too: only the lower and middle echelons of society survived and the local chiefs (the *basileis*) with power bases independent of the palaces.

This chapter has argued that the underlying reason for the thriving of the Euboean Gulf coast settlements in this LH IIIC period is that with the collapse of the land-based networks focused on the palaces, the coastal and maritime networks that had characterized the prepalatial period were reestablished. Using the galleys they had access to, coastal settlements took over the previous palatial trade routes. A cultural koine on the Euboean Gulf coasts is suggested by the similar pictorial pottery; since pottery with similar themes is found also in the southeastern Mediterranean (Rhodes, Kos) and since light-on-dark pottery, popular in the southeastern Mediterranean, is found along the coasts of the Euboean Gulf, long-distance links between the two areas are likely. Imports are now found spread throughout settlements or cemeteries, suggesting decentralized access and a fairly egalitarian and, at the same time, relatively wealthy society. Since there are a number of large settlements along the Euboean Gulf coasts in LH IIIC, settlement organization may have been heterarchical rather than hierarchical, much like it was in the prepalatial period.

9

CONCLUSIONS

Mycenaean scholarship started with Schliemann's excavations of Grave Circle A at Mycenae and has since been dominated overwhelmingly by a focus on the rich palatial cultures of the Peloponnese and the southern central mainland. Exactly how great the influence of the palaces on modern scholarship is, becomes clear when Feuer (2011, 510) summarizes Kilian's criteria for what constitutes Mycenaean civilization (Kilian 1990, 445–447), without noting how every one of them reflects palatial circumstances, times, and sites. This book focuses on some of the non-palatial areas outside the Peloponnese and investigates the various ways in which the Mycenaean core areas (especially the palatial polity of Thebes in Central Greece) interacted with the more provincial areas along the Euboean Gulf coasts.

To date, events in those non-palatial areas are usually described in terms of reactions to the palaces: the palaces are viewed as agents determining the course of history, the provinces as passively reacting or even as passive victims of palatial expansion. When this is not the case, as in Tartaron's recent book (2013) on *Maritime Networks in the Mycenaean World*, the land-based palaces are mostly absent from the discourse: while emphasizing the important position of the coasts in Greek prehistory, in only one case study does Tartaron examine these coastal areas in conjunction with the interior, land-based palaces. In his explanation, Korphos-Kalamianos is a territory contested between the old power of Kolonna and the new palatial power of Mycenae, which is responsible for the sea-facing Cyclopean walls at Korphos-Kalamianos. The walls at Korphos-Kalamianos are thus seen as tangible evidence for palatial reactions to a non-palatial island power. This book has suggested that this is not an isolated case, but that the palaces and the coastal areas on the margins of the palatial territories developed together, and reacted to each other, throughout the Late Bronze Age in Central Greece as well.

I have followed a coastscape approach, viewing the Euboean Gulf coasts as separate from the interior hinterland in ethos and cultural development, to emphasize the differences in trajectory. Whereas the Euboean Gulf coasts followed the same trajectory as the interior in the early Mycenaean period, in the palatial and postpalatial periods they are in opposite phases. This book has explained the unusual trajectory of the coasts on two levels: changes in cultural and social-political network structure and orientation, as revealed by pottery types, make clear why the coasts declined during the palatial periods of LH IIIA-B and flourished anew during the postpalatial period, while I have invoked agency of elites (the Theban *wanax*, the postpalatial coastal warrior elites), as seen in visual expressions of self-advertisement, to explain why network structure and orientation changed to begin with.

In the beginning of the Late Bronze Age, the Euboean Gulf coasts followed the developments in the Argolid and other centers of Mycenaean civilization: burials attest to a warrior ethos shared with emerging elites elsewhere, imported lustrous pottery suggests an emphasis on ceremonial drinking and feasting, and imported goods from farther afield play a role in the self-advertisements of these early elites as "men of the world." Weak ties and the manipulation of networks were of crucial importance in the status creation of the early Mycenaean elites. An emphasis on the individual, visible in graves as well as in depictions of individual "heroes" dueling, is linked to swords (equally individualized as Harrell has demonstrated for the Shaft Graves [Harrell 2012, 2014]) and swordsmanship. A number of early Mycenaean centers dot the coastal landscape in this period. I have argued that these centers arose due to the exploitation of long-distance links, which allowed for the dispersion of "exotic" goods and new fashions to spread rapidly throughout the Mycenaean world.

In contrast to this, there is very little evidence for early Mycenaean settlement outside of these centers of elites. It is generally recognized that this is due to the similarity of most pottery of the period to standard MH pottery, making it difficult to tell the two periods apart, especially when working with surface survey material. I have argued that this reveals the nature of early Mycenaean networks: the elite network, through which new lustrous pottery was distributed, was apparently highly exclusionary: peer–polity interaction and the sharing in lustrous pottery did not extend to lesser sites. This model not only explains why at most sites lustrous pottery is absent; it also explains why even at sites where lustrous pottery is found, it forms but a small fraction of the total pottery count: this ware was limited to elites, who used the new pottery in drinking ceremonies. The emergence of multiple elite centers suggests the emergence of a decentralized (scale-free) network type.

Only in LH IIIA1, typical Mycenaean cultural markers are found throughout the countryside, suggesting that the elite networks now opened up, allowing (or encouraging) smaller sites to link to them and participate in the Mycenaean culture. The spread of small prestige goods to other sites may have been in part due to a strategy of the highest elites – those who won the local power struggles of the early Mycenaean period – to form alliances with lower-level regional elites in order to compete on the regional level; part of it is undoubtedly due to regional settlements actively seeking out identification with Mycenaean high culture. As the power struggles of the early Mycenaean period diminished, ideologies changed from a warrior ethos to more consolidated forms of power as expressed in cult or civic symbols.

This is visible in the disappearance of warrior graves and a change in imagery, from overtly martial to more symbolic, on seal stones, possibly reflective of a transition in political organization from chiefdoms to early states. The enthusiastic adoption of LH IIIA-B Mainland Popular Group seals by elites and sub-elites in provincial areas is suggestive of provincial aspirations to elite status.

In the palatial period (LH IIIA2-B), the coasts of the Euboean Gulf area were not thriving as before: despite the emergence of elites in the early Mycenaean period, and despite the completion of Mycenaeanization, we do not recognize any prominent centers of even just regional significance in the palatial period. I argue that the cause of this is a realignment of networks: the coastal (maritime) network was broken up by an increasingly centralized network emanating from the hub of Thebes and cutting through the former coastal links. This network was land based, like the palace itself. The first signs of this reorientation are visible in changes in pottery types at Chalkis between LH IIA and IIB-IIIA.

The concentration of imports and workshops at Thebes, the cessation of industrial activity and dearth of imports elsewhere in Boeotia, and the enormous size of the Theban citadel compared to, for example, Mycenae and Tiryns all point to extreme centralization. The Theban network was increasingly centralized, with Thebes co-opting existing links and monopolizing production and distribution of elite goods. Sites on the Euboean Gulf coasts were affected by this in a number of different ways. Some sites on the mainland coast were actively "promoted" by the palaces, receiving fortification walls, and become visible only in the LH IIIA-B periods. The Cyclopean walls at Larymna are an example of this: Larymna functioned as the easternmost extension of a series of forts extending east from Orchomenos and meant to protect the drainage works of the Kopaic Basin. Most sites, on either side of the Euboean Gulf, did not receive such investment and suffered from the disruption of the maritime network. Kalapodi was in this period incorporated by Orchomenos, judging from the seals found at the sanctuary, even as evidence for settlement in the vicinity of Kalapodi dwindles; Mitrou may have been destroyed before being brought under control of one of the palaces.

A possible reason for this network restructuring is provided by the imports found in LH IIIA2-B contexts at Thebes. The contexts suggest that in this period exotic imports were reworked at the palace ("domesticated"). This suggests an attempt by palatial elites to control the consumption (and "production") of exotic imports, which may have various reasons; one possible reason proposed in this book is that, since import itself could not be controlled as there were always independent traders, the palaces dictated the value of what was imported by requiring reworking in palatial workshops.

Considering the importance of ships for the Mycenaean palatial elites in LH IIIA2-B, it is perhaps surprising that ships are rarely shown in monumental art, specifically frescoes. The only exceptions are at Pylos, from where we also have the richest textual records. The texts suggest the importance of the recently invented Mycenaean galleys for the palatial elites; yet the few ships that are depicted on frescoes are of the older, traditional Minoan type. Possible reasons for this include the conservatism of fresco art or the predominantly ceremonial place ships held in the official visual programs of palatial propaganda. I have suggested that the limited value of ships as vehicles for the communication of elite ideals may be the reason for their rarity in palatial art. This value is limited because ships are not that clearly associated with the palace (they are manned by crews from coastal centers, where they are built), nor are they visible throughout the polity. In addition, the groups of heavily armed rowers from the coastal centers would constitute a force to be reckoned with, should they ever turn against the palatial order (Wedde 2005).

After the palaces collapsed, the Euboean Gulf coasts thrived. I have proposed a reason rooted in a change in network structure and orientation: with the collapse of the palaces, the land-based networks emanating from the palaces fell apart. Since these palatial networks had been highly centralized, the loss of the palatial hub left surrounding settlements in a vacuum. The settlements on the Euboean Gulf, however, quickly reestablished the prepalatial coastal and maritime networks and, using the galleys they had access to, took over the previously palatial trade routes. A cultural koine on the Euboean Gulf coasts is suggested by the similar pictorial pottery; since pottery with similar themes is found also in the southeastern Mediterranean (Rhodes, Kos) and since light-on-dark pottery, popular in the southeastern Mediterranean, is found along the coasts of the Euboean Gulf, long-distance links between the two areas are likely. Kalapodi was part of the cultural koine and seems to have functioned as cult place for the elites of the Euboean Gulf coasts.

Imports are now found spread throughout the settlement of Lefkandi, suggesting a more egalitarian society; since these imports are found casually discarded, the society may have been relatively wealthy with relatively easy access to imports. Possibly this is because the "imports" represent personal possessions of the sailors based in Lefkandi. Similarly, at the cemetery at

Perati imports are spread over a large number of tombs, suggesting decentralized access. Since there are a number of large settlements along the Euboean Gulf coasts in LH IIIC, settlement organization may have been more heterarchical, in a decentralized system. The history of imports throughout the Late Bronze Age is in fact revealing: in LH I-II and LH IIIC, at least 20 percent of sites with extra-Aegean imports are located in the Euboean Gulf area (Parkinson 2010, 23). This strengthens the suggestion that the Euboean Gulf area followed trends set by Mycenae in LH I-II, and was underway to create local and regional centers. In the LH IIIA-B period, however, Euboean Gulf sites did not acquire any imports, in line with the general picture of decline that we have noted. In LH IIIC, the Euboean Gulf sites dominated extra-Aegean trade and exchange, profiting from their location and their sailor-warrior culture centered on galleys.

The palatial era thus appears as an anomaly in the longer-term history of the Late Bronze Age Euboean Gulf area, an interlude that was caused by palatial attempts to monopolize trade routes by co-opting preexisting links. In the pre- as well as postpalatial period, the Euboean Gulf coastal settlements capitalized on their strategic position on a major maritime route and thrived by forging and maintaining long-distance links.

At a number of LH IIIC settlements, indirect evidence exists for resistance against the previous palatial system in the form of painted pottery or different settlement organization. At Kynos, Lefkandi, and Kalapodi (and also at Volos and Perati), pictorial kraters glorified warriors and ships: a sailor-warrior culture existed and the elites at these settlements identified with warriors on ships. These sailor-warriors were part of the general chaos of the closing years of the Bronze Age and may have been part of the same phenomenon as the "Sea Peoples," and although they used the standard Mycenaean galleys, their weaponry (small shields, short spears) was not palatial. The incurved shields, attested in depictions from Volos and Kynos, seem precursors of the Geometric Dipylon shields rather than having similarities to older Mycenaean shields. Thus the earlier tension between land-based palaces and coastal settlements was flipped in favor of the coastal settlements, and the warrior ethos characterizing the early Mycenaean period returned in the postpalatial period.

To summarize, after the early Mycenaean period, social rise and fall happened along the Euboean Gulf coasts in opposite phase compared to that of the Mycenaean heartland. Initially (LH I–II), the coastal areas followed the same trajectory as the Mycenaean heartland: a warrior ethos and the creation of new long-distance ties led to the emergence of elites at several prominent centers in the early Mycenaean period. A change in ideology resulted in a gradual devaluation (or at least disappearance of overt expressions) of the warrior ethos in the LH IIIA1 period, when elites identified with seals and ostentatious pottery rather than with swords and boar's tusk helmets. From the palatial period onward, however, the coastal areas were in opposite phase from the Mycenaean palaces: when the palaces thrived, the Euboean Gulf coasts showed a relatively poor material record and the promise of the early Mycenaean centers remained unfulfilled, whereas after the collapse of the palaces, the coasts thrived.

During the postpalatial period, the ethos of the coastal elites seems similar to that of the prepalatial elites of the early Mycenaean period: a warrior ethos prevailed. In the postpalatial period, this was explicitly a sailor-warrior ethos. It is notable that the coastal settlements thrived in unsettled times when they followed this warrior ethos. Moreover, it is notable that they thrived when they created and maintained coastal and maritime networks: it seems likely that the fate of these coasts was intimately intertwined with their ability to exploit the maritime route through the Euboean Gulf. It is perhaps no surprise, then, that in the Early Iron Age Lefkandi was one of the very few settlements in all of the Greek mainland area that maintained long-distance contacts with Cyprus and the Levant, had a level of culture that exceeded the mere subsistence level, and was involved in modeling and painting clay boat models and pictorial scenes. Ultimately, it may well have been the employment of galleys coupled with its advantageous location which made Lefkandi the single most important Early Iron Age site in Greece.

This study has proposed the utility of combining network theory (or "network thinking") with agency theory to begin to explain the relation between the Mycenaean palaces (or palatial areas) and provinces, the coasts on the fringes of the palatial territories in Central Greece. A regional study with a social-historical emphasis, this book proposes explanations that are in many cases transferable to other Mycenaean regions. The destruction and decline of thriving coastal centers such as Mitrou is paralleled at Agios Stephanos and Iklaina, as is their limited postpalatial recovery. The investment of a palatial site in a marginal coastal site, as happened at Larymna, is similar to Mycenae's investment at Korphos-Kalamianos. The reason that postpalatial Messenia suffered such strong depopulation and decline is that, like Thebes, Pylos was a hub in an extremely centralized network so that when the palace collapsed, the entire network collapsed with it and all of Messenia was strongly affected. And the postpalatial return of the warrior ethos is paralleled in Achaea and Elis. The Euboean Gulf area thus constitutes a useful case study of interaction.

BIBLIOGRAPHY

Abramovitz, K. 1980. "Frescoes from Ayia Irini, Keos. Parts II–IV," *Hesperia* 49, 57–85.

———. 2006. "The Palace of Iolkos and Its End," in S. Deger-Jalkotzi and I.S. Lemos (eds.), *Ancient Greece: From the Mycenaean Palaces to the Age of Homer*, Edinburgh, 465–481.

Åkerström, Å. 1968. "A Mycenaean Potter's Factory at Berbati near Mycenae," in *Atti e Memorie del I Congresso Internazionale di Micenologia, Roma, 27 settembre–3 ottobre 1967* (Incunabula Graeca 25), Rome, 48–53.

Aprile, J.D. 2013. "Crafts, Specialists, and Markets in Mycenaean Greece. The New Political Economy of Nichoria: Using Intrasite Distributional Data to Investigate Regional Institutions," *AJA* 117, 429–436.

Aravantinos, V. 1999. "Κέντρο και περιφέρεια στη Μυκηναϊκή Βοιωτία," in Α᾽ Διεθνές Διεπιστημονικό Συμπόσιο «Η Περιφέρεια του Μυκηναϊκού Κόσμου», Λαμία, 25–29 Σεπτεμβρίου, 1994/1st International Interdisciplinary Colloquium "Periphery of the Mycenaean World," Lamia, 25–29 September, 1994, 235.

———. 2010. *The Archaeological Museum of Thebes*, John S. Latsis Public Benefit Foundation (e-book: www.latsis-foundation.org/megazine/publish/ebook.php?book=64&preloader=1).

Aravantinos, V., B. Burke, B. Burns, I. Fappas, and S. Lupack. 2009. "Eastern Boeotia Archaeological Project 2009," *Teiresias: A Review and Bibliography of Boiotian Studies* 39, 11–15.

———. 2012. "The Eastern Boeotia Archaeological Project, 2007–2008," in A. Mazarakis-Ainian (ed.), *AETHSE: Third Archaeological Meeting of Thessaly and Central Greece*, Volos, 1059–1068.

Aravantinos, V.L., L. Godart, and A. Sacconi. 2001. *Thèbes: fouilles de la Cadmée I. Les tablettes en Linéaire B de la Odos Pelopidou, Edition et commentaire*, Pisa & Rome.

Avila, R. 1983. "Das Kuppelgrab von Volos-Kapakli," *Prähistorische Zeitschrift* 58, 15–60.

Barabási, A.-L. 2002. *Linked: How Everything Is Connected to Everything Else and What It Means for Business, Science, and Everyday Life*, New York.

Barabási, A.-L. and R. Albert. 1999. "Emergence of Scaling in Random Networks," *Science* 286, 509–512.

Baran, P. 1964. "On Distributed Communications Networks," *IEEE Transactions on Communications Systems* 12, 1–9.

Basch, L. 1986. "The Aegina Pirate Ships of c. B.C. 1700," *Mariner's Mirror* 72, 415–437.

Bass, G. F. 1967. *Cape Gelidonya: A Bronze Age Shipwreck* (Transactions of the American Philosophical Society 57), Philadelphia.

Bell, J. 1992. "On Capturing Agency in Theories about Prehistory," in J.C. Gardin and C. Peebles (eds.), *Representations in Archaeology*, Bloomington, 30–55.

Bendall, L.M. 2003. "A Reconsideration of the Northeastern Building at Pylos: Evidence for a Mycenaean Redistributive Center," *AJA* 107, 181–231.

Bennett, J. 2007. "Representations of Power in Mycenaean Pylos. Script, Orality, Iconography," in F. Lang, C. Reinholdt, and J. Weilhartner (eds.), *ΣΤΕΦΑΝΟΣ ΑΡΙΣΤΕΙΟΣ. Archäologische Forschungen zwischen Nil und Istros. Festschrift für Stefan Hiller zum 65. Geburtstag*, Vienna, 11–22.

Billigmeier, J.-C. and J. A. Turner. 1981. "The Socio-Economic Roles of Women in Mycenaean Greece: A Brief Survey from Evidence of the Linear B Tablets," in H.P. Foley (ed.), *Reflections of Women in Antiquity*, New York, London, and Paris, 1–18.

Bintliff, J.L. and A.M. Snodgrass. 1985. "The Cambridge/Bradford Boeotian Expedition: The First Four Years," *JFA* 12, 123–161.

1988. "Mediterranean Survey and the City," *Antiquity* 62, 57–71.

Forthcoming. "Natural and Human Ecology: Geography, Climate and Demography," in I. Lemos and A. Kotsonis (eds.), *A Companion to the Archaeology of Early Greece and the Mediterranean. Blackwell Companions to the Ancient World*, Oxford and Chichester.

Bintliff, J., P. Howard, and A. Snodgrass. 1999. "The Hidden Landscape of Prehistoric Greece," *JMA* 12 (2), 139–168.

2007. *Testing the Hinterland: The Work of the Boeotia Survey (1989–1991) in the Southern Approaches to the City of Thespiai*, Cambridge.

Blegen, C.W. 1949. "Hyria," *Hesperia Suppl.* 8, 39–42.

Blegen, C.W. and M. Rawson. 1973. *The Palace of Nestor at Pylos in Western Messenia*, Princeton.

Bourdieu, P. 1977. *Outline of a Theory of Practice*, Cambridge.

1990. *The Logic of Practice*, Stanford.

Bouzek, J. 1994. "Late Bronze Age Greece and the Balkans: A Review of the Present Picture," *BSA* 89, 217–234.

Brecoulaki, H. 2004. Review of Brysbaert 2008, *The Power of Technology in the Bronze Age Eastern Mediterranean: The Case of the Painted Plaster*, *BMCR* 2010.12.27.

2004. "Restoration and Re-Study of the Mycenaean Wall Paintings," The Pylos Regional Archaeological Project: 14th Season Preliminary Report to the 7th Ephoreia of Prehistoric and Classical Antiquities, Olympia, on the Results of Museum Study, September 2003–October 2004 (http://classics.uc.edu/prap/reports.html).

2005. "Conservation and Re-study Project of Mycenaean Wall-Paintings," The Pylos Regional Archaeological Project: 15th Season Preliminary Report to the 7th Ephoreia of Prehistoric and Classical Antiquities, Olympia, on the Results of Museum Study, September 2004–October 2005 (http://classics.uc.edu/prap/reports.html).

2006. "Wall-Paintings from the Palace," Summary of Research at the Palace of Nestor between September 2005 and October 2006 (http://classics.uc.edu/prap/reports.html).

2007. "The Wall-Paintings," Summary of Research at the Palace of Nestor between September 2006 and October 2007 (http://classics.uc.edu/prap/reports.html).

Brecoulaki, H., S.R. Stocker, J.L. Davis, and E.C. Egan. 2015. "An Unprecedented Naval Scene from Pylos: First Considerations," in H. Brecoulaki, J.L. Davis, and S.R. Stocker (eds.), *Mycenaean Wall Painting in Context: New Discoveries and Old Finds Reconsidered: Proceedings of the International Conference in Athens, Greece in February 2010* (Meletemata 72), Athens, 260–291.

Brecoulaki, H., C. Zaitoun, S.R. Stocker, J.L. Davis, A.G. Karydas, M. Perla Colombini, and U. Bartolucci. 2008. "An Archer from the Palace of Nestor: A New Wall-Painting Fragment in the Chora Museum," *Hesperia* 77, 363–397.

Broodbank, C. 1989. "The Longboat and Society in the Cyclades in the Keros-Syros Culture," *AJA* 93, 319–337.

2000, *An Island Archaeology of the Early Cyclades*, Cambridge.

Brumfiel, E.M. 2000. "On the Archaeology of Choice. Agency Studies as a Research Stratagem," in M.-A. Dobres and J. Robb (eds.), *Agency in Archaeology*, London and New York, 249–255.

Brysbaert, A. 2008. *The Power of Technology in the Bronze Age Eastern Mediterranean: The Case of the Painted Plaster* (Monographs in Mediterranean Archaeology 12), London.

Brysbaert, A. (ed.) 2011. *Tracing Prehistoric Social Networks through Technology*, New York, London.

Buchholz, H.-G. and V. Karageorghis. 1973. *Prehistoric Greece and Cyprus. An Archaeological Handbook*, London.

Bulle, H. 1907. *Orchomenos I: Die älteren Ansiedlungsschichten*, Munich.

Burke, B. 2005. "Materialization of Mycenaean Ideology and the Ayia Triada Sarcophagus," *AJA* 109, 403–422.

    2007. "The Eastern Boeotia Archaeological Project (EBAP)," *Teiresias: A Review and Bibliography of Boiotian Studies* 37, 25–27.

Burke, B., B. Burns, A. Charami, and O. Kyriazi. 2013. "Eastern Boeotia Archaeological Project: Preliminary Report on Excavations 2011–2013," *Teiresias: A Review and Bibliography of Boiotian Studies* 43, 9–25.

Burns, B. 2010. *Mycenaean Greece, Mediterranean Commerce, and the Formation of Identity*, Cambridge.

Cambitoglou, A. and J.K. Papadopoulos. 1991. "Excavations at Torone," *Mediterranean Archaeology* 4, 147–171.

    1993. "The Earliest Mycenaeans in Macedonia," in C.W. Zerner (ed.), *Proceedings of the International Conference Wace and Blegen Held at the American School of Classical Studies at Athens, Athens, December 2–3, 1989, Pottery as Evidence for Trade in the Aegean Bronze Age 1939–1989*, Amsterdam, 289–302.

Casson, L. 1958. "Hemiolia and Triemiolia," *JHS* 78, 14–18.

Castleden, R. 2005. *Mycenaeans*, London and New York.

Catling, H.W., J.F. Cherry, R.E. Jones, and J.T. Killen. 1980. "The Linear B-Inscribed Stirrup-Jars and West Crete," *BSA* 75, 51–113.

Cavanagh, W.C. 2008. "Death and the Mycenaeans," in C.W. Shelmerdine (ed.), *The Cambridge Companion to The Aegean Bronze Age*, Cambridge, 327–341.

Cavanagh, W. and C. Mee. 1995. "Mourning Before and After the Dark Age," in C. Morris (ed.), *Klados: Essays in Honor of J. N. Coldstream*, London, 45–61.

    1998. *A Private Place: Death in Prehistoric Greece* (SIMA 125), Göteborg.

Chadwick, J. 1976. *The Mycenaean World*, Cambridge.

Charami, A., B. Burke, and B. Burns. 2015. "Eastern Boeotia Archaeological Project 2015 Report," *Teiresias. A Review and Bibliography of Boiotian Studies* 45, 6-12.

Cline, E. 1994. *Sailing the Wine Dark Sea* (BAR Int. Series 591), Oxford.

    2007. "Rethinking Mycenaean International Trade with Egypt and the Near East," in M.L. Galaty and W.A. Parkinson (eds.), *Rethinking Mycenaean Palaces II. Revised and Expanded Second Edition*, Los Angeles, 190–200.

Coleman, J.E. 1985. "'Frying Pans' of the Early Bronze Age Aegean," *AJA* 89, 191–219.

Cosmopoulos, M.B. 2001. *The Rural History of Ancient Greek City States: The Oropos Survey Project* (BAR-IS 1001), Oxford.

    2009. "Iklaina Archaeological Project: 2009 Season Internet Report," www.iklaina.org/annual (2009 Report), 1–15.

    2010. "Iklaina Archaeological Project: 2010 Internet Report," www.iklaina.org/annual (2010 Report), 1–15.

    2011. "Iklaina Archaeological Project: 2011 Field Report," www.iklaina.org/annual (2011 Report), 1–14.

    2012. "Iklaina Archaeological Project: 2012 Field Report," www.Iklaina.org/annual (2012 Report), 1–8.

    2015. "A Group of New Mycenaean Frescoes From Iklaina, Pylos," in H. Brecoulaki, J.L. Davis, and S.R. Stocker (eds.), *Mycenaean Wall Painting in Context: New Discoveries and Old Finds Reconsidered: Proceedings of the International Conference in Athens, Greece in February 2010* (Meletemata 72), Athens, 249–259.

Costin, C. 1991. "Craft Specialization: Issues in Defining, Documenting, and Explaining the Organization of Production," in M.B. Schiffer (ed.), *Archaeological Method and Theory* 3, Tucson, 1–56.

Crielaard, J.-P. 2000. "Homeric and Mycenaean Long-Distance Contacts: Discrepancies in the Evidence," *BABesch* 75, 51–63.

——— 2006. "Basileis at Sea: Elites and External Contacts in the Euboean Gulf Region from the End of the Bronze Age to the Beginning of the Iron Age," in S. Deger-Jalkotzi and I. Lemos (eds.), *Ancient Greece: From the Mycenaean Palaces to the Age of Homer*, Edinburgh, 271–297.

Crielaard, J.P., F. Songu, M. Chidiroglou, and M. Kosma. 2012. "The Plakari Archaeological Project. Project Outline and Preliminary Report on the First Field Season," *Pharos. Journal of the Netherlands Institute at Athens* 18, 83–106.

Crouwel, J.H. 1981. *Chariots and Other Means of Land Transport in Bronze Age Greece*, Amsterdam.

——— 1999. "Fighting on Land and Sea in Late Mycenaean Times," in R. Laffineur (ed.), *POLEMOS. Le contexte guerrier en Égée a l'Âge du Bronze. Actes de la 7è Rencontre égéenne international (Liège, 14–17 avril 1998)* (Aegaeum 19), Liège and Austin, 455–463.

——— 2006. "Late Mycenaean Pictorial Pottery," in D. Evely (ed.), *Lefkandi IV: The Bronze Age. The Late Helladic IIIC Settlement at Xeropolis* (BSA Suppl. 39), London, 233–255.

——— 2009. "Pictorial Pottery of the Latest Bronze Age and the Early Iron Age," in S. Deger-Jalkotzy and A.E. Bächle (eds.), *LH IIIC Chronology and Synchronisms III. LH IIIC Late and the Transition to the Early Iron Age. Proceedings of the International Workshop Held at the Austrian Academy of Sciences at Vienna February 23rd and 24th, 2007*, Vienna, 41–60.

Cullen, T., L. Talalay, and Ž. Tankosić. 2011: "The Emerging Prehistory of Southern Euboea," in D.W. Rupp and J.E. Tomlinson (eds.), *Euboea and Athens. Proceedings of a Colloquium in Memory of Malcom B. Wallace, Athens 26–27 June 2009* (Publications of the Canadian Institute in Greece 6), Athens, 29–51.

Cullen, T., L. Talalay, D. Keller, L. Karimali, and W. Farrand. 2012: *The Prehistory of the Paximadhi Peninsula, Euboea*, Philadelphia.

Dakoronia, F. 1987. "War-Ships on Sherds of LH IIIC Kraters from Kynos," in H. Tzalas (ed.), *Tropis II. 2nd International Symposium on Ship Construction in Antiquity*, Delphi, 117–122.

——— 1993. "Homeric Towns in East Lokris. Problems of Identification," *Hesperia* 62, 115–127.

——— 1996a. "Mycenaean East Lokris," in E. De Miro, L. Godart, and A. Sacconi (eds.), *Atti e memorie del secondo congresso internazionale di micenologia* 3, Rome, 1167–1173.

——— 1996b. "Kynos...Fleet" [*sic*], in H. Tzalas (ed.), *Tropis IV. 4th International Symposium on Ship Construction in Antiquity, Center for the Acropolis Studies, Athens, 28, 29, 30, 31 August 1991. Proceedings*, Athens, 159–171.

——— 1999. "Representations of Sea-Battles on Mycenaean Sherds from Kynos," in H. Tzalas (ed.), *Tropis V: Proceedings of the 5th International Symposium on Ship Construction in Antiquity*, Athens, 119–128.

——— 2002a. "Ανατολική Λοκρίδα: Η Ιστορία της μέσα από τα Μνημεία και τις Αρχαιολογικές Έρευνες," in F. Dakoronia, D. Kotoulas, E. Balta, V. Sythiakaki, and G. Tolias, *Λοκρίδα. Ιστορία και Πολιτισμός*, 19–112.

——— 2002b. "Further Finds from Kynos," in H. Tzalas (ed.), *Tropis VII. Seventh International Symposium on Ship Construction in Antiquity, Pylos, 26, 27, 28, 29 August 1999*, Athens, 283–290.

——— 2003. "The Transition from Late Helladic IIIC to the Early Iron Age at Kynos," in S. Deger-Jalkotzy and M. Zavadil (eds.), *LH IIIC Chronology and Synchronisms. Proceedings of the International Workshop Held at the Austrian Academy of Sciences at Vienna May 7th and 8th, 2001*, Vienna, 37–51.

——— 2006. "Mycenaean Pictorial Style at Kynos, East Lokris," in E. Rystedt and B. Wells (eds.), *Pictorial Pursuits: Figurative Painting on Mycenaean and Geometric Pottery. Papers from Two Seminars at the Swedish Institute at Athens in 1999 and 2001* (Acta Instituti Atheniensis Regni Sueciae, series 4, 53), Stockholm, 23–29.

——— 2007a. "LH IIIC Middle Pottery Repertoire of Kynos," in: S. Deger-Jalkotzy and M. Zavadil (eds.), *LH III C Chronology and Synchronisms II: LH IIIC Middle. Proceedings of the*

International Workshop Held at the Austrian Academy of Sciences at Vienna October 29th and 30th, 2004, Vienna, 119–127.

2007b. "Rare Burial Gifts from Mycenaean Chamber Tombs in North-East Phokis," in E. Alram-Stern and G. Nightingale (eds.), *Keimelion: Elitenbildung und elitärer Konsum von der mykenischen Palastzeit bis zur homerischen Epoche. Akten des internationalen Kongress vom 3. bis 5. Februar 2005 in Salzburg*, Vienna, 59–64.

Dakoronia, F. and S. Dimaki. 1998. "Καλαπόδι," *ArchDelt* 53 B'2, 394–395.

Dakoronia, F. and P. Kounouklas. 2009. "Kynos' Pace to the Early Iron Age," in S. Deger-Jalkotzy and A.E. Bächle (eds.), *LH IIIC Chronology and Synchronisms III. LH IIIC Late and the Transition to the Early Iron Age. Proceedings of the International Workshop Held at the Austrian academy of Sciences at Vienna February 23rd and 24th, 2007*, Vienna, 61–76.

Dakouri-Hild, A. 2010. "Thebes," in E.H. Cline (ed.), *The Oxford Handbook of the Bronze Age Aegean (ca. 3000–1000 BC)*, Oxford, 690–711.

2012. "Making *la Différence*: The Production and Consumption of Ornaments in Late Bronze Age Boeotia," in M.-L. Nosch and R. Laffineur (eds.), *KOSMOS. Jewellery, Adornment and Textiles in the Aegean Bronze Age. Proceedings of the 13th International Aegean Conference/13e Rencontre égéenne internationale, University of Copenhagen, Danish National Research Foundation's Centre for Textile Research, 21–26 April 2010* (Aegaeum 33), Leuven/Liège, 471–481.

Davaras, C. 2003. "The Mochlos Ship Cup," in J.S. Soles and C. Davaras (eds.), *Mochlos IC. Period III. The Neopalatatial Settlement on the Coast: The Artisans' Quarter and the Farmhouse at Chalinomouri. The Small Finds* (Prehistory Monographs 9), Philadelphia, 3–15.

Davis, E.N. 1986. "Youth and Age in the Thera Frescoes," *AJA* 90, 399–406.

Davis, J.L. and J. Bennet. 1999. "Making Mycenaeans: Warfare, Territorial Expansion, and Representations of the Other in the Pylian Kingdom," in R. Laffineur (ed.), *POLEMOS. Le contexte guerrier en Égée a l'Âge du Bronze. Actes de la 7è Rencontre égéenne international (Liège, 14–17 avril 1998)* (Aegaeum 19), Liège and Austin, 105–120.

Day, P.M. and H.W. Haskell. 1995. "Transport Stirrup Jars from Thebes as Evidence of Trade in Late Bronze Age Greece," in C. Gillis, C. Risberg, and B. Sjöberg (eds.), *Trade and Production in Premonetary Greece: Acquisition and Distribution of Raw Materials and Finished Products. Proceedings of the 6th International Workshop, Athens 1996*, Jonsered, 87–107.

De Solla Price, D.J. 1965. "Networks of Scientific Papers," *Science* 149 (3683), 510–515.

Deger-Jalkotzy, S. 1994. "The Post-Palatial Period of Greece: An Aegean Prelude to the 11th Century B.C. in Cyprus," in V. Karageorghis (ed.), *Cyprus in the 11th Century B.C.: Proceedings of the International Symposium, Nicosia 30–31 October 1993*, Nicosia, 11–30.

1995. "Mykenische Herrschaftsformen ohne Paläste und die griechische Polis," in R. Laffineur and W.-D. Niemeier (eds.), *Politeia. Society and State in the Aegean Bronze Age. Proceedings of the 5th International Aegean Conference/5e Rencontre égéenne internationale, University of Heidelberg, Archäologisches Institut, 10–13 April 1994*, (Aegaeum 12), Liège, 367–377.

2006. "Late Mycenaean Warrior Tombs," in S. Deger-Jalkotzy and I.S. Lemos (eds.), *Ancient Greece From the Mycenaean Palaces to the Age of Homer*, Edinburgh, 151–179.

2008. "Decline, Destruction, Aftermath," in C.W. Shelmerdine (ed.), *The Cambridge Companion to the Aegean Bronze Age*, Cambridge, 387–415.

Deger-Jalkotzy, S. and O. Panagl. 2006. *Die neuen Linear B-Texte aus Theben*, Vienna.

Del Freo, M. 2009. "The Geographical Names in the Linear B Texts from Thebes," *Pasiphae* 3, 41–68.

Demakopoulou, K. and D. Konsola. 1981. *Archaeological Museum of Thebes*, Athens.

Desborough, V.R.d'A. 1964. *The Last Mycenaeans and Their Successors: An Archaeological Survey c.1200-c.1000 BC.*, Oxford.

Dickers, A. 2001. *Die spätmykenischen Siegel aus weichem Stein: Untersuchungen zur spätbronzezeitlichen Glyptik auf dem griechischen Festland und in der Ägäis*, Rahden.

Dickinson, O.T.P.K. 1977. *The Origins of Mycenaean Civilisation* (SIMA 49), Göteborg.

Dobres, M.-A. and J.E. Robb. 2000. "Agency in Archaeology. Paradigm or Platitude?" in M.-A. Dobres and J.E. Robb (eds.), *Agency in Archaeology*, London and New York, 3–17.

Dornan, J.L. 2002. "Agency and Archaeology: Past, Present, and Future Directions," *Journal of Archaeological Method and Theory* 9, 303–329.

Doumas, C. 1992. *The Wall Paintings of Thera*, Athens.

Drews, R. 1988. *The Coming of the Greeks. Indo-European Conquests in the Aegean and the Near East*, Princeton.

   1993. *The End of the Bronze Age: Changes in Warfare and the Catastrophe ca. 1200 B.C.*, Princeton.

Driessen, J. 2000. *The Scribes of the Room of the Chariot Tablets: Interdisciplinary Approach to the Study of a Linear B Deposit* (Minos 16 Suppl.), Salamanca.

   2008. "Chronology of the Linear B Texts," in Y. Dhoux and A Morpurgo Davies (eds.), *A Companion to Linear B*, vol. 1, Louvain-la-Neuve, 69–79.

Driessen, J.M. and C.F. MacDonald. 1984. "Some Military Aspects of the Aegean in the Late Fifteenth and Early Fourteenth Centuries B.C.," *BSA* 79, 49–74.

Eder, B. 2007a. "The Power of Seals: Palaces, Peripheries and Territorial Control in the Mycenaean World," in I. Galanaki, H. Tomas, Y. Galanakis, and R. Laffineur (eds.), *Between the Aegean and Baltic Seas: Prehistory Across Borders. Proceedings of the International Conference Bronze and Early Iron Age Interconnections and Contemporary Developments between the Aegean and the Regions of the Balkan Peninsula, Central and Northern Europe. University of Zagreb, 11–14 April 2005* (Aegaeum 27), Liège, 35–45.

   2007b. "Im Spiegel der Siegel: Die nördlichen und westlichen Regionen Griechenlands im Spannungsfeld der mykenischen Paläste," in E. Alram-Stern and G. Nightingale (eds.), *Keimelion: Elitenbildung und elitärer Konsum von der mykenischen Palastzeit bis zur homerischen Epoche. Akten des internationalen Kongress vom 3. Bis 5. Februar 2005 in Salzburg*, Vienna, 81–124.

Emanuel, J.P. 2014. "Sea Peoples, Egypt, and the Aegean: The Transference of Maritime Technology in the Late Bronze-Early Iron Transition (LH IIIB-C)," *Aegean Studies* 1, 21–56.

Evely, D. (ed.) 2006. *Lefkandi IV: The Bronze Age. The Late Helladic IIIC Settlement at Xeropolis* (BSA Suppl. 39), London.

Farinetti, E. 2011. *Boeotian Landscapes: A GIS-Based Study for the Reconstruction and Interpretation of the Archaeological Datasets of Ancient Boeotia* (BAR Int. Series 2195), Oxford.

Felsch, R.C.S. 1981. "Mykenischer Kult im Heiligtum bei Kalapodi?" in R. Hägg and N. Marinatos (eds.), *Santuaries and Cults in the Aegean Bronze Age*, Stockholm, 81–90.

   (ed.) 1987. "Kalapodi. Bericht über die Grabungen im Heiligtum der Artemis Elaphebolos und des Apollon von Hyampolis 1978–1982," *AA*, 1–99.

   (ed.) 1996. *Kalapodi. Ergebnisse der Ausgrabungen im Heiligtum der Artemis und des Apollon von Hyampolis in der antiken Phokis, Band I*, Mainz.

Feuer, B. 2011. "Being Mycenaean: A View from the Periphery," *AJA* 115, 507–536.

Fortenberry, D. 1991. "Single Greaves in the Late Helladic Period," *AJA* 95, 623–627.

Fossey, J.M. 1988. *Topography and Population of Ancient Boiotia*, Chicago.

   1990a. *The Ancient Topography of Opountian Lokris*, Amsterdam.

   1990b. "Mycenaean Fortifications of the North East Kopaïs," in J.M. Fossey (ed.), *Papers in Boiotian Topography and History*, Amsterdam, 72–89.

Foxhall, L. 1995. "Bronze to Iron: Agricultural Systems and Political Structures in Late Bronze Age and Early Iron Age Greece," *BSA* 90, 239–250.

Galaty, M.L. 2007. "Wealth Ceramics, Staple Ceramics: Pots and the Mycenaean Palaces," in M.L. Galaty and W.A. Parkinson (eds.), *Rethinking Mycenaean Palaces II. Revised and Expanded Second Edition*, Los Angeles 74–86.

Galaty, M.L. 2010. "Wedging Clay: Combining Competing Models of Mycenaean Pottery Industries," in D.J. Pullen (ed.), *Political Economies of the Aegean Bronze Age: Papers from the Langford Conference, Florida State University, Tallahassee, 22–24 February 2007*, Oxford, 230–247.

Galaty, M.L. and W.A. Parkinson. 2007. "Introduction: Mycenaean Palaces Rethought," in M. L. Galaty and W.A. Parkinson (eds.), *Rethinking Mycenaean Palaces II. Revised and Expanded Second Edition*, Los Angeles, 1–17.

Galaty, M.L., W.A. Parkinson, D.J. Pullen, and R.M. Seifried. 2014. "Mycenaean -Scapes: Geography, Political Economy, and the Eastern Mediterranean World-System," in G. Touchais, R. Laffineur, and F. Rougemont (eds.), *PHYSIS. L'environnement naturel et la relation home-milieu dans le monde Égéen protohistorique. Actes de la 14e Rencontre égéenne internationale, Paris, Institut National d'Histoire de l'Art (INHA), 11–14 décembre 2012* (Aegaeum 37), Liège, 449–454.

Gauss, W. and R. Smetana. 2010. "Aegina Kolonna in the Middle Bronze Age," in A. Philippa-Touchais, G. Touchais, S. Voutsaki, and J. Wright (eds.), *Mesohelladika: La Grèce continentale au Bronze Moyen. Actes du colloque international organisé par l' École française d' Athènes, en collaboration avec l' American School of Classical Studies at Athens et le Netherlands Institute in Athens, Athènes 8–12 mars 2006* (BCH Supplements 52), Athens, 165–174.

Gell, A. 1998. *Art and Agency: An Anthropological Theory*, Oxford.

Giddens, A. 1979. *Central Problems in Social Theory: Action, Structure, and Contradiction in Social Analysis*, Los Angeles.

1984. *The Constitution of Society: Outline of the Theory of Structuration*, Cambridge.

Gillmer, T.C. 1985. "The Thera Ships as Sailing Vessels," *MM* 64, 125–133.

Gosden, C. and Y. Marshall. 1999. "The Cultural Biography of Objects," *World Archaeology* 31, 169–178.

Granovetter, M.S. 1973. "The Strength of Weak Ties," *American Journal of Sociology* 78 (6), 1360–1380.

Gray, D. 1974. *Seewesen (Archaeologia Homerica 1G)*, Göttingen.

Graziadio, G. 1991. "The Process of Social Stratification at Mycenae in the Shaft Grave Period: A Comparative Examination of the Evidence," *AJA* 95, 403–440.

Güntner, W. 2006. "Mycenaean Pictorial Vase Painters," in E. Rystedt and B. Wells (eds.), *Pictorial Pursuits. Figurative Painting on Mycenaean and Geometric Pottery. Papers from Two Seminars at the Swedish Institute at Athens in 1999 and 2001* (Acta Instituti Atheniensis Regni Sueciae, series 4, 53), Stockholm, 51–61.

Hallager, B. and E. Hallager, 1995. "The Knossian Bull – Political Propaganda in Neo-Palatial Crete?" in R. Laffineur and W.-D. Niemeier (eds.), *Politeia. Society and State in the Aegean Bronze Age. Proceedings of the 5th International Aegean Conference/5e Rencontre égéenne internationale, University of Heidelberg, Archäologisches Institut, 10–13 April 1994*, (Aegaeum 12), 547–556.

Hankey, V. 1952. "Late Helladic Tombs at Khalkis," *BSA* 47, 49–95.

1966. "Appendix II: A Late Helladic IIIA Tomb at Limni," *BSA* 61, 108–109.

Harding, A. 2006. "Facts and Fantasies from the Bronze Age," *Antiquity* 80, 463–465.

Harding, A., H. Hughes-Brock, and C.W. Beck. 1974. "Amber in the Mycenaean world," *BSA* 69, 145–172.

Harrell, K.M. 2012. "The Weapon's Beauty: A Reconsideration of the Ornamentation of the Shaft Grave Swords," in M.-L. Nosch and R. Laffineur (eds.), *KOSMOS. Jewellery, Adornment and Textiles in the Aegean Bronze Age. Proceedings of the 13th International Aegean Conference/13e Rencontre égéenne internationale, University of Copenhagen, Danish National Research Foundation's Centre for Textile Research, 21–26 April 2010* (Aegaeum 33), Leuven/Liège, 799–804.

2014. "The Fallen and Their Swords: A New Explanation for the Rise of the Shaft Graves," *AJA* 118, 3–17.

Haskell, H.W., R.E. Jones, P.M. Day, and J.T. Killen. 2011. *Transport Stirrup Jars of the Bronze Age Aegean and Eastern Mediterranean.* (Prehistory Monographs 33),. Philadelphia.

Helms, M.W. 1988. *Ulysses' Sail: An Ethnographic Odyssey of Power, Knowledge and Geographical Distance*, Princeton.

1993. *Craft and the Kingly Ideal: Art, Trade, and Power*, Austin.

Higgins, R. 1997. *Minoan and Mycenaean Art, New Revised Edition*, London and New York.

Hodder, I. 2011. "Human-Thing Entanglement: Towards an Integrated Archaeological Perspective," *Journal of the Royal Anthropological Institute* 17, 154–177.

Hood, S. 1978. *The Arts in Prehistoric Greece*, New Haven.

Hooker, J.T. 1967. "The Mycenae Siege Rhyton and the Question of Egyptian Influence," *AJA* 71, 269–281.

Hope Simpson, R. and O.T.P.K. Dickinson. 1979. *A Gazetteer of Aegean Civilisation in the Bronze Age, vol. I: The Mainland and Islands*, Göteborg.

Hope Simpson, R. and D.K. Hagel. 2006. *Mycenaean Fortifications, Highways, Dams and Canals* (SIMA 133), Sävedalen.

Hruby, J. 2012. "Identity and the Visual Identification of Seals," in M.-L. Nosch and R. Laffineur (eds.), *KOSMOS. Jewellery, Adornment and Textiles in the Aegean Bronze Age. Proceedings of the 13th International Aegean Conference/13e Rencontre égéenne internationale, University of Copenhagen, Danish National Research Foundation's Centre for Textile Research, 21–26 April 2010* (Aegaeum 33), Leuven/Liège, 389–395.

Iakovidis, S. 1969. Περάτι, Athens.

1989. Γλας I: Η Ανασκαφή 1955–1961, Athens.

1998. Γλας II: Η Ανασκαφή 1981–1991, Athens.

2001. *Gla and the Kopais in the 13th Century B.C.*, Athens.

Immerwahr, S.A. 1990. *Aegean Painting in the Bronze Age*, London.

Intzesiloglou, B.G. 2010. "A Gold Signet Ring, Three Seal Stones and a Scarab from the Mycenaean Tholos Tomb at Georgiko, Western Thessaly (Greece)," in W. Müller (ed.), *Die Bedeutung der minoischen und mykenischen Glyptik, VI. Internationales Siegel-Symposium aus Anlass des 50 jährigen Bestehens des CMS, Marburg, 9.–12. Oktober 2008*, Mainz, 239–247.

Jacob-Felsch, M. 1996. "Die spätmykenische bis frühproto-geometrische Keramik," in R.C.S. Felsch (ed.), *Kalapodi. Ergebnisse der Ausgrabungen im Heiligtum der Artemis und des Apollon von Hyampolis in der antiken Phokis, Band I*, Mainz, 1–213.

Jansen, A.G. 2002. *A Study of the Remains of Mycenaean Roads and Stations of Bronze-Age Greece*, Lewiston.

Jones, G.M. 1995. "Charred Grain from Late Bronze Age Gla, Boiotia," *BSA* 90, 235–238.

Jones, R.E. 1996. "Appendix: Chemical Analysis of Mycenaean and Submycenaean Pottery from Kalapodi," in R.C.S. Felsch (ed.), *Kalapodi. Ergebnisse der Ausgrabungen im Heiligtum der Artemis und des Apollon von Hyampolis in der antiken Phokis, Band I*, Mainz, 115–120.

Jung, R. 2010. "Der Charakter der Nordkontakte der minoischen und mykenischen Zivilisation um 1600 v.u.Z.," in H. Meller and F. Bertemes (eds.), *Der Griff nach den Sternen: Wie Europas Eliten zu Macht und Reichtum kamen, Internationales Symposium in Halle (Saale), 16.–21. February 2005*, Halle, 657–674.

Kahrstedt, U. 1937. "Die Kopaissee im Altertum und die 'Minyschen' Kanäle," *AA* 52, 1–19.

Kambanis, M.C. 1892. "Le desséchement du Lac Copais par les anciens," *BCH* 16, 121–137.

1893. "Le desséchement du Lac Copais par les anciens," *BCH* 17, 322–342.

Kenny, E.J.A. 1935. "The Ancient Drainage of the Copais," *Liverpool Annals of Archaeology and Anthropology* 22, 189–206.

Kilian, K. 1987. "Zur Funktion der mykenischen Residenzen," in R. Hägg and N. Marinatos (eds.), *The Function of the Minoan Palaces: Proceedings of the Fourth International Symposium at the Swedish Institute in Athens, 10–16 June, 1984*, Stockholm, 21–38.

1988. "Mycenaeans Up to Date. Trends and Changes in Recent Research," in E.B. French and K.A. Wardle (eds.), *Problems in Greek Prehistory. Papers Presented at the Centenary Conference of the British School of Archaeology at Athens, Manchester, April 1986*, Bristol, 115–152.

1990. "Mycenaean Colonization: Norm and Variety," in J.-P. Descoeudres (ed.), *Greek Colonists and Native Populations: Proceedings of the First Australian Congress of Classical Archaeology Held in Honour of Emeritus Professor A.D. Trendall, Sydney, 9–14 July 1985*, Oxford, 445–467.

Kilian-Dirlmeier, I. 1987. "Das Kuppelgrab von Vapheio (Lakonien): Die Beigabenausstattung in der Steinkiste: Untersuchungen zur Sozialstruktur in späthelladischer Zeit," *JRGZM* 34, 197–212.

——— 1988. "Jewellery in Minoan and Mycenaean 'Warrior Graves,' " in E.B. French and K.A. Wardle (eds.), *Problems in Greek Prehistory. Papers Presented at the Centenary Conference of the British School of Archaeology at Athens, Manchester, April 1986*, Bristol, 161–171.

——— 1993. *Die Schwerter in Griechenland (ausserhalb der Peloponnes), Bulgarien und Albanien (Prähistorische Bronzefunde)*, Wiesbaden.

——— 1997. *Alt-Ägina IV,3: Das mittelbronzezeitliche Schachtgrab von Ägina*, Mainz.

Kirkpatrick Smith, S. 2009. "Skeletal Evidence for Militarism in Mycenaean Athens," in L.A. Schepartz, S.C. Fox, and C. Bourbou (eds.), *New Directions in the Skeletal Biology of Greece (Hesperia Supplements 43)*, Princeton, 99–109.

Knappett, C. 2011. *An Archaeology of Interaction: Network Perspectives on Material Culture and Society*, Oxford.

Knappett, C. (ed.) 2013. *Network Analysis in Archaeology: New Approaches to Regional Interaction*, Oxford.

Knappett, C., Evans, T., and R. Rivers, 2008. "Modelling Maritime Interaction in the Aegean Bronze Age," *Antiquity* 82, 1009–1024.

——— 2011. "The Theran Eruption and Minoan Palatial Collapse: New Interpretations Gained from Modelling the Maritime Network," *Antiquity* 85, 1008–1023.

——— 2013. "What Makes a Site Important? Centrality, Gateways, and Gravity," in C. Knappett (ed.), *Network Analysis in Archaeology: New Approaches to Regional Interaction*, Oxford, 125–150.

Knauss, J. 1987. *Die Melioration des Kopaisbecken durch die Minyer im 2 Jt. V. Chr. – Wasserbau und Siedlungsbedingungen im Altertum* (Bericht Nr. 57, Institut für Wasserbau der Technischen Universität München), Munich.

——— 1990. *Wasserbau und Geschichte, Minysche Epoche – Bayerische Zeit (vier Jahrhunderte – ein Jahrzehnt)* (Bericht Nr. 63, Institut für Wasserbau der Technischen Universität München), Munich.

Knauss, J., B. Heinrich and H. Kalcyk. 1984. *Die Wasserbauten der Minyer in der Kopais – die älteste Flussregulierung Europas* (Bericht Nr. 50, Institut für Wasserbau der Technischen Universität München), Munich.

Knodell, A.R. 2013. *"Small-World Networks and Mediterranean Dynamics in the Euboean Gulf: An Archaeology of Complexity in Late Bronze Age and Early Iron Age Greece"* (unpublished PhD dissertation, Brown University).

Kontorli-Papadopoulou, L. 1999. "Fresco Fighting-Scenes as Evidence for Warlike Activities in the LBA Aegean," in R. Laffineur (ed.), *POLEMOS. Le contexte guerrier en Égée a l'Âge du Bronze. Actes de la 7è Rencontre égéenne international (Liège, 14–17 avril 1998)* (Aegaeum 19), Liège and Austin, 331–339.

Kopanias, K. 2012. "Raw Material, Exotic Jewellery or Magic Objects? The Use of Imported Near Eastern Seals in the Aegean," in M.-L. Nosch and R. Laffineur (eds.), *KOSMOS. Jewellery, Adornment and Textiles in the Aegean Bronze Age. Proceedings of the 13th International Aegean Conference/13e Rencontre égéenne internationale, University of Copenhagen, Danish National Research Foundation's Centre for Textile Research, 21–26 April 2010* (Aegaeum 33), Leuven/Liège, 397–406.

Kountouri, E., N. Petrochilos, D. Koutsoyiannis, N. Mamassis, N. Zarkadoulas, A. Vött, H. Hadler, P. Henning, and T. Willershäuser. 2012. "A New Project of Surface Survey, Geophysical and Excavation Research of the Mycenaean Drainage Works of the North Kopais: The First Study Season," *IWA Specialized Conference on Water and Wastewater 22–24 March 2012 Technologies in Ancient Civilizations Istanbul-Turkey*, 467–476.

Kramer-Hajos, M. 2008. *Beyond the Palace: Mycenaean East Lokris* (BAR IS 1781), Oxford.

——— 2012a. "Sailor-Warriors and the End of the Bronze Age along the Euboean Gulf," in A. Mazarakis Ainian and A. Doulgeri-Intzesioglou (eds.), *Proceedings of the 3rd*

Archaeological Meeting of Thessaly and Central Greece 2006-2008. From Prehistory to the Contemporary Period, Volos 12-15 March 2009, Volos, 811-821.

2012b. "The Land and the Heroes of Lokris in the *Iliad*," *JHS* 132, 87-105.

2015. "Mourning on the Larnakes at Tanagra: Gender, and Agency in Late Bronze Age Greece," *Hesperia* 84, 627-667.

Kramer-Hajos, M. and K.N. O'Neill. 2008. "The Bronze Age Site of Mitrou in East Lokris: Finds from the 1988-1989 Surface Survey," *Hesperia* 77, 163-250.

Kristiansen, K. and T.B. Larsson. 2007. "Contacts and Travels during the 2nd Millennium BC: Warriors on the Move," in I. Galanaki, H. Tomas, Y. Galanakis, and R. Laffineur (eds.), *Between the Aegean and Baltic Seas: Prehistory Across Borders. Proceedings of the International Conference Bronze and Early Iron Age Interconnections and Contemporary Developments between the Aegean and the Regions of the Balkan Peninsula, Central and Northern Europe. University of Zagreb, 11-14 April 2005* (Aegaeum 27), Liège and Austin, 25-34.

Kroll, H. 1984. "Zum Ackerbau gegen Ende der mykenischen Epoche in der Argolis," *AA* 99, 211-222.

Krzyszkowska, O. 2005a. *Aegean Seals: An Introduction*, London.

2005b. *Mycenaean Ivories from Tiryns*, Mainz.

Laffineur, R. 1990. "The Iconography of Mycenaean Seals and the Status of their Owners," in *Annales d'archéologie égéenne de l'Université de Liège* 6 (Aegaeum 6), Liège, 117-160.

1992. "Iconography as Evidence of Social and Political Status in Mycenaean Greece," in R. Laffineur and J.L. Crowley (eds.), *EIKΩN. Aegean Bronze Age Iconography: Shaping a Methodology. Proceedings of the 4th International Aegean Conference, University of Tasmania, Hobart, Australia, 6-9 April 1992*, Liège, 105-112.

2003. "Mycenaean Jewellery in the Periphery," in N. Kyparissi-Apostolika and M. Papakonstantinou (eds.), *Β' Διεθνές Διεπιστημονικό Συμπόσιο «Η Περιφέρεια του Μυκηναϊκού Κόσμου», 26-30 Σεπτεμβρίου, Λαμία 1999/2nd International Interdisciplinary Colloquium "Periphery of the Mycenaean World," 26-30 September, Lamia 1999*, Lamia, 81-85.

2010. "Thorikos," in E.H. Cline (ed.), *The Oxford Handbook of the Bronze Age Aegean (ca. 3000-1000 BC)*, Oxford, 712-721.

Lane, M. 2011. "Archaeological Reconnaissance of Unexplored Remains of Agriculture (AROURA): Fieldwork Report 2011" (www.umbc.edu/aroura/reports/AROURA2011_Annual_Report_201201.pdf).

2012. "Archaeological Reconnaissance of Unexplored Remains of Agriculture (AROURA): Interim Report, 2010-2011 Campaigns," *Teiresias* 42, 2-26.

Langdon, S. 2008. *Art and Identity in Dark Age Greece, 1100-700 B.C.E.*, Cambridge.

Lauffer, S. 1940. "Archäologische Funde im Kopaisgebiet 1939-1940," *AA* (1940) 184-188.

1971. "Topographische Untersuchungen im Kopaisgebiet 1970," *ArchDelt* 26 B, 239-245.

1974. "Untersuchungen im Kopaisgebiet 1971 and 1973," *ArchDelt* 29 B, 449-454.

1986. *Kopais I. Untersuchungen zur historischen Landeskunde Mittelgriechenlands*, Frankfurt.

Leidwanger, J., C. Knappett, P. Arnaud, P. Arthur, E. Blake, C. Broodbank, T. Brughmans, T. Evans, S. Graham, E.S. Greene, B. Kowalzig, B. Mills, R. Rivers, T.F. Tartaron, and R. Van de Noort. 2014. "A Manifesto for the Study of Ancient Mediterranean Maritime Networks," *Antiquity* (Project Gallery) 342.

Lemos, I.S. 1999. "Some Aspects of the Transition from the Late Bronze Age to the Early Iron Age in Central Greece," in F. Dakoronia (ed.), *Α' Διεθνές Διεπιστημονικό Συμπόσιο «Η Περιφέρεια του Μυκηναϊκού Κόσμου», Λαμία, 25-29 Σεπτεμβρίου, 1994/1st International Interdisciplinary Colloquium "Periphery of the Mycenaean World," Lamia, 25-29 September, 1994*, Lamia, 21-26.

2002. *The Protogeometric Aegean: The Archaeology of the Late Eleventh and Tenth Centuries BC*, Oxford.

2012. "Euboea and Central Greece in the Postpalatial and Early Greek Periods," *AR* 58, 19–27.

Lewartowski, K. 2000. *Late Helladic Simple Graves: A Study of Mycenaean Burial Customs* (BAR Int. Series 878), Oxford.

Lis, B., 2009. "The Sequence of Late Bronze/Early Iron Age Pottery from Central Greek Settlements. A Fresh Look at Old and New Evidence," in S. Deger-Jalkotzy and A. Bächle (eds.), *LH III Chronology and Synchronisms II: LH III C Middle. Proceedings of the International Workshop held at the Austrian Academy of Sciences at Vienna, October 29th and 30th, 2004*, Vienna, 373–390.

Lis, B. and Rückl, S. 2011. "Our Storerooms Are Full. Impressed Pithoi from Late Bronze/Early Iron Age East Lokris and Phokis and their Socio-Economic Significance," in W. Gauß, M. Lindblom, R.A.K. Smith, and J.C. Wright (eds.), *Our Cups Are Full: Pottery and Society in the Aegean Bronze Age. Papers Presented to Jeremy B. Rutter on the Occasion of his 65th Birthday* (BAR International Series 2227), 154–168.

Loader, N.C. 1998. *Building in Cyclopean Masonry, with Special Reference to the Mycenaean Fortifications on Mainland Greece* (SIMA Pocket-Book 148), Jonsered.

Lupack, S. 2008. "The Northeast Building of Pylos and An 1281," in A. Sacconi, M. Del Freo, L. Godart, and M. Negri (eds.), *Colloquium Romanum. Atti del XII colloquio internazionale di Micenologia, Roma, 20–25 Febbraio 2006 (Pasiphae II)*, Pisa and Rome, 467–484.

Luraghi, N. 2006. "Traders, Pirates, Warriors: The Proto-History of Greek Mercenary Soldiers in the Eastern Mediterranean," *Phoenix* 60, 21–47.

Maggidis, C. 2014. "Rediscovering a Giant," *Popular Archaeology Magazine* 16, http://popular-archaeology.com/issue/fall-09012014/article/rediscovering-a-giant.

Malafouris, L. 2008. "Is It 'Me' Or Is It 'Mine'? The Mycenaean Sword as a Body-Part," in J. Robb and D. Boric (eds.), *Past Bodies*, Oxford, 115–123.

Malkin, I. 2011. *A Small Greek World: Networks in the Ancient Mediterranean*, Oxford.

Malkin, I., C. Constantakopoulou, and K. Panagopoulou (eds.). 2009. *Greek and Roman Networks in the Mediterranean*, London and New York.

Maran, J. 2006. "Coming to Terms with the Past: Ideology and Power in Late Helladic IIIC," in S. Deger-Jalkotzy and I.S. Lemos (eds.), *Ancient Greece from the Mycenaean Palaces to the Age of Homer*, Edinburgh, 123–150.

Maran, J. and A. Van de Moortel. 2014. "A Horse-Bridle Piece with Carpatho-Danubian Connections from Late Helladic I Mitrou and the Emergence of a Warlike Elite in Greece during the Shaft Grave Period," *AJA* 118, 529–548.

Marinatos, N. 1995. "Divine Kingship in Minoan Crete," in P. Rehak (ed.), *The Role of the Ruler in the Prehistoric Aegean. Proceedings of a Panel Discussion Presented at the Annual Meeting of the Archaeological Institute of America New Orleans, Louisiana 28 December 1992. With Additions* (Aegaeum 11), Liège and Austin, 37–48.

McGeehan Liritzis, V. 1996. *The Role and Development of Metallurgy in the Late Neolithic and Early Bronze Age of Greece*, Jonsered.

McInerney, J. 2011. "Delphi and Phokis: A Network Theory Approach," *Pallas* 87, 95–106.

Mee, C.B. and W.G. Cavanagh. 1990. "The Spatial Distribution of Mycenaean Tombs," *BSA* 85, 225–243.

Merillees, R.S. 1992. "The Crisis Years: Cyprus – A Rejoinder," in W.A. Ward and M.S. Joukowsky (eds.), *The Crisis Years: The 12th Century B.C. From Beyond the Danube to the Tigris*, Dubuque, 87–92.

Milgram, S. 1967. "The Small World Problem," *Psychology Today* 1, 61–67.

Molloy, B. 2008. "Martial Arts and Materiality: A Combat Archaeology Perspective on Aegean Swords of the Fifteenth and Fourteenth Centuries BC," *World Archaeology* 40, 116–134.

2010. "Swords and Swordsmanship in the Aegean Bronze Age," *AJA* 114, 403–428.

Mommsen, H. and J. Maran, 2000–2001. "Production Places of Some Mycenaean Pictorial Vessels: The Contribution of Chemical Pottery Analysis," *OpAth* 25–26, 95–106.

Morgan, L. 1988. *The Miniature Wall Paintings of Thera*, Cambridge.

1995. "Of Animals and Men: The Symbolic Parallel," in C. Morris (ed.), *Klados: Essays in Honour of J. N. Coldstream* (BICS Suppl 63), London, 171–184.

1998. "The Wall Paintings of the North-East Bastion at Ayia Irini, Kea," in L.G. Mendoni and A. Mazarakis Ainian (eds.), *Kea-Kythnos: History and Archaeology* (Meletemata 27), Athens, 201–210.

2005. "New Discoveries and New Ideas in Aegean Wall Painting," in L. Morgan (ed.), *Aegean Wall Painting: A Tribute to Mark Cameron* (BSA Studies 13), London, 21–44.

Morris, S.P. 1989. "A Tale of Two Cities: The Miniature Frescoes from Thera and the Origins of Greek Poetry," *AJA* 93, 511–535.

2009-2010. "Prehistoric Torone: A Bronze Age Emporion in the Northern Aegean. Preliminary Report on the Lekythos Excavations 1986 and 1988–1990," *Mediterranean Archaeology* 22–23, 1–67.

Mountjoy, P.A. 1990. "Regional Mycenaean Pottery," *BSA* 85, 245–270.

1993. *Mycenaean Pottery: An Introduction*, Oxford.

1995. Thorikos Mine No. 3: The Mycenaean Pottery," *BSA* 90, 195–228.

1999. *Regional Mycenaean Decorated Pottery*, Rahden.

2005. "Mycenaean Connections with the Near East in LH IIIC: Ships and Sea Peoples," in R. Laffineur and E. Greco (eds.), *EMPORIA. Aegeans in the Central and Eastern Mediterranean: Proceedings of the 10th International Aegean Conference/10e rencontre égéenne internationale, Athens, Italian School of Archaeology, 14–18 April 2004*, (Aegaeum 25), Liège and Austin, 423–427.

2011. "A Bronze Age Ship from Ashkelon with Particular Reference to the Bronze Age Ship from Bademgediği Tepe," *AJA* 115, 483–488.

Mylonas, G. 1999. *Mycenae. A Guide to Its Ruins and Its History*, Athens.

Nakassis, D. 2012. "Prestige and Interest: Feasting and the King at Mycenaean Pylos," *Hesperia* 81, 1–30.

2013. *Individuals and Society in Mycenaean Pylos*, Leiden.

Nakassis, D., M.L. Galaty, and W.A. Parkinson. 2010. "State and Society," in E.H. Cline (ed.), *The Oxford Handbook of the Bronze Age Aegean*, Oxford, 239–250.

Nakassis, D. W.A. Parkinson, and M.A. Galaty. 2011. "Redistribution in Aegean Palatial Societies: Redistributive Economies from a Theoretical and Cross-Cultural Perspective," *AJA* 115, 177–184.

Nikita, K. and J. Henderson. 2006. "Glass Analyses from Mycenaean Thebes and Elateia: Compositional Evidence for a Mycenaean Glass Industry," *Journal of Glass Studies* 48, 71–120.

Nordquist, G. and H. Whittaker. 2007. "Comments on Kristian Kristiansen and Thomas B. Larsson: The Rise of Bronze Age Society. Travels, Transmissions and Transformations," *Norwegian Archaeological Review* 40, 75–84.

Nowicki, K. 2000. *Defensible Sites in Crete c. 1200–800 BC (LM IIIB/IIIC through Early Geometric)*, Liège.

2001. "Sea-Raiders and Refugees: Problems of Defensible Sites in Crete ca. 1200 BC," in V. Karageorghis and C. Morris (eds.), *Defensive Settlements of the Aegean and the Eastern Mediterranean after c. 1200 BC*, Nicosia, 23–40.

Oldfather, W.A. 1916. "Studies in the History and Topography of Lokris," *AJA* 20, 32–61.

Ortner, S.B. 1996. *Making Gender: The Politics and Erotics of Culture*, Boston.

Palaima, Th.G. 1991. "Maritime Matters in the Linear B Tablets," in R. Laffineur and L. Basch (eds.), *THALASSA. L'Egée préhistorique et la mer. Actes de la 3e Rencontre égéenne internationale de l'Université de Liège, Station de recherches sous-marines et océanographiques, Calvi, Corse, 23–25 avril 1990* (Aegaeum 7), 273–310.

1995. "The Nature of the Mycenaean Wanax: Non-Indo-European Origins and Priestly Functions," in P. Rehak (ed.), *The Role of the Ruler in the Prehistoric Aegean. Proceedings of a Panel Discussion Presented at the Annual Meeting of the Archaeological Institute of America New Orleans, Louisiana 28 December 1992. With Additions*, Liège and Austin, 119–139.

2003. "Reviewing the New Linear B Tablets from Thebes," *Kadmos* 42, 31–38.

2006. *"Wanaks* and Related Power Terms in Mycenaean and Later Greek," in S. Deger-Jalkotzy and I.S. Lemos (eds.), *Ancient Greece: From the Mycenaean Palaces to the Age of Homer*, Edinburgh, 53–71.

Pantou, P.A. 2010. "Mycenaean Dimini in Context: Investigating Regional Variability and Socioeconomic Complexities in Late Bronze Age Greece," *AJA* 114, 381–401.

Papadimitriou, N. 2001. *Built Chamber Tombs of Middle and Late Bronze Age Date in Mainland Greece and the Islands* (BAR Int. Series 925), Oxford.

2010. "Attica in the Middle Helladic Period," in A. Philippa-Touchais, G. Touchais, S. Voutsaki, J. Wright (eds.), *Mesohelladika: la Grèce continentale au Bronze Moyen. Actes du colloque international organisé par l' École française d' Athènes, en collaboration avec l' American School of Classical studies at Athens et le Netherlands Institute in Athens, Athènes 8-12 mars 2006. BCH Supplements 52.* Athens, 243–257.

Papadopoulos, A. 2009. "Warriors, Hunters and Ships in the Late Helladic IIIC Aegean: Changes in the Iconography of Warfare?" in C. Bachhuber and R.G. Roberts (eds.), *Forces of Transformation: The End of the Bronze Age in the Mediterranean. Proceedings of an International Symposium Held at St. John's College, University of Oxford 25-6 March 2006*, Oxford, 69–77.

Papadopoulos, Th.J. 1998. *The Late Bronze Age Daggers of the Aegean I: The Greek Mainland*, Stuttgart.

Papakonstantinou, M.-Ph. 1999. "The Grave Circle B of Antron. Preliminary Report," in P.B. Betancourt, V. Karageorghis, R. Laffineur, and W.D. Niemeier (eds.), *Meletemata, Studies in Aegean Archaeology Presented to Malcolm H. Wiener as He Enters His 65th Year* (Aegaeum 20), Liege, 626–631.

Papavasileios, G.A. 1910. *Περί των εν Ευβοία αρχαίων τάφων*, Athens.

Papazoglou-Manioudaki, L. 2012. *"Gold and Ivory Objects at Mycenae and Dendra Revealed. Private Luxury and/or* Insignia Dignitatis," in M.-L. Nosch and R. Laffineur (eds.), *KOSMOS. Jewellery, Adornment and Textiles in the Aegean Bronze Age. Proceedings of the 13th International Aegean Conference/13e Rencontre égéenne internationale, University of Copenhagen, Danish National Research Foundation's Centre for Textile Research, 21-26 April 2010* (Aegaeum 33), Leuven/Liège, 447–456.

Parkinson, W.A. 2007. "Chipping Away at a Mycenaean Economy: Obsidian Exchange, Linear B, and 'Palatial Control' in Late Bronze Age Messenia," in M.L. Galaty and W.A. Parkinson (eds.), *Rethinking Mycenaean Palaces II. Revised and Expanded Second Edition*, Los Angeles, 87–101.

2010. "Beyond the Peer: Social Interaction and Political Evolution in the Bronze Age Aegean," in D.J. Pullen (ed.), *Political Economies of the Aegean Bronze Age: Papers from the Langford Conference, Florida State University, Tallahassee, 22-24 February 2007*, Oxford and Oakville, 11–34.

Parkinson, W.A. and M.L. Galaty, 2007. "Secondary States in Perspective: An Integrated Approach to State Formation in the Prehistoric Aegean," *American Anthropologist* 109, 113–129.

Parkinson, W.A., D. Nakassis, and M.L. Galaty. 2013. "Crafts, Specialists, and Markets in Mycenaean Greece. Introduction," *AJA* 117, 413–422.

Peatfield, A. D. 1999. "The Paradox of Violence: Weaponry and Martial Art in Minoan Crete," in R. Laffineur (ed.), *POLEMOS. Le contexte guerrier en Égée a l'Âge du Bronze. Actes de la 7è Rencontre égéenne international (Liège, 14-17 avril 1998)* (Aegaeum 19), Liège and Austin, 67–74.

Petrakis, V.P. 2004. "Ship Representations on Late Helladic III C Pictorial Pottery: Some Notes," *Inferno* 9, 1–6.

2008. "*E-ke-ra2-wo ≠wa-na-ka:* The Implications of a Probable Non-Identification for Pylian Feasting and Politics," in L.A. Hitchcock, R. Laffineur, and J. Crowley (eds.), *DAIS: The Aegean Feast. Proceedings of the 12th International Aegean Conference,*

University of Melbourne, Centre for Classics and Archaeology, 25–29 March 2008 (*Aegaeum* 29), Liège, 391–398.

2011. "Politics of the Sea in the Late Bronze Age II-III Aegean: Iconographic Preferences and Textual Perspectives," in G. Vavouranakis (ed.), *The Seascape in Aegean Prehistory* (Monographs of the Danish Institute at Athens 14), Århus, Lancaster, and Oakville, 185–234.

Phialon, L. 2011. *L'Émergence de la civilization mycénienne en Grèce Centrale* (Aegaeum 32), Leuven/Liège.

Platon, N. 1949. "Ὁ τάφος τοθ Σταφύλου καὶ ὁ μινωϊκός ἀποικισμός τῆς Πεπαρήθου," *Kretika Chronika* 3, 534–573.

Podzuweit C. 2007. *Studien zur spätmykenischen Keramik, Tiryns XIV*, Wiesbaden.

Polikreti, K., J.M.A. Murphy, V. Kantarelou, and A.G. Karydas. 2011. "XRF Analysis of Glass Beads from the Mycenaean Palace of Nestor at Pylos, Peloponnesus, Greece: New Insight into the LBA Glass Trade," *JAS* 38, 2889–2896.

Popham, M.R. and E. Milburn. 1971. "Late Helladic IIIC pottery of Xeropolis (Lefkandi), a Summary," *BSA* 66, 333–352.

Popham, M.R. and L.H. Sackett (eds.) 1968. *Excavations at Lefkandi, Euboea 1964–1966. A Preliminary Report*, London.

Popham, M.R., D. Evely, and H. Sackett. 2006. "The Site and Its Excavation," in D. Evely (ed.), *Lefkandi IV: The Bronze Age. The Late Helladic IIIC Settlement at Xeropolis* (BSA Suppl. 39), London, 1–136.

Poursat, J.-C. 1977. *Les ivoires mycéniens. Essai sur la formation d'un art mycénien*, Athens and Paris.

Preston, L. 1999. "Mortuary Practices and the Negotiation of Social Identities at LM II Knossos," *BSA* 94, 131–143.

Privitera, S. 2013. *Principi, Pelasgi e pescatori. L'Attica nella Tarda Età del Bronzo* (Studi di Archeologia e di Topografia di Atene e dell' Attica), Athens and Paestum.

Pulak, C. 1997. "The Uluburun Shipwreck," in S. Swiny, R.L. Hohlfelder, and H.W. Swiny (eds.), *Res Maritimae: Cyprus and the Eastern Mediterranean from Prehistory to Late Antiquity*, Atlanta, 233–262.

1998. "The Uluburun Shipwreck: An Overview," *International Journal of Nautical Archaeology* 27, 188–224.

Pullen, D.J. and Th.F. Tartaron, 2007. "Where's the Palace? The Absence of State Formation in the Late Bronze Age Corinthia," in M.L. Galaty and W.A. Parkinson (eds.), *Rethinking Mycenaean Palaces II. Revised and Expanded Second Edition*, Los Angeles, 146–158.

Rebay-Salisbury, K., A. Brysbaert, and L. Foxhall (eds.) 2014. *Knowledge Networks and Craft Traditions in the Ancient World: Material Crossovers*, New York and London.

Rehak, P. 1984. "New Observations on the Mycenaean Warrior Goddess," *AA*, 535–545.

1994. "The Aegean 'Priest' on CMS I.223," *Kadmos* 33, 76–84.

1998. "The Mycenaean Warrior Goddess Revisited," in R. Laffineur (ed.), *POLEMOS. Le contexte guerrier en Égée a l'Âge du Bronze. Actes de la 7è Rencontre égéenne international (Liège, 14–17 avril 1998)* (Aegaeum 19), Liège and Austin, 227–239.

Rehak, P. and J.G. Younger. 2000. "Minoan and Mycenaean Administration in the Early Late Bronze Age: An Overview," in M. Perna (ed.), *Administrative Documents in the Aegean and Their Near Eastern Counterparts. Proceedings of the International Colloquium, Naples, February 29–March 2, 1996*, Torino, 277–301.

Renfrew, C. 1975. "Trade as Action at a Distance: Questions of Integration and Communication," in J.A. Sabloff and C.C. Lamberg-Karlovsky (eds.), *Ancient Civilization and Trade*, Albuquerque, 3–59.

1977. "Alternative Models for Exchange and Spatial Distribution," in T.K. Earle and J.E. Ericson (eds.), *Exchange Systems in Prehistory*, New York, 71–90.

Rosman, A. and P.G. Rubel. 1989. "Stalking the Wild Pig," in S. Kent (ed.), *Farmers as Hunters: The Implications of Sedentism*, Cambridge, 27–36.

Ruijgh, C.J. 1985. "Le mycénien et Homère," in Λ. Morpurgo Davies and Y. Duhoux (eds.), *Linear B: A 1984 Survey*, Louvain-la-Neuve, 143–190.

1995. "D'Homère aux origines proto-mycéniennes de la tradition épique. Analyse dialecto-logique du langage homérique, avec un excursus sur la création de l'alphabet grec," in J.P. Crielaard (ed.), *Homeric Questions. Essays in Philology, Ancient History and Archaeology, Including the Papers of a Conference Organized by the Netherlands Institute at Athens (15 May 1993)*, Amsterdam, 1–96.

2004. "The Source and the Structure of Homer's Epic Poetry," *European Review* 12 (4), 527–542.

Ruppenstein, F. 2010. "Einfache Radnadeln als Indikatoren europaweiter Fernbeziehungen zur Zeit der Deponierung der Himmelsscheibe von Nebra," in H. Meller and F. Bertemes (eds.), *Der Griff nach den Sternen: Wie Europas Eliten zu Macht und Reichtum kamen, Internationales Symposium in Halle (Saale), 16.–21 February 2005*, Halle, 641–653.

Rutter, J.B. 1983. "Some Thoughts on the Analysis of Ceramic Data Generated by Site Surveys," in D. Keller and D. Rupp (eds.), *Archaeological Survey in the Mediterranean* (BAR Int. Series 155), Oxford, 137–142.

2007. "How Different is LH IIIC Middle at Mitrou? An Initial Comparison with Kalapodi, Kynos, and Lefkandi," in S. Deger-Jalkotzy and M. Zavadil (eds.), *LH III C Chronology and Synchronisms II: LH IIIC Middle. Proceedings of the International Workshop Held at the Austrian Academy of Sciences at Vienna October 29th and 30th, 2004*, Vienna, 287–300.

Rutter, J.B. and C.W Zerner. 1984. "Early Hellado-Minoan Contacts," in R. Hägg and N. Marinatos (eds.), *The Minoan Thalassocracy: Myth and Reality. Proceedings of the Third International Symposium at the Swedish Institute in Athens, May 31–June 5, 1982*, Stockholm, 75–83.

Sackett, L.H., V. Hankey, R.J. Howell, T.W. Jacobsen, and M.R. Popham. 1966. "Prehistoric Euboea: Contributions toward a Survey," *BSA* 61, 33–112.

Sakellariou, A. 1971. "Scène de bataille sur un vase mycénien en pierre?" *Revue Archéologique* 1971, 3–14.

Salavoura, E. 2012. "Mycenaean 'Ear Pick': A Rare Metal Burial Gift, Toilette Or Medical Implement?" in M.-L. Nosch and R. Laffineur (eds.), *KOSMOS. Jewellery, Adornment and Textiles in the Aegean Bronze Age. Proceedings of the 13th International Aegean Conference/13e Rencontre égéenne internationale, University of Copenhagen, Danish National Research Foundation's Centre for Textile Research, 21–26 April 2010* (Aegaeum 33), Leuven/Liège, 345–351.

Sandars, N.K. 1961. "The First Aegean Swords and Their Ancestry," *AJA* 65, 17–29.

Sapouna-Sakellaraki, E. 1995. "A Middle Helladic Tomb Complex at Xeropolis (Lefkandi)," *BSA* 90, 41–54.

Sauvage, C. 2012. *Routes maritimes et systèmes d'échanges internationaux au Bronze récent en Méditerranée orientale* (Travaux de la Maison de l'Orient et de la Méditerranée 61), Lyon.

Schallin, A.-L. 1996. "The Late Helladic Period," in B. Wells and C. Runnels (eds.), *The Berbati-Limnes Archaeological Survey 1988–1990*, Stockholm, 123–177.

2002. "Pots for Sale: The LH IIIA and IIIB Ceramic Production at Berbati," in B. Wells (ed.), *New Research on Old Material from Asine and Berbati in Celebration of the Fiftieth Anniversary of the Swedish Institute at Athens*, Jonsered, 141–155.

Schliemann, H. 1881. *Orchomenos*, Leipzig.

Schofield, L. 2007. *The Mycenaeans*, Los Angeles.

Schofield, L. and R.B. Parkinson. 1994. "Of Helmets and Heretics: A Possible Egyptian Representation of Mycenaean Warriors on a Papyrus from El-Amarna," *BSA* 89, 157–170.

Schon, R. 2007. "Chariots, Industry, and Elite Power at Pylos," in M.L. Galaty and W.A. Parkinson (eds.), *Rethinking Mycenaean Palaces II. Revised and Expanded Second Edition*, Los Angeles, 133–145.

2010. "Think Locally, Act Globally: Mycenaean Elites and the Late Bronze Age World-System," in W.A. Parkinson and M.L. Galaty (eds.), *Archaic State Interaction: The Eastern Mediterranean in the Bronze Age*, Santa Fe, 213–236.

2011. "*Vox clamantis in campo*: Further Thoughts on Ceramics and Site Survey," in W. Gauß, M. Lindblom, R.A.K. Smith, and J.C. Wright (eds.), *Our Cups Are Full: Pottery and Society in the Aegean Bronze Age. Papers Presented to Jeremy B. Rutter on the Occasion of his 65th Birthday* (BAR International Series 2227), Oxford, 231–241.

Servais, J. 1968. "Le secteur mycénien sur le haut du Vélatouri," *Thorikos I 1963*, Brussels, 27–46.

1969. "Vases mycéniens de Thorikos au Musée de Genève," *Thorikos IV 1966/1967*, Brussels, 53–69.

Servais, J. and B. Servais-Soyez. 1984. "La tholos 'oblongue' (Tombe IV) et le tumulus (Tombe V) sur le Vélatouri," *Thorikos VIII 1972/1976*, Brussels, 15–71.

Shanks, M., and Tilley, C. 1987. *Re-Constructing Archaeology: Theory and Practice*, New York and London.

Shaw, M.C. 1980. "Painted 'Ikria' at Mycenae?" *AJA* 84, 167–179.

Shelmerdine, C.W. 2008a. "Background, Sources, and Methods," in C.W. Shelmerdine (ed.), *The Cambridge Companion to the Aegean Bronze Age*, Cambridge, 1–18.

2008b. "Mycenaean Society," in Y. Duhoux and A.M. Davies (eds.), *A Companion to Linear B: Mycenaean Greek Texts and Their World*, Louvain, 1, 115–158.

Shelton, K. 2010. "Citadel and Settlement: A Developing Economy at Mycenae, the Case of Petsas House," in D.J. Pullen (ed.), *Political Economies of the Aegean Bronze Age: Papers from the Langford Conference, Florida State University, Tallahassee, 22–24 February 2007*, Oxford, 184–204.

Sherratt, A. 1994. "The Emergence of Elites: Earlier Bronze Age Europe, 2500–1300 BC," in B. Cunliffe (ed.), *The Oxford Illustrated Prehistory of Europe*, Oxford, 244–276.

Sherratt, S. 2006a. "The Pottery in a Wider Context," in D. Evely (ed.), *Lefkandi IV. The Bronze Age. The Late Helladic IIIC Settlement at Xeropolis* (BSA Suppl. 39), 218–231.

2006b. "LH IIIC Lefkandi: An Overview," in D. Evely (ed.), *Lefkandi IV: The Bronze Age. The Late Helladic IIIC Settlement at Xeropolis* (BSA Suppl. 39), 303–309.

Siedentopf, H. 1991. *Alt-Ägina IV.2: Mattbemalte Keramik der Mittleren Bronzezeit*, Mainz.

Spencer, C. 1990. "On the Tempo and Mode of State Formation: Neoevolutionism Reconsidered," *Journal of Anthropological Archaeology* 9, 1–30.

Spitaels, P. 1982. "An Unstratified Late Mycenaean Deposit from Thorikos (Mine Gallery no. 3) Attica," in P. Spitaels (ed.), *Studies in South Attica I, Miscellanea Graeca* 5, Ghent, 83–96.

Spyropoulos, Th. 2015. "Wall Paintings from the Mycenaean Palace of Boiotian Orchomenos," in H. Brecoulaki, J.L. Davis, and S.R. Stocker (eds.), *Mycenaean Wall Painting in Context: New Discoveries and Old Finds Reconsidered: Proceedings of the International Conference in Athens, Greece in February 2010*, Athens, 355–368.

Stamatopoulou, M. 2011. "Thessaly (Archaic to Roman)," *AR* 57, 73–84.

Stanzel, M. 1991. *Die Tierreste aus dem Artemis-/Apollon-Heiligtum bei Kalapodi in Böotien/Griechenland*, Munich.

Steel, L. 2006. "Women in Mycenaean Pictorial Vase Painting," in E. Rystedt and B. Wells (eds.), *Pictorial Pursuits: Figurative Painting on Mycenaean and Geometric Pottery. Papers from two seminars at the Swedish Institute at Athens in 1999 and 2001* (Acta Instituti Atheniensis Regni Sueciae, series 4, 53), Stockholm, 147–155.

Steinmann, B. 2012. *Die Waffengräber der ägäischen Bronzezeit: Waffenbeigaben, soziale Selbstdarstellung und Adelsethos in der minoisch-mykenischen Kultur* (Philippika 52), Wiesbaden.

Stockhammer, Ph. 2007. "Kontinuität und Wandel: Die Keramik der Nachpalastzeit aus der Unterstadt von Tiryns" (unpublished PhD dissertation, University of Heidelberg).

Symeonoglou, S. 1985. *The Topography of Thebes from the Bronze Age to Modern Times*, Princeton.

Talalay, L.E., T. Cullen, D.R. Keller, and E. Karimali. 2005. "Prehistoric Occupation in Southern Euboea: An Overview," in N.M. Kennell and J.E. Tomlinson (eds.), *Ancient Greece at the Turn of the Millennium: Recent Work and Future Perspectives*, Athens, 21–44.

Tankosić, Ž. and M. Chidiroglou. 2010. "The Karystian Kampos Survey Project: Methods and Preliminary Results," in D.R. Keller(ed.), *Styria Gaia. Proceedings of the International Symposium "The Archaeology of Styra and Southern Euboea, Held at Styra, 3-5 July 2009* (Mediterranean Archaeology and Archaeometry 10-13), 11-17.

Tankosić, Ž. and I. Mathioudaki. 2009. "Agios Nikolaos Mylon. Some Speculations on the Bronze Age of Southern Euboea," in A. Mazarakis Ainian (ed.), *2ο Αρχαιολογικό Έργο Θεσσαλίας και Στερεάς Ελλάδας (2nd Archaeological Work of Thessaly and Central Greece), Πρακτικά Επιστημονικής Συνάντησης, Τμήμα Ιστορίας, Αρχαιολογίας, Κοινωνικής Ανθρωπολογίας Πανεπιστημίου Θεσσαλίας και ΥΠΠΟ, Βόλος 16-19.3.2006*, Volos, 941-949.

Tankosić, Ž. and I. Mathioudaki. 2011. "The Finds from the Prehistoric Site of Ayios Nikolaos Mylon, Southern Euboea, Greece," *BSA* 106, 99-140.

Tartaron, T.F. 2008. "Aegean Prehistory as World Archaeology: Recent Trends in the Archaeology of Bronze Age Greece," *Journal of Archaeological Research* 16, 83-161.

2010. "Between and Beyond: Political Economy in Non-palatial Mycenaean Worlds," in D.J. Pullen (ed.), *Political Economies of the Aegean Bronze Age: Papers from the Langford Conference, Florida State University, Tallahassee, 22-24 February 2007*, Oxford and Oakville, 161-183.

2013. *Maritime Networks in the Mycenaean World*, Cambridge and New York.

Tartaron, T.F., D.J. Pullen, R.K. Dunn, L. Tzortzopoulou-Gregory, A. Dill, and J.I. Boyce. 2011. "The Saronic Harbors Archaeological Research Project (SHARP): Investigations at Mycenaean Kalamianos, 2007-2009," *Hesperia* 80, 559-634.

Taylour, W. D. and R. Janko. 2008. *Ayios Stephanos: Excavations at a Bronze Age and Medieval Settlement in Southern Laconia*, London.

Televantou, C. 1994. *Ακρωτήρι Θήρας. Οι τοιχογραφίες της Δυτικής Οικίας* (Athens Archaeological Society Monograph 143), Athens.

Thomas, N.R. 1999. "The War Animal: Three Days in the Life of the Mycenaean Lion," in R. Laffineur (ed.), *POLEMOS. Le contexte guerrier en Égée a l'Âge du Bronze. Actes de la 7è Rencontre égéenne international (Liège, 14-17 avril 1998)* (Aegaeum 19), Liège and Austin, 297-312.

Tournavitou, I. 2012. "Fresco Decoration and Politics in a Mycenaean Palatial Centre: The Case of the West House at Mycenae," in M.-L. Nosch and R. Laffineur (eds.), *KOSMOS. Jewellery, Adornment and Textiles in the Aegean Bronze Age. Proceedings of the 13th International Aegean Conference/13e Rencontre égéenne internationale, University of Copenhagen, Danish National Research Foundation's Centre for Textile Research, 21-26 April 2010* (Aegaeum 33), Leuven/Liège, 723-729.

Treherne, P. 1995. "The Warrior's Beauty: The Masculine Body and Self-Identity in Bronze-Age Europe," *Journal of European Archaeology* 3, 105-144.

Van de Moortel, A. 2006. "Mitrou: Season II," *Newsletter of the Department of Classics at the University of Tennessee.*

2007. "Mitrou: Season III," *Newsletter of the Department of Classics at the University of Tennessee.*

2009. "The Late Helladic IIIC – Protogeometric Transition at Mitrou, Lokris," in S. Deger-Jalkotzy and A.E. Bächle (eds.), *LH IIIC Chronology and Synchronisms III. LH IIIC Late and the Transition to the Early Iron Age. Proceedings of the International Workshop Held at the Austrian academy of Sciences at Vienna February 23rd and 24th, 2007*, Vienna, 359-372.

2013. "Mitrou 2013: New Light on the Early Mycenaean Elite," *Newsletter of the Department of Classics at the University of Tennessee.*

Van de Moortel, A. and E. Zahou. 2005. "2004 Excavations at Mitrou, East Lokris," *AEA* 7 (2003-2004), 39-48.

2011. "The Bronze Age-Iron Age Transition at Mitrou, in East Lokris: Evidence for Continuity and Discontinuity," in A. Mazarakis Ainian (ed.), *The "Dark Ages"*

Revisited. Acts of an International Symposium in Memory of William D.E. Coulson, University of Thessaly, Volos, Greece, 14–17 June 2007, Volos, 331–347.

Van Wijngaarden, G.-J. 1999. "Production, Circulation, and Consumption of Mycenaean Pottery (Sixteenth to Twelfth Centuries BC)," in J.P. Crielaard, V. Stissi, and G.-J. van Wijngaarden (eds.), *The Complex Past of Pottery: Production, Circulation and Consumption of Mycenaean and Greek Pottery (Sixteenth to Early Fifth Centuries BC)*, Amsterdam, 21–47.

Ventris, M. and J. Chadwick. 1973. *Documents in Mycenaean Greek*, Cambridge.

Vermeule, E.D.T. 1964. *Greece in the Bronze Age*, Chicago and London.

Vermeule, E. and V. Karageorghis. 1982. *Mycenaean Pictorial Vase Painting*, Cambridge.

Vitale, S. 2008. "Ritual Drinking and Eating at LH IIIA2 Early Mitrou, East Lokris. Evidence for Mycenaean Feasting Activities?" in L.A. Hitchcock, R. Laffineur, and J. Crowley (eds.), *Dais. The Aegean Feast. Proceedings of the 12th International conference/12e Rencontre égéenne international. University of Melbourne, Centre for Classics and Archaeology, 25–29 March 2008* (Aegaeum 29), Liège, 229–237.

———. 2009. "Making Mycenaeans in the 'Periphery.' " A Preliminary Report on the Late Helladic IIA to Late Helladic IIIB Pottery from Mitrou, East Lokris, and its Wider Historical Implications (unpublished conference paper delivered at the AIA Annual Meeting 2009).

———. 2011. "The Late Helladic IIIA2 Pottery from Mitrou and its Implications for the Chronology of the Mycenaean Mainland," in W. Gauß, M. Lindblom, R.A.K. Smith, and J.C. Wright (eds.), *Our Cups Are Full: Pottery and Society in the Aegean Bronze Age. Papers Presented to Jeremy B. Rutter on the Occasion of his 65th Birthday* (BAR International Series 2227), Oxford, 331–344.

———. 2013a. "Two LH IIIA1 Deposits From Mitrou, East Lokris: A Chronological, Typological, and Functional Analysis of the Pottery," in G. Graziadio, R. Guglielmino, V. Lenuzza, and S. Vitale (eds.), *Φιλική Συναυλία: Studies in Mediterranean Archaeology for Mario Benzi* (BAR International Series 2460), 123–133.

———. 2013b. "Local Traditions and Mycenaeanization in Central Greece: A Preliminary Report on the Late Helladic IIA to Late Helladic IIIB Pottery from Mitrou, East Lokris," in A. Mazarakis Ainian and A. Doulgeri-Intzesioglou (eds.), *Proceedings of the 3rd Archaeological Meeting of Thessaly and Central Greece 2006–2008. From Prehistory to the Contemporary Period, Volos 12–15 March 2009*. Volos, 1147–1158.

Voutsaki, S. 1995. "Social and Political Processes in the Mycenaean Argolid: The Evidence from the Mortuary Practices," in R. Laffineur and W.-D. Niemeier (eds.), *POLITEIA. Society and State in the Aegean Bronze Age. Proceedings of the 5th International Aegean Conference/5e Rencontre égéenne internationale, University of Heidelberg, Archäologisches Institut, 10–13 April 1994* (Aegaeum 12), Liège, 55–66.

———. 1997. "The Creation of Value and Prestige in the Late Bronze Age Aegean," *Journal of European Archaeology* 5, 34–52.

———. 2001. "Economic Control, Power and Prestige in the Mycenaean World: The Archaeological Evidence," in S. Voutsaki and J. Killen (eds.), *Economy and Politics in the Mycenaean Palace States. Proceedings of a Conference Held on 1–3 July 1999 in the Faculty of Classics, Cambridge* (The Cambridge Philological Society Suppl. 27), 195–213.

———. 2010a. "From the Kinship Economy to the Palatial Economy: The Argolid in the 2nd Millennium BC," in D.J. Pullen (ed.), *Political Economies of the Aegean Bronze Age: Papers from the Langford Conference, Florida State University, Tallahassee, 22–24 February 2007*, Oxford and Oakville, Oxford, 86–111.

———. 2010b. "Agency and Personhood at the Onset of the Mycenaean Period," *Archaeological Dialogues* 17, 65–92.

Vykukal, R.L. 2011. "Purpurae Florem of Mitrou: Assessing the Role of Purple Dye Manufacture in the Emergence of a Political Elite" (unpublished Master's Thesis, University of Tennessee).

Wachsmann, S. 1998. *Seagoing Ships and Seamanship in the Bronze Age Levant*, College Station.

Wallace, M., D. Keller, J. Wickens, and R. Lamberton. 2006. "The Southern Euboea Exploration Project: 25 Years of Archaeological Research," in M. Chidiroglou and A. Chatzidimitriou (eds.), *Antiquities of Karystia / Αρχαιότητεςτης Καρυστίας*, Karystos, 18–49.

Walton, M.S., A. Shortland, S. Kirk, and P. Degryse. 2009. "Evidence for the Trade of Mesopotamian and Egyptian Glass to Mycenaean Greece," *Journal of Archaeological Science* 36, 1496–1503.

Warren, P. 1979. "The Miniature Fresco from the West House at Akrotiri, Thera, and Its Aegean Setting," *JHS* 99, 115–129.

Watts, D.J. and Strogatz, S.H. 1998. "Collective Dynamics of 'Small-World' Networks," *Nature* 393 (6684), 440–442.

Wedde, M. 1999. "War at Sea: The Mycenaean and Early Iron Age Oared Galley," in R. Laffineur (ed.), *POLEMOS. Le contexte guerrier en Égée a l'Âge du Bronze. Actes de la 7è Rencontre égéenne international (Liège, 14–17 avril 1998)* (Aegaeum 19), Liège and Austin, 465–476.

  2000. *Towards a Hermeneutics of Aegean Bronze Age Ship Imagery*, Mannheim and Möhnesee.

  2005. "The Mycenaean Galley in Context: From Fact to Idée Fixe," in R. Laffineur and E. Greco (eds.), *Emporia. Aegeans in the Central and Eastern Mediterranean: Proceedings of the 10th International Aegean Conference/10e rencontre égéenne internationale, Athens, Italian School of Archaeology, 14–18 April 2004*, Liège, 29–37.

  2006. "Pictorial Evidence for Partial System Survival in the Greek Bronze to Iron Age Transition," in E. Rystedt and B. Wells (eds.), *Pictorial Pursuits: Figurative Painting on Mycenaean and Geometric Pottery. Papers from two seminars at the Swedish Institute at Athens in 1999 and 2001* (Acta Instituti Atheniensis Regni Sueciae, series 4, 53), Stockholm, 255–269.

Weingarten, J. 2010a. "Corridors of Power: A Social Network Analysis of the Minoan 'Replica Rings,' " in W. Müller (ed.), *Die Bedeutung der minoischen und mykenischen Glyptik* (CMS Beiheft 8), Mainz, 395–412.

  2010b. "Minoan Seals and Sealings," in E.H. Cline (ed.), *The Oxford Handbook of the Bronze Age Aegean (ca. 3000–1000 BC)*, Oxford, 317–328.

West, M.L. 1988. "The Rise of the Greek Epic," *JHS* 108, 151–172.

Whitley, J. 2002. "Objects with Attitude: Biographical Facts and Fallacies in the Study of Late Bronze Age and Early Iron Age Warrior Graves," *CAJ* 12, 217–232.

  2002–2003. "Archaeology in Greece 2002–2003," *Archaeological Reports* 49, 1–88.

  2012. "Agency in Greek Art," in T.J. Smith and D. Plantzos (eds.), *A Companion to Greek Art*, Oxford, 579–595.

Winter-Livneh, R., T. Svoray, I. Gilead. 2012. "Secondary Burial Cemeteries, Visibility and Land Tenure: A View from the Southern Levant Chalcolithic Period," *Journal of Anthropological Archaeology* 31, 423–438.

Wood, M. 1987. *In Search of the Trojan War*, New York.

Wright, H.E. 1972. "Vegetation History," in W.A. McDonald and G.R. Rapp (eds.), *The Minnesota Messenia Expedition: Reconstructing a Bronze Age Regional Environment*, Minneapolis, 188–199.

Wright, J.C. 1995. "Empty Cups and Empty Jugs: The Social Role of Wine in Minoan and Mycenaean Societies," in P. McGovern, S. Fleming and S. Katz (eds.), *The Origins and Ancient History of Wine*, Amsterdam, 287–309.

  2001. "Factions and the Origins of Leadership and Identity in Mycenaean Society," *BICS* 45, 182.

  2004a. "Mycenaean Drinking Services and Standards of Etiquette," in P. Halstead and J.C. Barrett (eds.), *Food, Cuisine and Society in Prehistoric Greece*, Oxford, 90–104.

  2004b. "A Survey of Evidence for Feasting in Mycenaean Society," in J.C. Wright (ed.), *The Mycenaean Feast* (American School of Classical Studies at Athens), Princeton, 13–58.

2004c. "The Emergence of Leadership and the Rise of Civilization in the Aegean," in J.C. Barrett and P. Halstead (eds.), *The Emergence of Civilisation Revisited* (Sheffield Studies in Aegean Archaeology 6), Oxford, 64–89.

2008. "Early Mycenaean Greece," in C.W. Shelmerdine (ed.), *The Cambridge Companion to the Aegean Bronze Age*, Cambridge, 230–257.

Younger, J.G. 1979. "Semi-Precious Stones to the Aegean," *Archaeological News* 8, 40–44.

1997. "The Stelai of Mycenae Grave Circles A and B," in R. Laffineur and P. Betancourt (eds.), *TEXNH. Craftsmen, Craftswomen and Craftsmanship in the Aegean Bronze Age / Artisanat et artisans en Égée à l'âge du Bronze. Proceedings of the 6th International Aegean Conference / 6e Rencontre égéenne internationale, Philadelphia, Temple University, 18–21 April 1996* (Aegaeum 16), 229–239.

2010. "Mycenaean Seals and Sealings," in E.H. Cline (ed.), *The Oxford Handbook of the Bronze Age Aegean (ca. 3000–1000 BC)*, Oxford, 329–339.

2011. "A View from the Sea," in G. Vavouranakis (ed.), *The Seascape in Aegean Prehistory* (Monographs of the Danish Institute in Athens 14), Athens, 161–183.

2012. "Mycenaean Collections of Seals: The Role of Blue," in M.-L. Nosch and R. Laffineur (eds.), *KOSMOS. Jewellery, Adornment and Textiles in the Aegean Bronze Age. Proceedings of the 13th International Aegean Conference/13e Rencontre égéenne internationale, University of Copenhagen, Danish National Research Foundation's Centre for Textile Research, 21–26 April 2010* (Aegaeum 33), Leuven/Liège, 749–753.

Zangger, E., M.E. Timpson, S.B. Yazvenko, F. Kuhnke, and J. Knauss. 1997. "The Pylos Regional Archaeological Project: Part II: Landscape Evolution and Site Preservation," *Hesperia* 66, 549–641.

INDEX

Achaea, 61, 103, 108, 164–165, 185
administration, 77, 82, 98–100, 179
    Mycenaean, 70, 82, 92, 126, 127
    Theban, 96, 112
administrator, 10, 19, 93, 95, 99
Aegina, 36, 49, 60, 63, 115
Aetolia, 96, 98–99
agate, 41, 85, 86, 88–92, 94, 141
agency, 18, 28–31, 125, 126, 145
    agency theory, 5, 30, 185
    of elites, 125, 128, 181
    of objects, 30–31, 122
    of swords, 38, 103
agent, 4, 5, 29, 30, 180
Agia Irini, 43, 49–51, 134
Agia Marina (Kopais), 117, 119
Agia Triada (Crete), 78, 79
Agia Triada (Elis), 164
Agia Triada (near Mitrou), 64, 73, 94, 104
Agios Ioannis (Kopais), 119, 120
Agios Mamas, 66
Agios Nikolaos (South Euboea), 7
Agios Stephanos, 147, 185
Agios Vasileios, 13, 147
Agnanti, 26, 118
agrimi. *See* goat
Aidepsos, 5, 15, 59, 61
Akrotiri, 23, 50–55, 78, 79, 109, 128–130, 132,
    134, 140, 149
alabaster, 33, 60, 86
alabastron, 42, 60, 74, 108, 109
alluvium, 15
altar
    at Kalapodi, 9, 170
    on ships, 140
    with griffins, 85
Amarynthos, 8, 61, 110, 161, 162, 168

amber, 27, 33, 40–42, 55, 70–73, 81, 86, 145
amethyst, 41
amulet, 175, 176
Anatolia, 46
ancestors, 104
anchorage, 15, 133
Anthedon, 15, 110, 112, 126, 145, 147, 166, 167,
    172
Anthia (Messenia), 79, 84
antler, 46, 143
Antron (Glypha), 66, 67
Apollo, 9, 42
Aravantinos, Vassilios, 10
Archaeological Reconnaissance of
    Uninvestigated Remains of Agriculture,
    10, 116
archers, 80, 161, 169
architecture, 12, 65, 111
    monumental architecture, 9, 49, 107, *See*
    also monumental building; Cyclopean
    masonry
    palatial architecture, 10, 82
Argolid, 1–4, 17, 28, 39–41, 46, 54, 56, 61, 62, 64,
    71, 83–85, 88, 93, 96, 98, 100, 112–114, 117,
    123, 124, 142–145, 153, 157, 167, 176, 178, 181
Argos, 86, 112, 142, 167
Arma, 7
AROURA. *See* Archaeological
    Reconnaissance of Uninvestigated
    Remains of Agriculture
arrow, 39, 43, 47, 102, 152
arrowheads, 33, 41, 42, 45, 80–82, 102, 153, 161
Artemis, 9
Ashkelon, 132, 137, 157
Asia Minor, 172
Asine, 84, 86, 112, 142, 157, 167
Atalanti, 72, 96

Athens, 45, 60, 83, 150, 157, 166, 178
Attica, 1, 8, 12–14, 43, 44, 59–61, 83, 85, 88, 96, 98, 108, 153, 164, 175, 178
Avlonari, 164

Bademgediği Tepe, 157, 172, 173
balance scales, 42
Balkans, 47, 62, 66, 71
Barabási, Albert- László, 19, 25
Baran, Paul, 20, 22
basileus, 163, 173, 179
battle, 34, 39, 45, 47, 48, 76, 80, 103, 104, 131, 132, 138
    at sea, 50, 131, 152, 153, 155–159, 165, 171
battle costume, 45
Battle in the Glen (ring), 35, 50, 55
battle scene, 33, 35, 36, 44, 47, 78, 100, 105, 133, 137
battlefield, 55, 79, 101
bead, 9, 27, 33, 41–43, 66, 70–73, 76, 81, 86, 99, 106, 141, 143, 146
bell curve, 21
Bell, James, 29
Berbati, 83, 84, 157, 167
Berbati Valley, 167
betweenness centrality, 23, 62, 63, 109, 113
Bintliff, John, 5, 58
boar hunt, 10, 80
boar's tusk, 33, 41, 141, *See also* helmet:boar's tusk helmet
Boeotia, 1, 4, 5, 10–11, 13, 14, 16, 17, 31, 58, 61, 63, 85, 93, 98, 108, 110, 112, 115, 123, 143, 145, 153, 165, 166, 172, 176, 178, 182
bone, 49, 141, 143, 153
Bouzek, Jan, 132
bow (ship), 50, 130–133, 152, 172
bow-and-arrow, 43, 52, 161
bowsprit, 134
brailed rig, 131, 132, 157, 158
brailed sail. *See* brailed rig
Brauron, 78, 94
bridge (network), 23
bridle piece, 46–48, 66, 176
bronze, 33, 36, 40–42, 44, 45, 49, 50, 67, 81, 102, 103, 105, 111, 134, 143, 153, 164, 174–177
Broodbank, Cyprian, 14, 23–25, 27, 134, 135, 148
bull leaper, 10
bull leaping, 78
Bulle, Heinrich, 10
bureaucracy. *See* administration
Burke, Brendan, 11
Burns, Bryan, 11, 143–145

cabin (on ship), 134, 140
Cambridge/Bradford Boeotian Expedition, 5
Cape Gelidonya shipwreck, 131
captain, 48, 55, 140, 147, 164, 173
cargo, 27, 130, 132, 157, 174, 178
carnelian, 79, 86, 88–91, 93, 94
Carpathian Basin, 66
carrying capacity, 23, 26
cartouche, 176
Catalogue of Ships (*Iliad*), 161
cemetery, 1, 5, 6, 9, 11, 12, 26, 41, 70, 73, 74, 79, 115, 118, 122, 125, 126, 143, 153, 164, 173, 176, 179, 183
Central Europe, 46, 66, 67, 88
Central Greece, 2–4, 7, 11, 19, 24, 26, 28, 39, 42, 56–59, 62, 66, 70, 71, 88, 95, 98, 107, 112, 146, 166, 168, 178, 180, 185
central place, 23
centralization, 23, 56, 111, 112, 123, 142, 178, 182
ceremonial drinking, 12, 50, 54, 181, *See also* drinking ceremonies
Chalkidike, 61
Chalkis, 5, 14–18, 41, 54, 59–62, 64, 71, 72, 74, 75, 96–98, 101, 108–113, 125, 126, 142, 164, 170, 172, 182
Chalkis-Trypa, 41, 59, 60, 64, 96, 97, 109
chamber tomb, 5, 9, 12, 40, 41, 42, 43, 62, 64, 73–74, 81, 87, 88, 104, 106, 108, 115, 116, 142, 164, 176
    built chamber tomb, 11
Chantsa (Kopais), 119
Charami, Alexandra, 11
chariot, 46–48, 55, 78–80, 82–84, 87, 105, 138–139
    depicted on frescoes, 10, 80, 104, 137, 138, 147
    depicted on pottery, 76, 82–84, 100, 164
    depicted on seals, 47, 78–80, 82, 84, 85, 105
    depicted on stelae, 138
chariot driving, 165
chariot model, 83
chariot racing, 139
charioteer, 139, 162, 163
CHELP. *See* Cornell Halai and East Lokris Project
chiefdom, 70, 126, 182
cist tomb, 62, 64, 74
citadel, 31, 60, 112, 117, 119, 122, 132, 137, 138, 143, 182
    of Gla, 10, 120
city state, 7
Cline, Eric, 146, 177
cluster (network), 14, 23, 25, 176
clustering (network), 20, 21

coast, 4, 8, 11–15, 27, 43, 56, 64, 73, 96, 107, 108,
    110, 111, 120, 131–133, 147, 148, 155, 159, 164,
    166, 168, 171–173, 175, 179–182, 185
  as liminal zone, 13
coastal centers, 15, 65, 126, 135, 139, 144, 146,
    147, 183, 185
coastal communities, 13, 145, 146, 171, 172
coastal plains, 15
coastal settlements, 14, 15, 144, 145, 157, 159,
    165, 179, 184–185
coastal societies, 19, 145
coastal worlds, 14, 24
coastscape, 4, 13, 180
collapse of palaces, 4, 100, 124, 148, 152, 153,
    157, 160, 163–166, 168, 170–173, 175, 176,
    178, 183, 185
comb, 44, 86
communication speed (in a network), 22, 23
conspicuous consumption, 29, 39, 45, 50, 54
continuity
  between Bronze and Early Iron Age, 9, 173,
    174, *See also* Early Iron Age
  between LH IIIB and IIIC, 159
  between MH and LH III, 58, 64
core area, 1, 4, 14, 39, 56, 98–100, 122, 125, 180,
    184
Corinth, 83
Corinthia, 13, 178
Cornell Halai and East Lokris Project, 7, 58
Cosmopoulos, Michael, 7
Crete, 8, 14, 27, 36, 39, 44, 53, 60, 66, 68, 71, 78,
    79, 84, 93–94, 101, 109, 115, 116, 154, 157,
    172, 174
crew, 27, 130, 134, 138, 139, 183
Crielaard, Jan Paul, 7, 154
Crouwel, Joost, 83, 149, 151
crow's nests, 159
crystal, 41, 94
cumulative advantage. *See* preferential
    attachment
cupellation, 12
Cyclades, 14, 15, 24, 25, 39, 44, 49, 50, 66, 134,
    135, 138, 159
Cyclopean masonry, 31, 107, 117, 119, 121, 180,
    182, *See also* architecture; monumental
    building
Cypro-Minoan script, 12
Cyprus, 11, 27, 71, 76, 83, 130, 141, 161, 175, 178,
    185

dagger, 33, 35, 36, 42–45, 53, 80, 85, 101, 103, 162
Dakoronia, Fanouria, 8, 42, 44, 161, 170
Dakouri-Hild, Anastasia, 143
Daskaleio-Kavos, 23, 148

Daulosis-Kastraki (Kopais), 118
Davaras, Costis, 140
de Ridder, T.A., 10
deadeyes, 129, 132
deck, 131–134, 152, 157, 158, 173
deer, 43, 46, 47, 49, 85, 94, 149, 150, 171
Deger-Jalkotzy, Sigrid, 163, 165
degree of separation, 20–22
Dendra, 45, 82, 86, 142
DEPAS. *See* Dickinson Excavation Project
    and Archaeological Survey of Glas
depopulation, 56, 67, 115, 153, 165, 185
destruction, 9, 46, 114, 115, 120, 122–123, 126,
    143, 144, 147, 179, 185
Dickinson Excavation Project and
    Archaeological Survey of Glas, 10
Dickinson, Oliver, 26, 41
Dimini, 11, 84, 88, 126
Dipylon vase, 162
divine status, 87, 149
Dodecanese, 103, 172–174
Doris, 98
drain tiles, 126
drainage works (Kopais), 118–120, 122–124,
    182
Dramesi, 15, 40–41, 54, 60, 160, 171
drinking ceremonies, 12, 49, 171, 181,
    See also ceremonial drinking
dromos, 12, 40, 42, 43, 73
Drosia, 15
duel, 34–37, 39, 45, 46, 55, 79, 84, 87, 91, 101,
    105, 152, 162

Early Iron Age, 7, 9, 12, 15, 31, 173, 185
Early Iron Age (transition to), 1, 9, 174, 176,
    See also continuity
ear-scoop, 42, 44
East Lokris, 5, 6, 8, 13, 14, 15, 26, 122
Eastern Boeotia Archaeological Project, 7
Eastern Korinthia Archaeological Survey, 59
EBAP. *See* Eastern Boeotia Archaeological
    Project
economy, 23, 123
edge (network), 19, *See also* link
Egypt, 11, 27, 46, 146, 159, 175, 178
Egyptian reliefs, 159, *See also* Medinet Habu
    relief
Elateia, 1, 12, 88
Eleon, 5, 7, 11, 110, 126
Eleusis, 60, 137, 174
Elis, 98, 108, 164, 185
elite burial, 41, 80, 143
elite centers, 12, 65, 70, 74, 75, 106, 112, 115, 147,
    181

elite competition, 40, 125, 145
elite culture, 54
elite ideals, 183
elite identity, 66, 139, 154, 171
elite network, 62–65, 69, 106, 181
elite status, 40, 43, 82, 124, 139, 182
elite vessels, 41
elite warriors, 36, 44, 46, 49
elites, 4, 10, 19, 29, 31, 39–41, 44, 47, 50, 54, 58,
    63, 66–67, 70–71, 73, 75–76, 78, 81–82, 85,
    88, 92, 95, 99, 100, 102, 103, 106, 115,
    124–125, 139, 142–144, 146, 148, 150, 152,
    156, 163, 165, 168, 170–172, 181–184, *See
    also* palatial elites; postpalatial elites;
    prepalatial elites
  coastal elites, 145, 170, 173, 185
  early Mycenaean elites, 9, 46, 53, 54, 60, 66,
    94, 99, 181
  emergence of, 12, 43, 69, 74, 182, 184
  emerging elites, 9, 39, 41, 43, 49, 58, 63–67,
    69, 127, 181, *See also* Mitrou
  Near Eastern elites, 46
  provincial elites, 95, 99
emporion, 62
cntanglement, 30, 48, 68, 82
eparchia, 13
Epirus, 103
epos, 36, 51, 53, 156
Eretria, 15, 78, 94
Erita (priestess at Pylos), 104
ethos of the sword. *See* warrior ethos
Euboea, 7, 8, 12–17, 41, 44, 58, 59, 61, 63, 71, 96,
    98, 110, 114, 125, 153, 163, 164, 172
  Central Euboea, 5, 11, 14, 41, 110
  North Euboea, 5, 14, 16, 26
Euripos, 11, 14, 40, 41, 61, 112, 152, 163, 166
Eutresis, 110, 166, 167
Evely, Don, 114
exotica, 29, 30, 69, 75, 85, 112, 142, 144–146, 148,
    See also import; luxury goods; prestige
    goods

farmland, 23, 123
feasting, 33, 49–50, 68, 170, 181
Felsch, Rainer, 9
female status, 80, 104
Feuer, Bryan, 180
figurine, 9, 44, 153
fishermen, 160
fishing, 160
Flotilla Fresco (Akrotiri), 51, 53, 132
fortification, 113, 118
  along Kopais, 115, 118–122, 125, 126, 182
  along the Euripos, 112

at Gla, 117
at Haliartos, 118
at Larymna, 120
at Lefkandi, 40, 154
at Mycenae, 119
fortification walls, 107, 126, 154, 182
Fossey, John, 5, 58, 118, 119
fractals, 65
free will, 28
fresco, 4, 10, 31, 43, 45, 48–53, 76, 80, 83–85,
    103–105, 115, 118, 128–138, 147, 149, 154,
    161–163, 183
Further Province (of Pylos), 127, 146
Furtwängler, Adolf, 10

galley, 130–141, 145, 147–148, 156–161, 164, 168,
    171–174, 176, 178, 179, 183–185
Gazi, 132, 137, 157
geodesic (network), 19
geophysical survey, 10, 120
Georgiko (Thessaly), 86
Gerokomeion Hill (Thebes), 142
Gialtra, 14–17
Giddens, Anthony, 29
Gla, 5, 10, 107, 112, 116–123, 124, 127, 142
glass, 27, 86, 96, 141–143, 146, 175, 176
Glypha, 63, 64, 67, 74
goat, 51, 78–80, 88, 149
gold, 11, 31, 33–35, 37–45, 47, 49, 55, 56, 63, 66,
    77–81, 85–89, 91, 94, 99, 101, 104, 136,
    141–143, 151, 161, 174–176
Golemi, 72, 115
Goumourades, 7, 15
Gouvalari, 84, 92
graffiti, 160
graph (network), 19, 20, 22, 23, 27–28
grave circle, 67
Grave Circle A (Mycenae), 33–35, 80, 91, 138,
    180, *See also* Shaft Graves (Mycenae)
Grave Circle B (Mycenae), 40, 67, 77, 80,
    See also Shaft Graves (Mycenae)
grave stele, 33–36, 38, 46, 78, 138
gravity feature (network model), 26
greave, 45
Greek Archaeological Service, 5, 8
griffin, 43, 63, 78, 79, 81, 85–88, 149–151, 161, 170
grooming, 42, 44, 90

habitus, 29, 30, 39, 69, 128, 145
Hagel, Dietmar, 118
Halai, 7
Haliartos, 118
Hall 64 (Pylos), 103, 129, 132, 133
Hankey, Vronwey, 41, 59

harbor, 8, 9, 11, 27, 110, 116, 130
Harrell, Katherine, 38, 92, 181
headland, 15
heartland. *See* core area
heirloom, 30, 89, 95, 99
helmet, 34, 35, 52, 53, 55, 140, 159, 160, 172
    boar's tusk helmet, 39, 41, 45, 47, 48, 51–54,
        80, 143, 185
    hedgehog helmet, 159, 162, 173
Helms, Margaret, 47
helmsman, 53, 131, 140, 152, 155, 157
heterarchical organization, 11, 12, 22, 74, 75,
        126, 171, 175, 179, 184
Hiller, Stefan, 133
hills, 11, 13, 15, 73, 104, 107, 118
hinterland, 4, 13, 64, 70, 74, 75, 161, 169,
        171, 180
Hither Province (of Pylos), 133
Hope Simpson, Richard, 26, 41, 118
horns of consecration, 10, 52
horse, 46, 55, 139
    depicted on pottery, 83
    depicted on seals, 78, 79, 84
    depicted on stelae, 46, 138
horse burial, 12, 43
horse model, 83
horse-and-chariot, 33, 46–47, 79, 83
horse-bridle piece, 66
hub, 22–24, 27, 28, 62, 64–65, 67, 70, 74–76,
        109, 111–113, 125, 166, 175, 176, 178–179, 182,
        183, 185
hunt, 43, 47, 48, 55, 78, 80, 103,
        104, 165
hunter, 43, 47–49, 85, 100, 103, 134, 141, 162,
        163, 169
hunting, 33, 36, 39, 43, 45, 47–49, 79, 84, 85,
        136–138
Hylike, 14, 118
Hymettus, 60

Iakovidis, Spiridon, 10
iconographic analysis, 31
iconography, 28, 31, 34, 36, 38, 43, 44, 46–48,
        52, 55, 76, 78, 80, 84, 91, 92, 103–104, 128,
        130, 136, 138, 146, 151, 171, 173
identity, 4, 24, 28, 30, 31, 36, 55, 66, 69, 70, 75,
        100, 104, 133, 139, 151, 159, 171, *See also*
        elite identity; warrior identity
ideology, 4, 5, 18, 31, 76–78, 80, 82, 84, 104, 105,
        133, 137–140, 144, 165, 171, 182, 184, *See also*
        warrior ideology
Iklaina, 123, 133, 138, 147, 185
ikria, 129, 137, 140
Iliad, 36, 50, 53, 85, 161

import, 9, 24, 84, 116, 142–144, 174–179, 181,
        182, 184, *See also* exotica
    at Lefkandi, 174, 183
    at Mycenae, 177
    at Perati, 174–177, 184
    at Pylos, 146
    at Thebes, 141, 142, 182
    Baltic, 33, 54
    control of, 110, 144, 147, 166, 183, *See also*
        palatial control
    exotic imports, 4, 11, 110, 128, 183
    extra-Aegean, 66, 116, 176, 184
    from Anatolia, 33, 54
    from Balkans, 66, 174
    from Canaan, 142
    from Carpathian Basin, 46
    from Crete, 33, 40, 54, 109, 112
    from Cyprus, 12, 142, 172, 174, 176
    from Egypt, 12, 54, 142, 146, 173, 176
    from Italy, 174
    from Laconia/Kythera, 60
    from Melos, 174
    from Mesopotamia, 141, 142, 146
    from Naxos, 174
    from Near East, 141, 173
    from Syria, 142
    from Syria-Palestine, 141, 164, 176
    from the Cyclades, 40, 176
    from the Levant, 12
    from the Saronic Gulf, 174
    Kassite, 142
    Mitanni, 94, 142
    of ivory, 143
    of pottery, 63
    of raw materials, 176, 178
    of tin and copper, 103
import consumption, 4, 29, 128, 143, 144, 183
ingots, 15, 27
inscribed stirrup jars, 112, 116
insularity, 14
interaction, 4, 18, 19, 23–28, 30, 48, 64, 65, 68,
        107, 181, 185
iron, 164, 175
ISJs. *See* inscribed stirrup jars
Island Sanctuaries Group, 87
Italy, 11, 174
ivory, 11, 31, 33, 42, 48, 55, 85–87, 141, 143, 150,
        151, 174, 178

javelin, 86, 152, 155, 161–162, 164

Kadesh, 159, 162
Kadmeion, 39, 141
Kakovatos, 71, 84

Kalapodi, 1, 5, 8, 9, 26, 42–45, 54, 72, 73, 86–94, 97, 101, 104, 115, 118, 122, 124–126, 153, 154, 157, 160–162, 168–171, 182–184
Kanghadi (in Achaea), 165
Karageorghis, Vassos, 83, 162
Karystos, 7, 110
Kastro (near Gla), 117
Kastro (near Volos), 11, 12, 126
Kastron/Topolia (Kopais), 119
katavothra, 113, 116–119, 122, 124
Kazanaki, 11
Kazarma, 79, 84, 91
keel, 130
Keller, Donald, 7
Keos, 60
Kilian, Klaus, 133, 180
Knappett, Carl, 68
knife, 39, 42, 80, 101, 164, 175–177
Knodell, Alex, 7, 10, 25, 27, 110, 112
Knossos, 78–80, 82, 85, 95, 101, 111, 146, 150
    Arsenal, 102
    Room with the Chariot Tablets, 78, 82
knowledgeable social actor, 29, 126, 128, 145
koine, 5, 24, 75, 161, 163, 168–171, 179, 183
Kokkalia, 9, 42, 72, 87–89, 115
Kokkinonyzes (near Kynos), 42, 64, 72
Kolaka-Agios Ioannis, 73, 118, 126
Kolonna, 36, 39, 44, 49, 51, 55, 111, 135, 160, 180
Kopaic Basin, 3, 116–119, 122, 182
Kopais, 14, 73, 113, 116–120, 122, 125
Kopanias, Konstantinos, 142
Korphos-Kalamianos, 111, 121, 144, 180, 185
Kos, 71, 157, 172, 179, 183
Kosma, Maria, 7
Kotrona, 7, 15
krater, 33, 49, 154, 164–165, 169
    Aeginetan, 49
    chariot krater, 82–84
    pictorial, 31, 76, 84, 130, 137, 151, 153–157, 159–162, 164, 169, 170, 172–175, 178, 184
Kreusis, 110
Kroll, Helmut, 123
kylikes, 74, 87, 167, 170
Kynos, 1, 5, 8, 11, 15–17, 26, 42, 62, 64, 72, 74, 94, 114, 126, 131, 151–162, 168–172, 184
Kyparissi, 26

Laconia, 13, 39, 43, 60, 61, 88, 147, 178
Laffineur, Robert, 40, 81, 85
lake, 14, 116–118, 122, See also Hylike; Kopais
Lamian Gulf, 14
lance, 34, 50, 55, 161, 164
Lane, Michael, 10, 116
lapis lazuli, 92, 94, 118, 141, 143

"large world", 22
larnax, 11, 100
Larymna, 15, 107, 120–122, 124–126, 145, 147, 182, 185
Laureion, 12, 178
lawagetas, 133, 135
lead, 12, 41, 50, 100, 118, 143, 159, 174, 178
Lefkandi, 1, 5, 8, 11, 40–41, 54, 60, 61, 67, 83, 94, 96–98, 114, 126, 149–154, 159–163, 165–172, 174–176, 183–185
Leiden-Ljubljana Ancient Cities of Boeotia Project, 5
Lelantine Plain, 15, 17
Lemos, Irene, 8, 11, 163
Levant, 11, 27, 159, 176, 178, 185
libation, 9
Lichas, 15
liminal zone, 13
Limni, 14, 15–17, 73, 126
Linear A, 136
Linear B, 12, 126, 136
    archives, 146
Linear B tablets, 7, 10–12, 23, 82, 104, 110, 115, 126, 135, 138, 163
Linear B texts, 96, 133, 134, 136, 137, 183
link, 4, 19–24, 27–28, 47, 50, 60, 61, 63–65, 70, 72, 93, 108, 123, 125, 163, 171–172, 176, 178, 182, 184
    long range, 21, 65, 176, See also long distance ties
    weighted, 28
link connectivity, 23
lion, 36, 48, 79, 85, 87, 91, 151, 161
    carved in ivory, 150
    depicted on dagger, 33, 43, 85, 103, 161
    depicted on frescoes, 151
    depicted on pottery, 151
    depicted on seals, 37, 79, 80, 84–85, 87–91, 94
Lion Gate (Mycenae), 31, 151
Lis, Bartłomiej, 169
litharge, 12
Loader, Claire, 117
Lokris, 5, 7, 98
long distance links. See long distance ties
long distance ties, 21, 47, 54, 65–66, 69, 71, 75, 125, 126, 136, 143, 176, 179, 181, 183–185, See also link; weak ties
longboat, 51, 134, 135
Longos, 15
Loukisia, 62, 64, 74
Loutra Aidepsou, 15
luxury goods, 27, 31, 43, 54, 150, 177, 178, See also exotica; import; prestige goods

Maggidis, Christofilis, 10, 120

Magnesia peninsula, 67

Mainland Popular Group. *See* seal:Mainland Popular Group

Manika, 15, 44, 61

Marathon, 12, 40, 43, 54, 74

maritime access, 4, 14

maritime route, 14, 61, 111, 125, 160, 175, 184, 185

maritime traffic, 11, 110, 112

masculine status, 43

mast, 51, 128–130, 134, 136, 157–158, 172

Medeon, 88, 99

Medinet Habu relief, 133, 158, 159, 162

Megaplatanos-Sventza, 97

megaron, 12, 85, 123, 126, 133, 137, 138, 152

melathron, 10, 119

Melidoni, 15–17, 26

Melos, 172

Menelaos, 85

Menidi, 86

Mesozoic soils, 107

Messenia, 1, 39, 43, 46, 56, 71, 79, 88, 93, 98, 124, 129, 133, 144, 147, 153, 165, 167, 185

metal, 8, 24, 27, 77, 132, 143, 144, 178

metal working, 12, 82, 153

Midea, 95, 96, 98, 112, 142, 167

Miletos, 172

mirror, 81, 89, 92, 164

Mitrou, 15–17, 26, 40, 41, 46, 54, 60, 64, 65, 66, 67, 71, 73, 94, 142, 145–147, 151–154, 159, 170, 171

  amber at, 71, 72

  bridle piece at, 46, 47, 66, 176

  Building B, 152

  Building D, 114, 139, 152

  built tomb at, 40, 42, 48, 71, 73, 74, 101

  chamber tombs at, 62, 64, 74

  emerging elites at, 40, 41, 47, 58, 66, 72

  feasting at, 49

  fieldwork at, 1, 5, 7, 8, 58

  LH IIIB decline, 114–115, 122, 123, 126, 182, 185

  pottery, 8, 9, 59, 61–64, 67, 68, 169–171

  seals at, 96, 97, 99

Mitrou Archaeological Project, 8

mold (for jewelry), 11, 126, 136, 141

mold (for sword), 36

Molloy, Barry, 38, 102, 103

monumental building, 9, 114, *See also* architecture; Cyclopean masonry

Morris, Sarah, 51, 53

mound, 8, 11, 15, 18, 114, 154, 163

Mount Kandili, 14

Mount Ptoon, 14, 16

mountains, 13–14, 79, 116

Mountjoy, Penelope, 62

MPG. *See* seal:Mainland Popular Group

Mycenae, 1, 10, 17, 36, 37, 41, 46, 54, 67, 71–72, 75, 78–84, 86–88, 95, 96, 98, 104, 105, 111, 112, 116, 127, 129, 137, 138, 140, 142–143, 146, 150, 151, 157, 159, 161, 167, 169, 172, 175–177, 180, 182, 184, 185, *See also* Grave Circle A; Grave Circle B; Shaft Graves; Treasury of Atreus; workshop

  citadel, 112, 119, 122

  Cult Center, 76, 80

  House of the Oil Merchant, 137

  Lion Gate, 31, 151

  Petsas House, 167

  Ramp House, 88

  road system, 83, 139

  Room with the Fresco, 76, 80, 103

  tholos tombs, 81

  Tsountas House, 80

Mycenaeanization, 1, 40, 56, 74, 106, 182

NASK. *See* Norwegian Archaeological Survey in the Karystia

na-u-do-mo (shipwrights), 135

Nauplion, 83, 112, 142

Near East, 15, 47, 83, 162

nearest neighbor, 20, 25, 65

network, 5, 19–28, 107, *See also* elites; palatial network; postpalatial network; prepalatial network; small world network

  centralized, 21, 22, 111, 112, 128, 166, 175, 176, 182, 185

  changes in, 19, 31

  coastal, 108, 112, 113, 125, 126, 170, 171, 182, 183

  collapse of, 24, 179, 185

  condensation of, 22, 112

  connected, 27

  connectivity of, 23

  decentralized, 20–22, 28, 62, 64, 67, 75, 125, 128, 171, 176, 177, 181

  diameter, 4, 24

  directed, 28

  distributed, 20, 22–23, 67, 75

  exclusionary, 64–65, 181

  land-based, 109, 125, 179, 182, 183

  maritime, 60, 67, 109, 179, 180, 182, 183, 185

  mesh-like, 20–22, 62

  orientation, 4, 30, 112, 125, 128, 181–183

  palatial, 125, 126, 178, 183

  prepalatial, 66

  reconstruction, 26

  scale-free, 20–22, 24, 62, 75, 82, 112, 125, 181

  simple, 27

  social network, 19, 24

network (cont.)
  structure, 4, 22, 24, 30, 32, 70, 72, 74, 75, 112, 125, 166, 181–183
  topology, 19, 24, 27, 128
  type, 4, 19, 20, 62, 72, 111, 167
  undirected, 27
  unweighted, 27
  vulnerability, 22–23, 75, 166
  weighted, 28
  network actors, 4, 5, 19, 28, 64, 69
network analysis, 19, 24, 32
network architecture, 19, 20, 21
network dynamics, 19, 27, 62
"network glasses", 19, 27, 62, *See also* network thinking
network growth, 24, 67, 113
network model, 25–28, 76, 109, 112, 166, 181
network science, 24
network theory, 4, 7, 24, 25, 28, 31, 56, 125, 185
network thinking, 25, 26, 28, 185, *See also* "network glasses"
Nichoria, 46, 86, 90–93, 137, 144
Niemeier, Wolf-Dietrich, 9
node, 4, 19–24, 27–28, 61, 62, 64–67, 75, 112, 113, 125, 166, 171, 176
node connectivity, 23
node degree, 20–23, 75
Norwegian Archaeological Survey in the Karystia, 7

oars, 132, 135, 157, 160, 161, 172
object biography, 30
obsidian, 174
Odysseus, 164
offering table (at Kalapodi), 9
olive oil, 27, 112, 120
Onchestos, 118
Orchomenos, 5, 10, 12, 14, 18, 43, 48, 67, 85, 86, 98, 105, 107, 108, 112, 115–116, 118–127, 137, 138, 146, 163, 166, 167, 170, 178, 182
ore, 12, 153, 178
Oropos, 16
Oropos Survey Project, 7
Oxilithos (Euboea), 96, 97, 99

Pagasitic Gulf, 11
Palaima, Thomas, 135
Palaiokastro, 8
palatial area, 4, 31, 84, 95, 103, 122, 123, 125, 126, 165, 178, 180, 185
palatial control, 83, 98, 103, 105, 112, 124, 126, 141, 142, 144–146, 152, 167, 173
palatial culture, 13, 83, 99, 125, 136, 180

palatial elites, 31, 48, 66, 81–84, 100, 105, 124–126, 128, 136, 138, 139, 144, 151, 183
palatial expansion, 147, 180
palatial gap, 152, 163, *See also* Mitrou:LH IIIB decline
palatial officials, 84, 140, 141, 145, 147
palatial period, 1, 4, 7, 13, 17, 18, 48, 77, 98, 101, 103, 104, 107, 114, 118, 125, 128, 130, 137, 138, 142, 143, 145, 151, 152, 157, 161, 163, 165, 170, 175–177, 181, 182, 184, 185
palatial power, 31, 82, 123, 139, 150, 151, 180
palatial sphere, 100, 105, 122, 145
Palioura, 164
Pantou, Panagiota, 11, 12
Papadimitriou, Nikolas, 40
Parkinson, William, 116, 142, 174, 175, 177
path (network), 19, 20, 21, 27
path length (network), 20, 22
Patras, 164
pattern propagation, 65, 67
Pazaraki (near Larymna), 120, 121
Pefkakia, 11
Peleset, 162, *See also* Sea Peoples
Peloponnese, 40, 61, 84–85, 87, 88, 91, 93, 100, 108, 153, 164, 178, 180
penteconter, 160, 161
Perati, 12, 83, 142, 153, 156, 164, 166, 168, 172, 174–178, 184
peripheral area, 26
periphery, 100, 107, 125, 163
Petalian Gulf, 12
Pevkakia Magoula, 62
Phaistos, 157
Pharos-Dexameni (near Chalkis), 142
phenomenological perspective, 13, 122
Phialon, Laetitia, 7
Philistines, 158, *See also* Peleset
Phokis, 42, 61, 74, 96, 98, 99, 153, 163
phrygana, 107
Phthiotis, 67
Phylakopi, 157, 172, 174
pirates, 53, 159
pithos, 160, 169
  impressed pithos, 8, 44, 153, 169–171
plain of Atalanti, 15, 17, 153
Plakari, 7
  Plakari Archaeological Project, 7
Poissonian distribution. *See* bell curve
polder, 10, 116–120, 122–124
Poligira (Kopais), 119
Politika (Euboea), 14, 15
polity, 18, 60, 64, 65, 69, 72, 75, 96, 99, 103, 108–110, 118, 122, 123, 126, 127, 139, 147, 167, 175, 180, 181, 183

pommels. *See* sword pommels
Popham, Mervyn, 11, 151, 154
ports. *See* harbors
postpalatial elites, 31, 152, 154, 162, 163, 181
postpalatial Messenia, 185
postpalatial period, 1, 4, 8, 12, 18, 31, 136, 148, 152, 153, 157, 159, 163, 165, 170–172, 175–178, 181, 184–185
postpalatial settlement, 152, 153, 172
postpalatial trade, 177
pottery, 4, 8, 17, 24, 40, 49, 58–64, 68, 70, 74, 75, 82–84, 105, 107, 108, 111, 113, 115, 116, 125, 149, 151–153, 161, 164, 166, 167, 169, 172, 173, 178, 181–182, 184
 for feasting, 49
 imported, 40
 LH IIB, 42
 LH IIIB, 11, 166
 lustrous, 56, 58–59, 61–63, 181
 MH pottery, 181
 Minoan, 33, 60–62
 palatial, 9, 60, 115, 126
 pictorial, 8, 9, 11, 82–84, 100, 137, 154, 164, 168–172, 179, 183
 skeumorphic, 99
PPA. *See* proximal point analysis
practice theory, 29
preferential attachment, 21, 67, 70, 75
prepalatial elites, 152, 162, 185
prepalatial period, 18, 70, 72, 125, 138, 142, 146, 152, 161, 171, 179, 184
prestige goods, 63–65, 67, 69, 112, 126–128, 132, 136, 142, 144–146, 148, 181, *See also* exotica; import; luxury goods
 at Thebes, 110, 116
 in burials, 10
Privitera, Santo, 8
production, 126, 143, 167, *See also* workshops
 attached, 139
 household production, 8
 of bronze, 154
 of luxury items, 139, 141, 146, 182, 183
 of pottery, 83, 84, 109, 166, 167
 of seals, 95
 of textile, 154, *See also* textile industry
propaganda, 31, 105, 138, 147, 183
Proskynas, 15
Prosymna, 84, 86, 142, 167
prothesis, 164
province, 4, 12, 31, 99, 123, 145, 180, 185
provincial areas, 1, 70, 88, 98, 122, 125, 175, 180, 182
proximal point analysis, 20, 25, 112
Psachna, 14, 15, 17

Pullen, Daniel, 13
purple dye, 9, 12, 146
Pylos, 23, 43, 49, 71, 78–80, 84, 85, 95, 103–105, 111, 124, 127–139, 144, 146, 147, 151, 161, 162, 165, 167, 183, 185
Pyrgos (Kopais), 8, 116, 119
Pyrgos Livanaton. *See* Kynos

quartz, 94, 141, 175, 176

Rachita (Vardates), 164
Rachmani, 99
raiding, 50, 51, 53, 54, 132, 135, 157, 159
ram (on ships), 157
Ramesses III, 158
Ramses II, 159
rational actor, 29, 145, *See also* knowledgeable social actor
raw materials, 19, 136, 148, 157, 174, 176, 178
razor, 33, 44, 164
refuge settlement, 154
regional center, 26, 41, 56, 184
Rehak, Paul, 86, 91, 92
resources, 4, 23, 71, 125, 126
 natural resources, 15
rhyton, 41, 53, 142
road, 13, 19, 41, 83, 120, 122, 139
Romanou, 136
roof tiles, 9, 10
Roustiana, 8
Routsi, 84, 86, 92, 101
Rovies, 14, 15–17
rowers, 55, 130–138, 147, 155, 157, 172, 173, 183
rowers' stanchions, 131, 133, 160
rowers' galleries, 130, 160
Rückl, Štěpán, 169
Ruijgh, Cornelis, 53
ruler symbolism, 94
Rutter, Jeremy, 58

Sackett, Hugh, 5, 11, 26, 56, 113, 154
sailing route. *See* maritime route
sailor, 48, 55, 163, 173, 178
sailor-warrior, 155, 159, 164, 165, 170, 173, 174, 184–185
Salamis, 83, 86
sanctuary
 at Dimini, 12
 at Kalapodi, 1, 9, 97, 125, 154, 170, 171, 182
Saronic Gulf, 13, 14, 111
scarab, 175, 176, 178
Schliemann, Heinrich, 10, 115, 180
Schon, Robert, 59, 138, 139
scribe, 134, 135

Sea Peoples, 158–159, 162, 184

seafaring, 55, 124, 129, 137, 163, 165, 171

seal, 4, 9, 24, 31, 33, 34, 42–44, 55, 76–101, 103–106, 118, 138, 141, 142, 150, 161, 164, 176, 182, 184
   cylinder seal, 79, 86, 87, 94, 141–143
   gold cushion, 34, 37, 88, 91
   gold ring, 33, 35, 44, 47, 78, 79, 81, 88, 89, 94, 151, 161
   Hittite, 141
   Mainland Popular Group, 81, 94–100, 182
   metal ring, 86, 87
   Old Babylonian, 141

sealing, 23, 77–80, 82, 90, 93, 97, 99, 136

secondary burial, 42, 104

SEEP. *See* South Euboea Exploration Project

self-advertisement, 31, 181

Seraglio, 157, 172

settlement patterns, 15, 22, 24, 58

Shaft Graves (Mycenae), 11, 31, 33, 38–40, 43, 44, 46, 47, 49, 54, 63, 67, 71, 77, 78, 80, 84, 88, 93, 104, 181, *See also* Grave Circle A (Mycenae); Grave Circle B (Mycenae)

Shardana, 159, 162, *See also* Sea Peoples

Shaw, Maria, 128, 129, 140

shield, 33–35, 38, 43, 51, 52, 55, 60, 61, 80, 85, 152, 155, 159, 160, 162, 169, 174, 184
   Dipylon shield, 174, 184
   proto-Dipylon shield, 162, 174

ship, 15, 27, 48, 50, 53, 54, 128–141, 144, 183
   depicted in Egypt, 158
   depicted on frescoes, 50–51, 128–138, 140, 183
   depicted on larnax, 137
   depicted on pottery, 8, 51, 55, 130, 134, 137, 155, 156, 158
   depicted on seals, 78, 94
   depicted on stelae, 160
   doodled on clay tablet, 136
   in *Iliad*, 50, 161
   in Linear B tablets, 132–135
   on gold diadem, 136
   on mold, 136

ship model, 50, 132, 137, 160, 161, 185

shipwright, 134, 135

Siege Rhyton, 33, 52, 53, 161

silver, 12, 33, 40, 42, 44, 49, 52, 164, 178

silver mine, 178

Skala Atalantis, 15, 26

Sklavokambos, 78, 79

Skopelos, 42, 54

Skoubris cemetery (Lefkandi), 173

Skroponeri, 14, 15, 121

Skyros, 131, 157, 158

small world, 14, 21, 65, 69, 161, 172

small world network, 20–22, 28, 65, 72, 74, 75

smith, 134

Snodgrass, Anthony, 5

South Euboea Exploration Project, 7

spear, 35, 55, 184
   depicted in frescoes, 43, 51, 77, 103, 140
   depicted on dagger, 43
   depicted on pottery, 152, 160–162
   depicted on seals, 34, 35, 50
   in burial, 39, 43, 45, 164
   on Linear B tablets, 102

spearhead, 38, 40, 42, 81, 82, 164

Spercheios Valley, 67, 164

sphinx, 81, 86, 87, 149, 151, 161

spindle whorls, 42, 99, 153

Sporades, 42

Spyropoulos, Theodoros, 10, 11

Stag Rhyton, 33

Staphylos (Skopelos), 42

state, 4, 42, 70, 103, 126, 127, 167, 178, 182

status creation, 64, 181

status indicators. *See* status marker

status marker, 78, 99, 100

status symbol, 47, 99

steatite, 11, 81, 94, 99, 141, 164, 175

Steel, Louise, 47

Steinmann, Bernhard, 102

stem post, 131, 132, 136, 152, 158, 159, 172

stern, 134, 157, 160

stirrup jar, 60, 120, 131, 140, 157, 164, *See also* transport stirrup jar; inscribed stirrup jar

storage rooms, 10, 126

Strait of Oreoi, 15, 42, 63, 74

strength of weak ties, 28, 65

Stroviki (Kopais), 117, 119

structuration theory, 29

structure (society), 29

Submycenaean, 2, 97, 98, 165, 170

surface survey, 5, 7, 8, 26, 58–59, 114, 169, 181

sword pommels, 33, 55

swords, 33–39, 43–45, 55, 82, 101–103, 105, 156, 164, 165, 181, 184
   agency of, 30, 31, 38–39, 76, 103
   ceremonial, 101
   cut-and-thrust type, 165
   depicted in art, 36, 38, 43, 48, 77
   depicted in frescoes, 51, 55, 76, 103
   depicted on larnax, 36
   depicted on pottery, 76, 130, 155, 162
   depicted on seals, 34–35
   depicted on stelae, 36

in burials, 10, 33, 38, 39, 42–45, 55, 77, 80, 81, 92, 165
   killing of, 31, 39
   on Linear B tablets, 101
   single-edged, 37, 38, 102
   type A, 36, 37, 44, 101, 102
   type B, 37, 101, 102
   type C, 102
   type D, 102
   type F, 101–103, 164
   type G, 101–103, 164
   type Naue II, 102, 165
   types, 36, 101, 102
swordsmanship, 181
symbols of power, 9, 85, 124, 161
symposium, 155, 165

Tanagra, 5, 7, 11, 36, 90, 92–94, 96–98, 100, 104, 132, 137, 142
Tankosić, Žarko, 7
Tartaron, Thomas, 13, 14, 24, 27, 133, 136, 138, 180
technology transfer, 19
temple (at Kalapodi), 9, 87, 170
Tertiary deposits, 15
textile, 8
textile industry, 110, 153
Thebes, 1, 11, 12, 17, 18, 28, 43, 54, 66, 67, 71, 72, 74, 75, 78, 95–98, 107–116, 118, 122–126, 128, 136–138, 141–144, 146, 151, 166, 167, 172, 177, 178, 180, 182, 185, *See also* workshops
   amber from, 71, 72
   Arsenal, 141
   boat models from, 137
   built tomb at, 39
   chamber tombs, 41, 64, 71, 115, 116
   excavations, 5, 10
   frescoes, 105, 136, 137
   imports at, 142–143, 146, 172, 175–177, 182
   jewelry from, 11, 141
   Kadmeion, 11, 142
   Kordatzi "hoard", 141
   Linear B tablets from, 7, 96
   pottery from, 61, 108, 112, 116, 172
   scepterhead from, 85
   sealing from, 95, 96
   seals from, 86, 96–98, 118, 142
   swords from, 36
   territory, 14, 96, 108, 110–112, 118, 122, 166
   Treasure Room, 142
Thessaly, 63, 71, 74, 86, 96, 99, 109, 153
tholos tomb, 84, 85
   at Anthia, 79
   at Dendra, 86
   at Dimini, 88
   at Kazarma, 79, 80
   at Marathon, 12, 43
   at Menidi, 86
   at Mycenae, 81
   at Nichoria, 86
   at Orchomenos, 10, 115, 116
   at Oxylithos, 96, 97
   at Rachmani, 99
   at Routsi, 86, 101
   at Thorikos, 12, 40, 43
   at Tragana, 92, 136, 157
   at Vapheio, 79, 80, 86
   near Volos, 11, 56
Thorikos, 12, 40, 43, 54, 59, 60, 74, 142, 176, 178
Threpsiades, I., 10
ties. *See* link
Tiryns, 43, 48, 78, 80, 82–84, 95, 96, 98, 104, 112, 116, 117, 127, 137, 138, 142, 143, 146, 150, 152, 161, 163, 167, 169, 172, 175, 176, 182
Torone, 56, 61, 63, 66
trade network, 178–179
trade route, 105, 172, 179, 183, 184
Tragana, 84, 91, 136, 157, 160
transport stirrup jars, 8, 116, 172, *See also* inscribed stirrup jar
Treasury of Atreus, 10, 115, 143
Treasury of Minyas, 10, 115
Treherne, Paul, 44
"trickle down" of goods, 24, 64, 69, 74, 85, 144
trireme, 157
Troy, 15, 161
tumulus, 12, 40, 74
Turkey, 27
tweezers, 42, 44, 164

Ugarit, 76
Uluburun shipwreck, 27
Urals, 46
Urnfield cultures, 132, 158

Van de Moortel, Aleydis, 8
Vapheio, 53, 79, 84, 86, 88, 92
Vapheio Cup, 40, 49, 56, 58, 61, 62, 67, 68
Vardates. *See* Rachita (Vardates)
Varkiza, 84
Vermeule, Emily, 83, 162
vertices (network), 19
Vitale, Salvatore, 63
Vlichada, 7, 15

Volos, 8, 11, 14, 56, 61–63, 86, 126, 154, 161, 162, 165, 168, 169, 184
votive, 9, 170
Voudeni (in Achaea), 164
Voutsaki, Sofia, 92, 142

Wachsmann, Shelley, 129, 132, 134, 158
Wallace, Malcolm, 7
wanax, 82, 110, 124, 134, 135, 150, 166, 181
warrior, 33, 36–39, 42–50, 54, 55, 66, 70, 77, 79–82, 84, 85, 89, 100–106, 130, 138, 140, 156, 159–165, 171
  at sea, 53, 54, 132, 135, 155, 158, 173, 174, 184
  body, 30, 38, 44
  depicted on dagger, 103
  depicted on fresco, 10, 50–52, 55, 103, 105, 136, 163
  depicted on ivory, 143
  depicted on pottery, 8, 130, 131, 152, 155–162, 169, 173
  depicted on rhyton, 53
  depicted on seal, 34–36
  depicted on stele, 36
warrior aristocracy, 46, 47, 55, 80
warrior burial. *See* warrior grave
warrior class, 44, 163
warrior culture. *See* warrior ethos
warrior elites, 38, 39, 46, 54, 73, 80, 82, 84, 99, 105, 161, 170, 181
warrior ethos, 11, 33, 42, 43, 53–55, 78, 80, 81, 88, 100, 105, 154, 163, 165, 168, 171, 178, 181, 182, 184, 185

warrior grave, 40–42, 44, 45, 48, 56, 73, 78, 80–82, 85, 86, 88, 100, 101, 103, 105, 156, 163–165, 177, 182
warrior identity, 43, 49, 100, 106
warrior ideology. *See* warrior ethos
warrior package, 48, 50, 55, 78, 174
warrior status, 38, 41, 43
warrior tomb. *See* warrior grave
warrior values. *See* warrior ethos
Warrior Vase, 159
warships, 130, 136
weak ties, 28, 47, 64–66, 69, 71, 126, 128, 131, 181, *See also* long distance ties
Wedde, Michael, 78, 130, 134, 136
Weingarten, Judith, 93
West, Martin, 53
Whitley, James, 29, 156
workshops, 31, 77, 124, 126, 141, 145, *See also* production
  at Mycenae, 143, 167
  at Thebes, 11, 110, 141, 182
  for bronze, 105
  for pottery, 167, 169
  for seals, 82, 93, 94
  for textiles, 110
  Mastos workshop, 167
  palatial workshops, 82, 143–145, 147, 183
Wright, James, 54, 92

Xeste 3 (Akrotiri), 87, 149

Younger, John, 54, 91–93, 132

Zahou, Eleni, 8